MERCURY CONTAMINATION: A HUM
Patricia A. D'Itri and Frank M. D'Itri

POLLUTANTS AND HIGH RISK GROU
Edward J. Calabrese

METHODOLOGICAL APPROACHES TO DERIVING ENVIRONMENTAL AND OCCUPATIONAL HEALTH STANDARDS
Edward J. Calabrese

NUTRITION AND ENVIRONMENTAL HEALTH—Volume I: The Vitamins
Edward J. Calabrese

NUTRITION AND ENVIRONMENTAL HEALTH—Volume II: Minerals and Macronutrients
Edward J. Calabrese

SULFUR IN THE ENVIRONMENT, Parts I and II
Jerome O. Nriagu, Editor

COPPER IN THE ENVIRONMENT, Parts I and II
Jerome O. Nriagu, Editor

ZINC IN THE ENVIRONMENT, Parts I and II
Jerome O. Nriagu, Editor

CADMIUM IN THE ENVIRONMENT, Parts I and II
Jerome O. Nriagu, Editor

NICKEL IN THE ENVIRONMENT
Jerome O. Nriagu, Editor

ENERGY UTILIZATION AND ENVIRONMENTAL HEALTH
Richard A. Wadden, Editor

FOOD, CLIMATE AND MAN
Margaret R. Biswas and Asit K. Biswas, Editors

CHEMICAL CONCEPTS IN POLLUTANT BEHAVIOR
Ian J. Tinsley

RESOURCE RECOVERY AND RECYCLING
A. F. M. Barton

QUANTITATIVE TOXICOLOGY
V.A. Filov, A.A. Golubev, E.I. Liublina, and N.A. Tolokontsev

AIR AND WATER
POLLUTION CONTROL

AIR AND WATER POLLUTION CONTROL

A Benefit-Cost Assessment

A. MYRICK FREEMAN, III
Bowdoin College

A WILEY-INTERSCIENCE PUBLICATION
JOHN WILEY & SONS
New York • Chichester • Brisbane • Toronto • Singapore

Copyright © 1982 by John Wiley & Sons, Inc.

All rights reserved. Published simultaneously in Canada.

Reproduction or translation of any part of this work beyond that permitted by Section 107 or 108 of the 1976 United States Copyright Act without the permission of the copyright owner is unlawful. Requests for permission or further information should be addressed to the Permissions Department, John Wiley & Sons, Inc.

Library of Congress Cataloging in Publication Data:
Freeman, A. Myrick, 1936-
    Air and water pollution control.

    (Environmental science and technology, ISSN 0194-0827)
    Includes index.
    1. Environmental policy—Cost effectiveness.
    2. Air quality management—Cost effectiveness.
    2. Water quality management—Cost effectiveness.
I. Title. II. Series.

HC79.E5F697 1982   338.4'3363736'0973   82-8409
ISBN 0-471-08985-0
Printed in the United States of America

10 9 8 7 6 5 4 3 2 1

*to the seals
off Cat Ledges*

SERIES PREFACE

Environmental Science and Technology

The Environmental Science and Technology Series of Monographs, Textbooks, and Advances is devoted to the study of the quality of environment and to the technology of its conservation. Environmental science therefore relates to the chemical, physical, and biological changes in the environment through contamination or modification, to the physical nature and biological behavior of air, water, soil, food, and waste as they are affected by man's agricultural, industrial, and social activities, and to the application of science and technology to the control and improvement of environmental quality.

The deterioration of environmental quality, which began when man first collected into villages and utilized fire, has existed as a serious problem under the ever-increasing impacts of exponentially increasing population and of industrializing society. Environmental contamination of air, water, soil, and food has become a threat to the continued existence of many plant and animal communities of the ecosystem and may ultimately threaten the very survival of the human race.

It seems clear that if we are to preserve for future generations some semblance of the biological order of the world of the past and hope to improve on the deteriorating standards of urban public health, environmental science and technology must quickly come to play a dominant role in designing our social and industrial structure for tommorrow. Scientifically rigorous criteria of environmental quality must be developed. Based in part on these criteria, realistic standards must be established and our technological progress must be tailored to meet them. It is obvious that civilization will continue to require increasing amounts of fuel, transportation, industrial chemicals, fertilizers, pesticides, and countless other products; and that it will continue to produce waste products of all descriptions. What is urgently needed is a total systems approach to modern civilization through which the pooled talents of scientists and engineers, in cooperation with social scientists and the medical profession, can be focused on the development of order and equilibrium in the presently disparate segments of the human environment. Most of the skills and tools that are needed are already in existence. We surely have a right to hope a technology that has created such manifold environmental problems is also capable of solving them. It is our hope that this Series in Environmental Sciences and Technology will not only serve to make this challenge more explicit to the established professionals, but that it also will help to stimulate the student toward the career opportunities in this vital area.

Robert L. Metcalf
Werner Stumm

PREFACE

In early 1979, Paul Portney, who was then the staff economist at the U.S. Council on Environmental Quality, asked me if I would prepare a survey and critical review of the empirical literature on the benefits of air and water pollution control. He wanted me also to determine whether, in my judgement, it was possible on the basis of this literature to say what benefits the federal air and water pollution control policies had yielded. I had just published a book through Resources for the Future, Inc., describing and discussing the various models and techniques that were available to anyone who wished to estimate pollution control benefits (*The Benefits of Environmental Improvement: Theory and Practice*, Johns Hopkins University Press, 1979). So I welcomed the opportunity to see to what extent the tools made available by modern economic and econometric theory were actually being used by practitioners engaged in empirical benefit analysis.

The result of Paul's invitation was a report to CEQ submitted in December, 1979 and released by them in April, 1980 (*The Benefits of Air and Water Pollution Control: A Review and Synthesis*). This book is an expansion and updating of that report. I have added materials explaining to the noneconomist what we mean by the term *benefits*, and how we go about measuring benefits. I have also added discussions of those new benefit analyses that have become available since the completion of the earlier report for CEQ. In some instances this new information has led me to make revisions in my synthesis, or best judgment estimates, of the magnitude of pollution control benefits.

I am very grateful to Paul Portney for the initial stimulus to undertake this project and for a number of very helpful comments and suggestions in the course of the study. I want to acknowledge the financial support of the Council on Environmental Quality during the preparation of my report to them. But of course the views expressed there and in this book are my own and do not necessarily reflect the views of the Council when the report was

x   Preface

released (1980) or now. The Bowdoin College Faculty Research Fund provided support for preparing this book.

I also thank Trev Leger and John Wiley and Sons for giving me the opportunity to expand this work into book form. Jini Linkovich typed the manuscript with her usual skill and good cheer. Finally, I wish to thank a number of my colleagues who work in the field of environmental economics for helpful comments and suggestions as the work progressed. I especially wish to acknowledge the help of Alan Carlin, Thomas Crocker, Donald Gillette, Robert Horst, John Jaksch, Kay Jones, Lester Lave, Ben-Chieh Liu, Jon Nelson, Clifford Russell, Eugene Seskin, William Schulze, Richard Schwing, William Watson, and Ronald Wyzga. Of course, I bear sole responsibility for any errors, and for all judgements, interpretations, and conclusions.

A. MYRICK FREEMAN, III

Back River
Georgetown, Maine
May 1982

CONTENTS

1. **Introduction**   1

2. **Defining and Measuring Benefits**   8
   Types of Benefits, 8
   Stages in the Production of Benefits, 13
   Approaches to Determining Values, 16
   Market Approaches, 19

3. **Introduction to Air Pollution Control Benefits**   26
   A National Benefits Model, 27
   Trends in Air Quality, 29

4. **The Health Benefits of Air Pollution Control**   36
   Valuing Health, 37
   Stationary Sources, 43
   Mobile Sources, 77

5. **Vegetation, Materials, and Cleaning**   86
   Vegetation, 86
   Materials, 91
   Cleaning and Soiling, 100
   Acid Rain, 107

6. **Aesthetics**   110
   Benefits to Residential Property Values, 111
   Wage Differentials, 121

xii   Contents

7. **Air Pollution Control Benefits: A Summary** — 125
   Overlaps and Gaps in Estimating Benefits, 125
   Benefits and Costs Compared, 130

8. **Water Pollution Control and Recreation Benefits** — 132
   Methods for Estimating Recreation Benefits, 135
   A Review of Recreation Damage and Benefit Studies, 144
   Synthesis Estimates of Recreation Benefits, 158

9. **Water Pollution Control: Other Benefits, Conclusions** — 163
   Nonuser Benefits, 163
   Commercial Fisheries, 165
   Diversionary Uses, 166
   Benefits and Costs Compared, 169

10. **Conclusions** — 173
    Aggregate Benefits and the Macroeconomy, 174

Author Index — 179

Subject Index — 183

AIR AND WATER
POLLUTION CONTROL

1

INTRODUCTION

There is increasing concern in the United States today about the extent of regulation. The focus is not only on regulation of price, quantity, and service in transportation, communications, and other supposedly noncompetitive sectors of the economy, but also on regulations dealing with problems that economists have analyzed under the heading of external diseconomies: the impacts of air and water pollution on health, recreation, productivity, and amenities; the risk to workers of accident and ill health due to occupational hazards; and so forth. This concern with the extent of regulation primarily has to do with the relationship between regulatory costs and benefits. Most of the legislation authorizing regulation in environmental quality, occupational safety and health, and product safety has not placed major emphasis on the benefit–cost relationship as a criterion in regulatory decision making. In fact, consideration of benefit–cost relationships is ruled out in some cases—for example, the establishment of national primary air quality standards. Thus regulatory agencies have had little incentive, until recently, to develop comprehensive and well-documented measures of benefits and costs.

But now serious questions are being asked about whether the major federal programs to control air and water pollution have been worth the cost. President Reagan has assured that such questions will be asked about proposals for new federal regulations by issuing Executive Order 12291 in February, 1981. This order requires that agencies prepare for each proposed regulation a regulatory impact analysis which includes a complete description and, where possible, a monetary valuation of all the beneficial and adverse consequences to be expected if the regulation is adopted. Many agencies have found themselves to be ill prepared to deal with this new interest in measuring the benefits of existing and future regulatory programs.

The major purpose of this book is to assess the present state of knowledge about the national benefits of air and water pollution control programs. There have been a number of efforts to estimate various aspects of the damages caused by air and water pollution or the benefits that might be expected to

2 Introduction

accrue from controlling pollution discharges to air and water. Some of these studies have been based on new primary data sources, while others have attempted to draw inferences from secondary sources. Some of these studies have had good data but used poor theory; others have used good theory but have had poor data. It is difficult to draw any conclusions on the basis of the individual studies because of noncomparability in the data bases, in the methodological frameworks employed, and in the assumptions as to baseline conditions. But when an effort is made to place all of these studies on a comparable basis, it does appear possible to reach some conclusion concerning the nature and magnitude of the benefits of pollution control.

This book is based largely on an earlier research project carried out for the U.S. Council on Environmental Quality (Freeman, 1979a). The major objectives of that research were: first, to provide a survey and critical review of the existing literature on air and water pollution control giving estimates of national benefits or damages; second, where possible, to place all of these benefit or damage estimates in a common framework with respect to such factors as the postulated change in pollution and the year and price level, so as to facilitate comparisons; and third, to draw upon this body of past research to obtain defensible and consistent estimates of the benefits of controlling air and water pollution. In this book, these estimates are then compared with cost measures in an effort to inform the ongoing debate about environmental regulation.

It is not my objective—nor could it be, given the existing state of knowledge—to determine whether the existing set of environmental regulations is optimal in the sense of equating marginal benefits and marginal costs across all control activities for all substances. It is not reasonable to hope to provide such detailed information to guide individual decisions, either at a national or regional level. Such comprehensiveness and precision are difficult to achieve with studies based on existing empirical techniques and data sets. Rather, what are presented here are national aggregate measures of pollution and polluting effects. Typically the data are for aggregates of polluting substances. And the estimates refer to the benefits of nonmarginal changes in pollution, not accurate point estimates of marginal benefits.

I turn now to a discussion of the concept of benefits and the analytical framework within which benefit measures are formulated and interpreted. First, it is important to draw a distinction between the *concept of benefits* and the *effects* of environmental pollution. Pollutants can have effects on people directly or indirectly through a variety of channels. For example, pollutants can affect human health as measured by morbidity and mortality rates. Pollutants can affect activities—such as water-based recreation. Or they can affect the availability of goods and services through their influence on agricultural productivity or the rates of deterioration of materials. Controlling pollution means reducing the magnitude of these effects.

Each of these types of effects has an economic aspect. The values that people place on reducing the adverse effects of pollution constitute economists' measure of benefits. The basis for determining these values is taken to be individuals' preferences. The benefit of an environmental improvement is the sum of the monetary values assigned to the effects of that improvement by all individuals directly or indirectly affected by the action. These monetary values can be defined in terms of the individuals' willingness to pay to obtain the effects of the environmental improvement, or in terms of the sums individuals would have to receive as compensation in order to induce them to accept voluntarily the adverse effects of pollution. In practice, there is likely to be little difference between the two conceptual approaches. They will be assumed to be equivalent in this book.

It is also important to distinguish between *benefits* and *damages*. Benefits are the value of some improvement from a "dirty" status quo. Damages represent what is lost in money terms because the emission of pollutants has degraded the environment from some natural, "clean" state. Benefits and damages are mirror images of each other. The benefits of eliminating all pollutants are equal in magnitude to the damages incurred because of the existing level of pollutants. The benefit terminology is preferred because it is more applicable to policy decisions regarding potential environmental improvements. However, many of the studies reviewed in this book have used the damage terminology.

Although measuring benefits involves the use of economic theory and technique, benefit estimates must be built on a foundation of knowledge of the physical and biological effects of pollution. For example, estimates of the health benefits from air pollution control must be based on scientific knowledge of the relationship between pollutant concentrations and human health. Estimates of recreation and fishery benefits stemming from water pollution control require knowledge of the relationship between pollutant levels and biological productivity. Lack of knowledge of these relationships may, in some instances, be the major barrier to the accurate empirical estimation of pollution control benefits.

There are three basic approaches to determining the values that individuals place on improvements in environmental quality. One is simply to ask individuals, through surveys and direct questioning. The second is to place proposals for alternative levels of improvement in environmental quality to referendum vote. Under certain circumstances, the outcome of the voting process will be consistent with, and therefore reveal information about, the underlying demand for environmental improvement. The third approach

4 Introduction

involves analyzing data from market transactions in goods and services related to environmental quality. Under certain circumstances, the willingness to pay for environmental improvements can be estimated from market data about the demands for goods and services that have substitute or complementary relationships with environmental quality. All of the empirical techniques actually used in an effort to obtain quantitative estimates of benefits involve some variation on one of these basic approaches. These approaches and their application will be discussed in more detail in Chapter 2. For further discussion of the principles of benefit estimation, see Freeman (1979b).

Since the benefits of a pollution control policy are measured by the dollar value of the change in environmental quality, some choice must be made about the postulated range over which environmental quality has changed. The conceptually correct measure of the benefits of a policy would compare environmental quality levels *with* and *without* some specified degree of control, holding all other things equal, including the patterns of production, technology, and demand which determine the generation of pollutants. Thus one should compare an actual observed outcome resulting from the policy with a hypothetical or counterfactual position reflecting the same underlying economic conditions and differing only with respect to the impact of the environmental policy.

A major issue today is the impact of already-adopted environmental policies. To measure the benefits of existing policy, one should compare the actual environmental quality in the appropriate year, for example, 1978, with that environmental quality which would have been experienced in 1978 in the absence of any legislation restricting or controlling pollution, all other things being equal. To implement this measure, we would have to have some way of predicting what the levels of economic activity and discharges to the environment would have been in the absence of any controlling legislation. Economic models can be developed for this purpose; but it is beyond the scope of this study to do so.[1]

An alternative measure would be to compare environmental quality levels in, say, 1978 with actual environmental quality levels in the year in which the policy was adopted. This measure has the virtue of being based upon actual observations of environmental quality levels before and after the adoption of the policies. But in a growing economy, it is likely to lead to an underestimate of the conceptually correct or ideal measure. This is because in the absence of a control policy population growth and increases in

---

[1] For examples of this type of analysis, see U.S. Council on Environmental Quality (1978, pp. 419–421), and National Economic Research Associates (1980).

the level of economic activity would have resulted in higher pollution levels in later years.

The two measures described above look at the actual or realized impact of environmental policies at a particular point in time. An alternative measure would look at the benefits to be realized if and when policies actually achieved stated targets, such as national ambient air quality standards. Again, the conceptually correct measure would compare the hypothetical alternative of no policy with the world in which environmental quality targets had been met, other things held equal. Alternatively one could compare the actual environmental quality levels at the time of adoption of the policy with the stated targets or standards on the implicit assumption that the targets would be met immediately or at some specified future date.

Because of data limitations and the limited resources available for this study, neither of the conceptually preferred comparisons could be made. Instead, the benefits of air pollution control are measured in terms of the actual improvement in air quality between 1970, the year the Clean Air Act was passed, and 1978, the reference year for the study. Water pollution control benefits are measured in terms of the expected improvement in water quality between 1972, the year that the Federal Water Pollution Control Act was passed, and 1985, the year that the pollution control objectives of the act are to be attained. In the case of both air and water pollution control, these measures are likely to be underestimates of true benefits of the federal policies because the comparison is with prepolicy actual environmental quality levels rather than with the hypothetical "no policy but other things equal" levels.

Even the most careful estimates of benefits will contain inaccuracies due to errors in measurement and statistical estimation. It will often be necessary to make some assumptions regarding unknown parameters. Given the present state of the art and knowledge about damage and benefit relationships, these sources of error and uncertainty are especially important. The preferred approach to dealing with uncertainty is to adopt the framework and language of probability theory (Freeman, 1979b, pp. 30–32). This framework can be used to incorporate information on the error properties of statistical estimates and subjective probability statements as they affect the determination of expected values or most likely estimates, and the confidence intervals or ranges within which the true value is thought to lie with some probability.

Some of the benefit estimates reviewed in this book have used a formal or informal probability framework to establish most likely values and lower and upper bounds. Others have simply stated point estimates as if they were certain. The synthesis estimates I present below will be stated in terms of a range with lower and upper bounds. I will also state my judgment as to the most reasonable point estimate. The most reasonable point estimate can be interpreted as an expected value derived from a subjective probability distribution of possible values. The range could be interpreted as a 90% confidence around the expected value. In the language of the bookmaker, I would be willing to accept wagers at ten-to-one odds that the true values of benefits, if known, would be found to lie outside the stated ranges.

Neither the ranges nor the most reasonable point estimates are derived from a formal probability model. They are based on subjective judgments and estimates. For example, where two or more sources are used as the basis for a particular value, the point estimates can be interpreted as representing weighted averages of available sources, with the weights representing my subjective judgment of the reliability or accuracy of the source. The bases for these judgments will be described in more detail for each estimate. The most reasonable point estimate should not be cited or discussed independent of the range of upper and lower bounds, since to do so would convey an entirely false sense of accuracy or certainty about inherently inaccurate and uncertain values.

In Chapter 2 I discuss in more detail the concept of benefits and alternative techniques for their measurement. This is to prepare the reader for the discussion of the theoretical and empirical adequacy of the benefit estimates reviewed in the remainder of the book. Chapters 3 through 7 focus on air pollution control benefits. These chapters are devoted to an introduction to air pollution benefits (Chapter 3), benefits to human health (Chapter 4), impacts on structures, materials, and crops (Chapter 5), and amenities and aesthetics, including visibility (Chapter 6). Chapter 7 presents a summary of the estimates of air pollution control benefits, a comparison with the costs of air pollution control, and a discussion of the policy implications.

Chapters 8 and 9 deal with water pollution control benefits. Recreation, the largest, single category of water pollution control benefits, is the topic of Chapter 8. Chapter 9 presents a discussion of other categories of water pollution control benefits, a summary, and a comparison with water pollution control costs. The final chapter of this book includes a discussion of possible uses of estimates of national benefits of the form presented here, and an assessment of the present state of the art and research needs.

REFERENCES

Freeman, A. Myrick, III. *The Benefits of Air and Water Pollution Control: A Review and Synthesis of Recent Estimates.* A report to the U.S. Council on Environmental Quality, 1979a.

_____. *The Benefits of Environmental Improvement: Theory and Practice.* Baltimore: Johns Hopkins University Press, 1979b.

National Economic Research Associates, Inc. *Cost Effectiveness and Cost-Benefit Analysis of Air Quality Regulation. The Business Roundtable Air Quality Project,* Vol. 4. New York: Business Roundtable, 1980.

U.S. Council on Environmental Quality. *Environmental Quality.* Washington, D.C.: U.S. Government Printing Office, 1978.

2

DEFINING AND MEASURING BENEFITS

A reduction in the discharge of a pollutant and the resulting increase in some measure of environmental quality may operate through a variety of channels to benefit people in terms of their own preferences. Benefits can accrue to individuals either directly in the form of increases in the availability of goods and services (for example, improved health, better visibility, improved recreation opportunities), or indirectly through increases in production efficiency (for example, reduced materials damages or enhanced productivity of commercial fisheries) which lower the prices of goods normally purchased through markets. In the first section of this chapter, I present a classification of beneficial effects according to the physical and biological mechanisms involved and the economic channels through which benefits are conveyed to individuals.

In the second section, I examine the processes involved in the production of benefits, beginning with the regulatory policy which reduces the discharges of a polluting substance and ending with individuals' subjective valuation of the beneficial effects. This discussion helps to make clear the nature of the data required to support a benefit estimate and to clarify the roles of economists and physical and biological scientists in the benefit estimation process. Then I briefly review the major approaches to estimating monetary measures of values, or willingness to pay. Specific benefit estimation techniques will be discussed in more detail as necessary in later chapters where estimates of various categories of benefits are examined.

TYPES OF BENEFITS

This section presents a way of categorizing, or classifying, the variety of possible beneficial effects of improvements in environmental quality. Of course, any classification system contains a certain element of arbitrariness.

Types of Benefits

The usefulness of this classification scheme is that it provides a link with the various approaches for estimating monetary values of beneficial effects. The two main categories of effects are those that operate through biological mechanisms (our own, as seen in human health, and those of other organisms) and those that do not. Each category of effect also can be described as conveying its benefits either through the market system in the form of higher incomes to producers and greater availability and lower prices of goods to consumers or through increases in the availability of goods and services not normally purchased through markets—for example, better health, improved environmental amenities such as visibility, and higher quality water based recreation opportunities. The former will be called *market effects*, while the latter will be called *nonmarket effects*. The two types of effects, and subtypes, and the economic channels through which they operate are summarized below and discussed in the following section:

Effects on Living Systems (Involving Biological Mechanisms)

1. Human health (nonmarket):
   a. mortality
   b. morbidity
2. Economic productivity of ecological systems (market):
   a. agriculture
   b. commercial fisheries
   c. forestry
3. Other ecological system effects impinging directly on human activities (nonmarket):
   a. sports fishing
   b. hunting
   c. wildlife observation
   d. water-based recreation
   e. home gardening and landscaping
   f. commercial, institutional, public landscaping (which are market effects to the extent that market prices or tax burdens are reduced)
4. Ecological system effects not directly impinging on humans (nonmarket)
   a. species diversity
   b. ecosystem stability

Effects on Nonliving Systems

1. Producers (market):
   a. damages to materials, for example, corrosion

10 Defining and Measuring Benefits

    b. soiling
    c. reduction in product quality
2. Households (nonmarket):
    a. damages to materials
    b. soiling
3. Changes in weather and climate (nonmarket)
4. Other (nonmarket):
    a. visibility
    b. tranquility

Effects on Living Systems

Human Health

Exposure to some forms of air pollution has been associated with increases in morbidity and mortality. Outbreaks of infectious diseases have been traced to contaminants in municipal water supplies. Certain chemicals in water supplies have been linked with elevated cancer mortality rates. The incidence and magnitude of the adverse health effects resulting from exposure to present ambient levels of pollutants have not been clearly established for many of these substances. But to the extent that adverse health effects can be traced to pollution, improvements in air or water quality can result in benefits in the form of better health. Since there is no market in which individuals can purchase decreases in morbidity and mortality directly, these are nonmarket effects.

Economic Productivity of Ecological Systems

This category refers to those cases where either natural or cultivated ecological systems are used to produce goods that will be sold in markets. Examples include agriculture, forestry, and commercial fisheries. Changes in environmental quality can affect the biological productivity of these systems and, therefore, the cost and supply of their products. In the arid West, runoff and return flows from irrigated fields carry dissolved salts leached from the soil. The result of irrigation in upstream areas is degraded water quality downstream. Repeated rediversion of river flow for irrigation purposes increases concentrations of total dissolved solids, which can reduce the productivity of the irrigation water for agriculture.

Agricultural productivity also can be affected by air pollutants. Sulfur dioxide and photochemical oxidants both have been linked with various forms of leaf damage and reduced photosynthesis rates. There also may be a long-term effect on agricultural productivity due to rising soil acidity caused by acid rain. The yields from forest lands also may be adversely affected by acid rain.

Lowered water quality can affect commercial fishery production adversely in a number of ways. In rivers it can reduce or eliminate spawning runs of commercially valuable species, such as salmon, shad, herring, and smelt. Toxic substances can affect the biological productivity of estuarine areas, which are the foundation of the biological food chain. The toxic substances can themselves directly reduce or eliminate populations of commercially valuable species, such as crabs and lobsters. The chemical and bacteria contents of surviving commercially valuable species can render them unfit for human consumption. Swordfish and tuna have been taken off the market because of high levels of mercury. Shellfish beds have been closed to commercial harvesting because of both bacteria and chemical contents.

If pollution is controlled and these effects are reduced, the increased productivity of agricultural lands and fisheries should be reflected in higher incomes to farm owners as well as in greater quantities and lower prices of agricultural products to consumers. These are market effects.

Other Ecological System Effects Impinging Directly on Human Activities

This category consists primarily of those outdoor recreation activities where involvement with nature is an integral part of the experience. This would include sports fishing, boating, camping, and wildlife observation, but not, for example, tennis or softball. If the control of air pollutants results in improved plant growth in natural areas, or if higher water quality improves the species composition of the aquatic environment, then the utility derived from associated recreation activities may be increased, and individuals may utilize these natural areas more frequently. Since these environmental services are not normally purchased in markets, these are nonmarket effects. If the costs of commercial and public gardening and landscaping are reduced by improved air quality, these are market effects to the extent that the lower costs are reflected in lower product prices or lower taxes.

Ecological System Effects Not Directly Impinging on Human Activities

This category includes changes in ecological system diversity and stability and the local or total extinction of species with no economic or recreational significance. These are clearly nonmarket effects.

Defining and Measuring Benefits

Effects on Nonliving Systems

Effects on Producers

Air and water pollution can affect producers in a variety of ways, all of which have the consequence of raising the costs of production. This in turn results in a decrease in profits and returns to fixed factors and/or an increase in product prices. Water pollution may lower the quality of water used as an input to the production process. This results either in lower productivity or increased costs incurred for mitigating activities, such as input water treatment. Air pollutants can cause physical deterioration of materials and structures, necessitating increased maintenance and repair costs and/or more frequent replacement. Suspended particulates can result in increased soiling of spaces, thus necessitating more frequent cleaning. Some manufacturing plants require special treatment of air to maintain the required cleanliness for certain operations, such as manufacture of sensitive measuring instruments. Finally, waterborne sediments may settle in navigation channels and anchorages. This can either reduce their effectiveness or necessitate more frequent and costly dredging. Improvements in environmental quality reduce the magnitude of these adverse effects and result in some combination of higher producers' incomes and/or lower consumers' prices. Thus they are market effects.

Effects on Households

Physically similar effects, such as soiling and materials damage, may be experienced by households. With an improvement in environmental quality, households may respond by incurring reduced cleaning and maintenance costs, or they might simply experience an improvement in their utility or welfare. These are nonmarket effects.

Effects on Weather and Climate

Whether through raising the level of carbon dioxide or particulates in the atmosphere or through ozone depletion, the discharge of some forms of pollutants may significantly affect weather and climate. The economic significance of climate change could be enormous. Climate change could affect human health directly; it could substantially alter production costs (for example, that of heating), and it could have enormous impact on the economic productivity of ecological systems. However, very little is known about the likely magnitude, or in some cases even the direction, of possible climatic change. These problems must be dealt with at the federal or even international level. Since these are potential consequences of future pollution, it does not seem likely that we have experienced any climatic improvement benefits due to control of pollutants to date. Therefore this type of benefit will not be discussed further in this book.

Other Effects

Both air and water pollutants can have or cause odors and tastes that affect individuals' utility and welfare without adversely affecting physiological health. Also, when smog impairs the view of a nearby mountain range, this could result in a loss of amenity values. Because aesthetic effects such as these are often not associated with the direct use of environmental resources, they pose difficult measurement and valuation problems. But to the extent that improvements in amenities yield utility gains that are reflected in willingness to pay, they are nevertheless every bit as real, in an economic sense, as the benefits of improved human health.

STAGES IN THE PRODUCTION OF BENEFITS

The process by which the benefits of environmental improvement are produced by pollution control policy has three distinct stages. The estimation of the benefits of environmental regulatory policy requires knowledge of the relationships involved in each of these stages. The stages are:

1. Pollution control policy leads to improvements in environmental quality. Regulations such as emission standards or effluent charges, if effective, induce polluters to reduce their discharges. Changes in the temporal and spatial pattern of discharges lead to changes in the temporal and spatial patterns of air and water quality.

2. Changes in environmental quality result in changes in the types and levels of human uses of the environment. These changes may be reflected in physiological and physical changes in humans and other living species or in nonliving things, for example, materials and structures. Or they may be reflected in altered patterns of human activity, for example, recreation.

3. Changes in human uses of the environment affect utility or welfare. These changes can, in principle, be measured in monetary equivalents, that is, willingness to pay.

The first stage is almost entirely noneconomic in nature because it involves a variety of physical, chemical, and biological processes and relationships. The third stage is wholly within the realm of economics because it involves demand and production theory and the theory of economic value. The second stage involves the interface between the noneconomic and economic stages of the production of benefits. Understanding this stage is essential if empirical estimates of benefits are to be made. Yet this seems to be the least understood of the three stages and is, perhaps, the most serious present barrier to successful benefit estimation.

Figure 2.1 shows the application of this three-stage framework to water quality benefits associated with improvement in ambient water quality. A variety of substances are discharged to water bodies. These discharges can affect physical, chemical, and biological indicators of water quality, such as dissolved oxygen, temperature, algae levels, and fish populations. Changes in these indicators can be predicted with water quality models. The resulting water quality, as measured by these indicators, can affect human use of the water body. This includes withdrawal uses—for example, industrial or municipal water supply and irrigation—or in-stream uses—for example, fishery production or recreation. The major difficulty in this stage arises from the fact that only rarely is the level of use a simple function of a single water quality indicator like dissolved oxygen. Rather, uses such as commercial fisheries and recreation depend in complex ways on the whole range of physical, chemical, and biological water quality indicators.

The third stage in estimating water quality benefits involves determining the monetary values that people place on such things as improved recreation opportunities, increases in fish production, and availability of particular species of fish. Regarding the analysis of this stage, there is a well-developed theory of economic value. The theory provides a number of approaches for estimating these values under different circumstances. These will be discussed below.

Figure 2.2 shows a similar application of the framework to the abatement of air pollution. Understanding Stage 1 is the task of the atmospheric scientists who study photochemistry, atmospheric dispersion and transport, and the like. They must provide the air quality models to relate changes in emissions to changes in the ambient concentrations of the substances of interest.

Developing an understanding of the effects changes in air quality have on agricultural productivity and materials damages is a technical problem for botanists, plant physiologists, and materials engineers. But economic models are also necessary because the effects and their valuation also depend on human responses—changes in cropping patterns, materials substitutions, and a variety of mitigating activities. These must be analyzed properly if we are to have an accurate picture of the effects of air pollution on human activity and welfare. Similarly, we must look to the biomedical sciences for information on the health effects of air pollution. But a full understanding of the relationship between air pollution and the health status of the U.S. population requires a comprehensive epidemiological analysis which controls for socioeconomic influences and other confounding variables, such as diet, life

Stages in the Production of Benefits 15

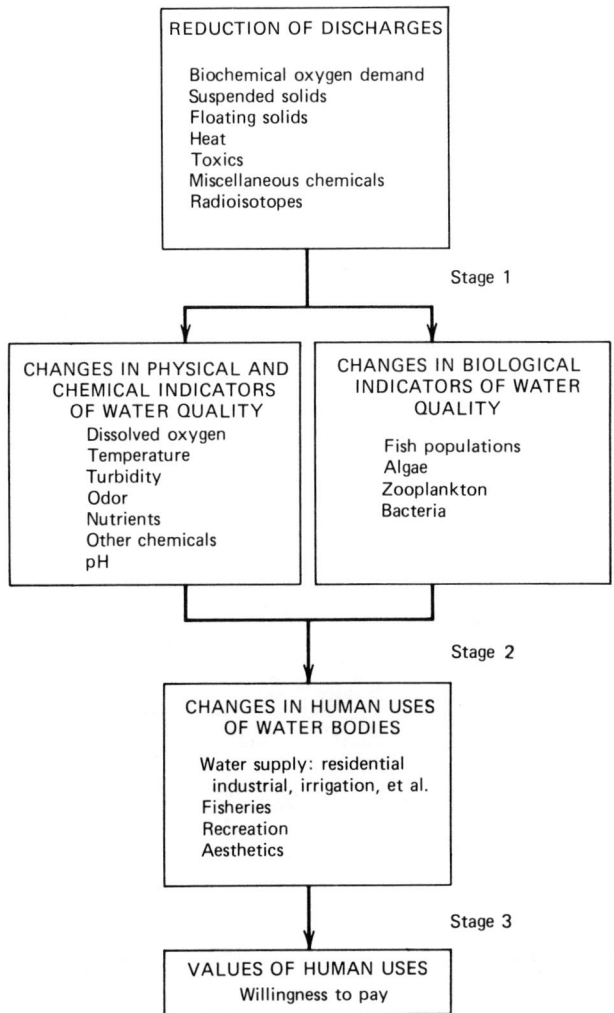

Figure 2.1. The production of benefits from improved ambient water quality.

style, and occupational exposures to harmful substances (Freeman, 1982). Economists have played and will continue to play an important, if controversial, role in the analysis of the health effects of air pollution.

The estimation of the values of improved air quality is a task for economists. I turn now to a discussion of the concept of benefits and a review of alternative approaches to determining monetary values.

16   Defining and Measuring Benefits

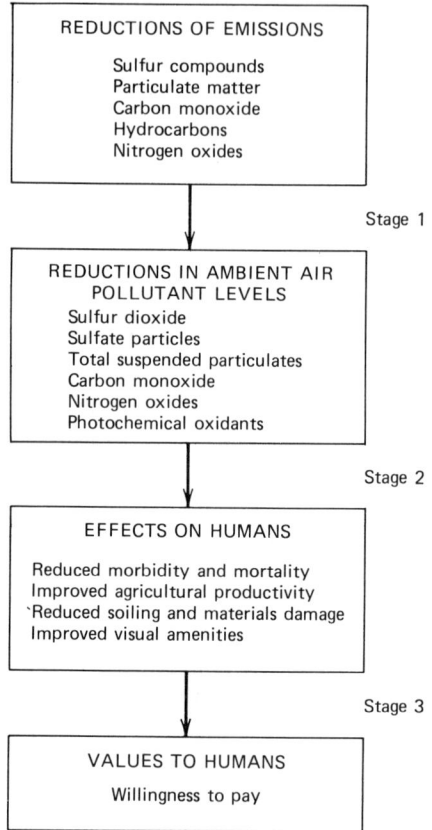

Figure 2.2. The production of benefits from improved ambient air quality.

APPROACHES TO DETERMINING VALUES

The benefit of an environmental improvement for an individual is a monetary measure of the increase in his or her welfare or utility. Since it is generally agreed among economists that utility cannot be directly measured in any meaningful way, how is this monetary equivalent to be determined? Fortunately there is a conceptual basis for determining this monetary value. It rests on the plausible assumption that when confronted with two alternative situations an individual can indicate which she prefers—or state that she is indifferent between them. If one situation is preferred, it must be because it conveys more utility. And if there is indifference, the two situations must convey the same utility.

Suppose there is an environmental improvement that will move the individual from Situation A to Situation B. The benefit of this change can be measured in either of two ways. The first is to determine the maximum sum of money the individual would be willing to pay rather than do without the environmental improvement. This maximum sum, called WTP for short, is the amount that would make her indifferent between paying for and having the improvement (Situation B) and staying at Situation A but not having to pay anything. WTP is the amount of money loss that would just offset the gain in utility due to moving to Situation B.

The second approach is to determine the amount of money the individual would accept (WTA) as an alternative to receiving the environmental improvement. WTA is the sum that would make her indifferent between Situation B on the one hand and Situation A plus the money on the other. It is the sum that has the same effect on utility as the environmental improvement.[1]

In principle WTP and WTA need not be exactly equal. WTP is constrained by the individual's income. The individual could not pay more than her income for the improvement. Yet there is in principle no upper limit on the amount that she could require as compensation for foregoing the improvement. A priori reasoning does not provide an objective basis for selecting one of these approaches as better in all circumstances. However, fortunately for empirical benefit estimation, it has been determined that these two approaches will give virtually equal answers to most of the empirically relevant benefit questions to be asked. The differences between the two approaches can be safely ignored provided that the WTP measure is small relative to total income, say, no more than 10% of income (Willig, 1976). All of the benefit estimates presented in this book fall well within this limit.

The definition of benefits as willingness to pay implies the existence of a demand curve for the effects of the environmental improvement. In the conventional economic analysis of a good that can be bought in a market, the demand curve shows the quantity of the good that the individual would purchase at any given market price. For example, if X in Figure 2.3 could be purchased at a price of P_1, this individual would purchase X_1 units. If the price were lower, the individual would purchase a larger quantity.

Demand curves of this type exist in principle for all goods, whether or not they can be bought in a market. But for nonmarket goods such as the amenities associated with environmental improvement, the demand curve can be given a different interpretation. For any given quantity of X available at a point in time, the demand curve shows the maximum amount the individual would pay for a small increase in X, that is, the *marginal*

---

[1] For a more formal discussion of these two approaches, see Freeman (1979, Chapter 3).

18   Defining and Measuring Benefits

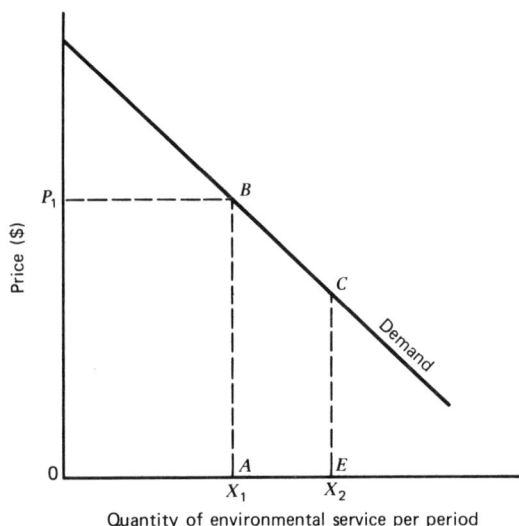

Figure 2.3.   The demand curve for an environmental service and willingness to pay.

willingness to pay. If the available quantity were X_1 in Figure 2.3, the individual would be willing to pay P_1 for a small increase in X. This is the benefit, or more precisely the marginal benefit, of an increase in X.

The willingness to pay for a nonmarginal increase in X, for example, to X_2, can be calculated as follows. Starting at X_1, the WTP for a one-unit increase in X is the vertical distance to the demand curve, or P_1. The WTP for the second unit, given that $X_1 + 1$ is now available, is the vertical distance to the demand curve at this point—slightly less than P_1. Continue this exercise with one-unit increases in X until X_2 is reached. The total WTP for the whole increase is the sum of the WTPs for each step along the way. This total WTP is approximated by the area under the demand curve between X_1 and X_2, or the area ABCE in Figure 2.3.[2] The total benefit to all the people in the economy is the sum of the WTPs for all affected individuals.

To estimate the benefits of an environmental improvement, we must obtain information, either by direct or indirect means, on the demand curve for the beneficial environmental effect. If the services of the environment could be purchased in a perfectly functioning market, estimating the demand curve would be a fairly straightforward problem in econometrics. However, environmental quality cannot generally be bought or sold in markets. This is in part because only one level of quality can be provided at a time, and

---

[2]For a more rigorous derivation of this result, see Freeman (1979, Chapter 3).

individuals are not free to vary independently the level of environmental services they consume. Also, once a given level of environmental quality is provided to some individuals, it may not be possible to prevent others from enjoying its services without paying the price for those services. These characteristics of environmental services lead to market failure. Without a market, there are no price and quantity data from which a demand function can be estimated.

In those cases in which market processes have failed to reveal these values directly, the techniques for estimating benefits involve a kind of detective work, that is, piecing together the clues about the values individuals place on environmental services. People leave these clues behind as they respond to other economic signals. There are three basic alternative approaches to determining the values which individuals place on improvements in environmental quality. They are: (1) *market approaches,* involving substitute and complementary relationships between market goods and environmental goods; (2) *surveys* in which people simply are asked to state their values or preference orderings for alternative levels of environmental quality; and (3) examination of *voting data* where the level of environmental quality has been an issue. Each approach is, in principle, capable of revealing information about individuals' preferences and values. Each also has limitations and problems in application.

MARKET APPROACHES

For those environmental improvements that lead to market effects, the application of a market approach in determining benefits is straightforward and often quite simple. For example, suppose that a decrease in the smog level in an area leads to an increase in the production of spinach. Provided that the price of spinach hasn't changed, the benefit is the increase in the market value of output (price times additional quantity). Or if an improvement in air quality leads to a reduction in the frequency with which a factory paints its exterior walls, the savings in the cost of painting can be taken as a measure of the benefit, at least as a first approximation.

As long as there are no significant effects on market prices, simple calculations of cost savings or value of increased production can be used to calculate benefits to agriculture, commercial fisheries, forestry, and materials and cleaning costs for producers. If price effects are significant, then consumers may capture some of the benefits of increased productivity through lower market prices. In these cases economic models must be developed to determine the producers' and consumers' benefits (Freeman, 1979, Chapter 4, especially pp. 63–68).

In those categories of nonmarket effects that do not entail increases in the outputs of marketed goods, there still may be impacts reflected in market prices and quantities for other goods and services that are substitutes or complements for the environmental good. In these cases market information can still be used in an indirect fashion to estimate values and benefits. For example, an improvement in water quality at a lake makes it a better site for boating and fishing. The increase in recreation activity is a reflection of the benefit of water quality improvement. The fact that people must incur time and money costs to travel to and from the lake provides a basis for imputing a money value to the improved water quality. Just how this calculation is performed will be described in Chapter 8. Other examples of indirect approaches based on market data include the use of differences in property values to reveal the values of differences in air quality across an urban area and the use of wage differentials to infer the value of differences in environmental amenities between cities or of differences in riskiness. These approaches will be described in more detail in later chapters.

Surveys

The second approach is simply to ask individuals, through surveys and direct questioning, what value they place on a specified change in environmental quality or how much quality they would "purchase" at a given stated price. Surveys of this type are sometimes called *bidding games*. One problem with this approach is how to induce individuals to give unbiased answers to questions about their willingness to pay. Where an individual believes that his share of the cost of providing improved environmental quality will be in some way proportional to his revealed willingness to pay for it, he has an incentive to understate his willingness to pay in order to reduce his repayment obligation. On the other hand, where assurances are given that tax burdens will not be affected by the answers given, the individual has an incentive to overstate his willingness to pay in an effort to assure that a given level of quality is provided or that quality is provided at a high level. These considerations introduce what is known as *strategic bias* into the data on willingness to pay.

In addition to these strategic biases, there is some evidence that certain structural characteristics of surveys have the potential for biasing responses. For example, in order to make the questions seem realistic, some surveys have stated that the vehicle for repayment will be an increase in the sales tax, or a surcharge on electric utility bills. If the respondents have some attitudes concerning the chosen means of repayment, this could introduce *vehicle bias* into responses. Also, in many surveys the questioner announces a value and then adjusts it upward or downward in fixed increments depending on the response. The starting point can introduce a bias.

It appears to be possible, however, to design survey questions so as to eliminate the incentives for biased response. The general approach is to design the survey instrument so as to minimize the occurrence of any linkage between a subject's response and either an actual repayment or an actual outcome. But devices to eliminate incentives for biased responses also have a second effect. They reduce the incentive to provide *accurate responses* (Freeman, 1979, Chapter 5). An accurate response is one that is consistent with the behavior that would be revealed if the good in question could actually be offered in a market. In the real world, an individual who takes an action inconsistent with his basic preferences, perhaps by mistake, incurs a cost or a loss of utility. In the purely hypothetical survey situation, there is no cost to being wrong, and therefore no incentive to undertake the mental effort to be accurate. The more hypothetical the situation posed to the individual, that is, the farther removed the situation is from his normal everyday experience, the less likely is the answer to be accurate.

Another set of problems has to do with perceptions and how to portray accurately the hypothetical situation to respondents. For example, if the purpose of the survey is to estimate the benefits of a specified water quality improvement, the questioner must find a way to describe the improved water quality accurately and in sufficient detail so that all respondents are reacting to similar perceptions of water quality improvement. Some of the best survey studies have combined photographs with descriptive textual material (for example, Brookshire, Ives, and Schulze, 1976; Randall, Ives, and Eastman, 1974; and Brookshire et al., 1979). But there are limits to the ability of both words and pictures to convey effectively all of the aesthetic dimensions associated with environmental improvements.

In summary, at the theoretical level the problems of bias, accuracy, and perceptions must give one pause about the effectiveness of surveys in measuring willingness to pay. However, at the practical level there is very little evidence concerning the seriousness or the magnitude of the errors introduced by these three problems. It would be very useful to have comparative studies of benefit estimates derived by alternative techniques. Very few of these have been done.[3] In the meantime, information derived from such surveys can be considered useful but not definitive.

---

[3]See Knetsch and Davis (1966) and Brookshire et al. (1982). Both of these studies have compared survey results with results from market approaches and found fairly close correspondence between the two.

Voting Behavior

A third approach is to place proposals that consist of alternative environmental quality levels and associated tax increases to referendum vote. Under certain circumstances the outcome of the voting process will be consistent with, and therefore reveal information about, the underlying demand curve for improved environmental services. The outcome of a referendum in any one jurisdiction only reveals whether the proposed level of environmental quality and the associated tax burden is preferable to the status quo for a majority of voters. However, if the outcomes of elections or referenda in a large number of jurisdictions are observed simultaneously, it can be assumed that they approximate the median preferences in each jurisdiction. Then each jurisdiction can be taken as a sample unit, and the data on the quantity of the good or service, price or tax share, and socioeconomic characteristics such as income, education, and occupation can be pooled and analyzed by multiple regression techniques to determine the relevant price and income elasticities of demand. Examples of this approach include Bergstrom and Goodman (1973) and Borcherding and Deacon (1972).

While these two studies suggest the feasibility of obtaining information on the demand for some kinds of public services from observations of political choices, the approach appears to have limited applicability to environmental quality services and the associated benefits of environmental improvements. The voting data must include both a stated level of environmental improvement and a tax cost to be imposed on voters. These procedures would be capable of generating information on the demand for environmental improvement only in those cases where the costs of pollution control would be financed from revenues raised within the political jurisdiction, that is, out of the pockets of voters.

Many of the important environmental problems for which benefit data are desired do not fit this description, at least in the United States. If some portion of pollution control costs is borne by the private sector or by some level of government other than the voting jurisdiction, then the link between the vote on environmental improvement and the tax share or price is broken, and the vote cannot be interpreted as revealing anything about the economic demand for improving environmental quality. Also the voting approach would only be applicable where both the benefits and costs of a pollution control policy fell entirely within the applicable political jurisdiction.

Assigning Arbitrary Prices or Values

Where it is impossible or impractical to determine actual values from individuals, politically responsible decision makers may wish to assign their own shadow prices or values to the effects of improvements in environmental quality. For example, the National Academy of Sciences used a value per life saved of $200,000 in estimating the benefits of reducing emissions from automobiles (National Academy of Sciences, 1974). Empirical benefit estimates derived from any of the three approaches described above still involve an element of judgment about the reliability of the data base and the empirical technique. This fourth approach acknowledges the judgment element in valuation and makes the value judgment explicit. Such judgments have more credence when there is some empirical justification for the values chosen. Because these judgments are typically made in administrative agencies rather than in Congress or state legislatures, they are termed *bureaucratic shadow prices.*

Problems in Estimating Benefits

A clear understanding of Stages 1 and 2 is necessary if monetary benefits are to be estimated. Yet there are a number of serious problems that impede the development of information on the relationships between the discharges of specific substances and the possible adverse physical, physiological, chemical, and biological effects. The analyst may lack information on the possible consequences of discharging a particular substance. Or apparent adverse effects may be observed—for example, ill health in a population—but the causes are unknown. Appropriate environmental policies cannot be designed or evaluated in the absence of information on the links between pollutants and their effects.

One type of problem in developing this information arises because of the stochastic nature of discharges and environmental processes. Discharge rates may vary systematically or stochastically because of, for example: changes in plant operating conditions; changes in demands for plant output, such as electricity; or existence of batch processes and slug discharges. Even for a given rate of discharge, natural system processes—which translate discharges into environmental quality—commonly vary over time because of stochastic or systematic variation in natural systems conditions, for example, wind speed and direction, temperature, solar input, or streamflow. This variation poses difficult problems for the analysis of both Stages 1 and 2. Some effects may be systematically related to extremes in exposure, while others might be related to arithmetic means or to cumulative exposures over time.

A second problem concerns perceptions of environmental quality and their relationships to human uses of the environment. This is a particular problem for those categories of benefits known as recreation and aesthetics. Which measurable indicators of environmental quality best coincide with individuals' perceptions? How accurate are individuals' perceptions? Are perceptions altered by new information and public discussion of pollution problems? If so, in what way or ways? Finally, to the extent that perceptions and objective indicators of environmental quality diverge, which serve better to explain individuals' behavior with respect to uses of the environment?

A third problem is the possibility of synergistic and antagonistic relationships among polluting substances and their influences on human uses. These can complicate the identification of cause-and-effect relationships and the measurement of dose-response functions.

Pollution can cause changes in ecological systems that have no obvious or direct impact on the production or consumption activities of humans. In such cases there is no obvious way of attaching monetary values to these effects within the individual preference-based economic framework. Westman (1977) suggests that impacts that result in decreases in ecological functions be valued at the cost of replacing those functions. For example, if an air pollutant reduces nitrogen fixation in soils, the damage could be calculated on the basis of the costs of manufacturing and applying an equivalent amount of chemical nitrogen fertilizer. This could be an appropriate basis for valuation if the replacement activities were actually undertaken. But the ecological functions lost may have little or no value to humans *at the margin*, that is, for small perturbations from existing levels. In other words, those lost functions would not actually be replaced because replacement costs exceed benefits.

It seems preferable to acknowledge that these ecological impacts lie outside the economic rubric. To admit that economics has nothing to say on such questions would make clear our ignorance concerning the significance of these effects for human welfare and highlight the necessity for making explicit judgments about the value and significance of such effects when making decisions about environmental policy. If benefits estimates in terms of replacement costs were provided, decision makers would be encouraged to add them up with benefit measures derived according to willingness to pay and individual preferences. This would reduce the usefulness of the overall figures because they would no longer be based upon a common set of economic concepts, definitions, and analytical framework.

REFERENCES

Bergstrom, Theodore C., and Robert P. Goodman. "Private Demands for Public Goods," *American Economic Review*, 63, no. 3 (June, 1973), 280–296.

Borcherding, Thomas E., and Robert T. Deacon. "The Demand for Services of Nonfederal Governments," *American Economic Review*, 62, no. 5 (December, 1972), 891–901.

References

Brookshire, David S., Ralph C. d'Arge, William D. Schulze, and Mark A. Thayer. *Methods Development for Assessing Tradeoffs in Environmental Management, Vol. 2: Experiments in Valuing Nonmarket Goods.* Washington, D.C.: Environmental Protection Agency, 1979.

Brookshire, David S., Berry C. Ives, and William D. Schulze. "The Valuation of Aesthetic Preferences," *Journal of Environmental Economics and Management,* 3, no. 4 (December, 1976), 325–346.

Brookshire, David S., Mark A. Thayer, William D. Schulze and Ralph C. d'Arge. "Valuing Public Goods: A Comparison of Survey and Hedonic Approaches," *American Economic Review,* 72, no. 1 (March, 1982), 165–177.

Freeman, A. Myrick, III. *The Benefits of Environmental Improvement: Theory and Practice.* Baltimore: Johns Hopkins University Press, 1979.

———. "The Health Implications of Residuals Discharges: A Methodological Overview in V. Kerry Smith and John V. Krutilla, eds., *Explorations in Natural Resource Economics.* Baltimore: Johns Hopkins University Press, 1982.

Knetsch, Jack L., and Robert K. Davis. "Comparisons of Methods for Recreation Evaluation," in Allen V. Kneese and Stephen C. Smith, eds., *Water Research.* Baltimore: Johns Hopkins University Press, 1966.

National Academy of Sciences, Coordinating Committee on Air Quality Studies. *Air Quality and Automobile Emission Control, Vol. 4. The Costs and Benefits of Automobile Emission Control.* Washington, D.C.: National Academy of Sciences, 1974.

Randall, Alan, Berry Ives, and Clyde Eastman. "Bidding Games for Evaluation of Aesthetic Environmental Improvement," *Journal of Environmental Economics and Management,* 1, no. 2 (August, 1974), 132–149.

Westman, Walter E. "How Much Are Nature's Services Worth?" *Science,* 197 (September, 2, 1977), 960–964.

Willig, Robert D. "Consumer's Surplus Without Apology," *American Economic Review,* 66, no. 4 (September, 1976), 589–597.

3

INTRODUCTION TO AIR POLLUTION CONTROL BENEFITS

The Clean Air Act Amendments of 1970 established a major federal policy effort to control stationary and mobile sources of air pollution. In the following four chapters, I review and evaluate a number of previous efforts to estimate air pollution damages and pollution control benefits and use these studies to develop my own best judgment estimates of the most reasonable and high and low values of the benefits achieved by this law. The categories of benefits are: improved human health (both mortality and morbidity); reduced cleaning costs and soiling; reduced materials damages; improved agricultural productivity; and improved aesthetics and amenities, such as visibility. Finally, my estimates of benefits are compared with estimated pollution control costs in an effort to draw some inferences about the economic justification of the present policy. As will be seen, there are substantial uncertainties surrounding my estimate of benefits. The low and high estimates differ by an order or magnitude (a factor of 10). Nevertheless the available evidence supports the conclusion that the control of stationary sources has produced benefits substantially in excess of costs; while the mobile source control program appears to be economically unjustified, with costs well in excess of likely benefits.

The point of reference for this analysis is air quality levels in 1970, the year the Clean Air Act Amendments were passed. I estimate the annual benefits realized by the 1978 population because of improvements in air quality between 1970 and 1978. It must be recognized that this may be only a portion of the total benefits achieved by the implementation of air pollution control policies since 1970. In the absence of the federal law, it is likely that growth in population, production, and income and perhaps changes in fuel prices and availability would have led to increases in emissions and deterioration of air quality between 1970 and 1978. The benefits due to prevention of further degradation, if known, should be added to the abatement benefits estimated here.

A NATIONAL BENEFITS MODEL

The three stages in the production of benefits can be described algebraically by a set of three equations:

$$Q = Q(D) \tag{3.1}$$

$$X = X(Q) \tag{3.2}$$

$$V = V(X) \tag{3.3}$$

where
$D \equiv$ the rate of discharge of the pollutant
$Q \equiv$ a measure of ambient air quality
$X \equiv$ the level of some activity or use of the ambient air
$V \equiv$ the monetary value of the use of the ambient air, measured by individuals' willingness to pay.

Q varies inversely with D, while X and V are positive functions of Q and X respectively.

By substitution we have

$$V = f(D) \tag{3.4}$$

And the benefits B of a policy that brings about a reduction in discharges from D_1 to D_2 are

$$B = \Delta V = f(D_2) - f(D_1) \tag{3.5}$$

In the ex ante analysis of a proposed policy, it is necessary to use air quality models of dispersion, transportation, and transformation phenomena in order to predict the impact of a given reduction of emissions on the relevant measures of ambient air quality. In this ex poste analysis, it is possible to dispense with Equation 3.1 and to use the observed changes in air quality for benefit estimation. Of course, one must question whether observed changes in air quality were in fact a consequence of the policy in question rather than the result of other factors quite independent of the policy. Trends in various measures of air quality will be discussed in the next section.

The information contained in Equation 3.2 can also be expressed in the form of a damage function or dose–effect relationship showing the negative consequences on X of increases in pollution (decreases in Q). To be usable for benefit estimation, these relationships must incorporate not only information on per-unit damages or effects (for example, reduction in crop yield per acre or increase in morbidity per 100,000 of exposed population), but also information on the extent of exposure to changes in air quality (for example, numbers of acres or numbers of people affected). The benefit estimates of Chapters 4 through 7 are based primarily on estimates of per-unit damage functions combined with estimates of the numbers of affected people, areas of land, quantities of materials, and so forth.

The conversion of physical consequences into monetary benefit measures as in Equation 3.3 requires economic models of demand and willingness to pay. In general, economic reasoning suggests that the willingness to pay for an additional unit of X will be a decreasing function of X. In other words, the marginal willingness to pay for X will be positive but decreasing. Unfortunately, in many cases the economic models and data necessary to estimate and use willingness to pay functions are not available. A second-best approach in such instances is to use point estimates of marginal willingness to pay at a specific level of the environmental service or activity and to assume that this price, or shadow price, is a constant for all levels of environmental quality. This is equivalent to assuming that the demand curve of Figure 2.3 is horizontal. If the change in environmental quality is small, the error involved in this approximation is not likely to be serious.

In order to estimate the benefits of an air pollution control policy, ideally one should implement the model represented by Equations 3.1–3.3 separately for each substance controlled and category of benefits, and for each separate region or airshed affected by the policy. National benefits could then be calculated by summing the different categories of benefits in each region and then summing across all regions of the country. If this procedure is used, the estimate reflects the differences in the regional composition of air pollution and regional responses to federal policy as well as differences in the socioeconomic characteristics of regions that affect the uses made of the environment and values attached to them. The limited time and resources available for this project ruled out the fully disaggregated approach described here. Rather, although separate estimates are made for each major category of benefits, there is no effort to disaggregate on a regional basis. It is assumed, in effect, that the air quality is the same in all airsheds and changes by the same amount. And other regional differences in uses of the environment, etc. are assumed to be unimportant.

TRENDS IN AIR QUALITY

The first step in implementing the simplified national benefits estimation model is to determine the average change in air pollution levels for the nation as a whole for the relevant pollutants. As discussed earlier, the conceptually correct basis for estimating the benefits of an air pollution control policy is to compare actual pollution levels in the year of interest with a prediction of what pollution levels would have been in that year in the absence of policy. Given the resources available for this project, it is not possible to develop such a prediction. Rather, I will base the estimates of benefits on the actual reduction in the average levels of suspended particulates and sulfur dioxide between 1970 and 1978.

For purposes of policy design, it would be most helpful to have separate estimates of the benefits of controlling each of the major air pollutants, especially suspended particulates, sulfur compounds (sulfur dioxide and sulfate particles), carbon monoxide, nitrogen oxides, and photochemical oxidants. However, we do not presently have the knowledge of dose–response functions required to provide disaggregated estimates of benefits. One reason for this is the high degree of correlation in the levels of, and exposures to, some pairs of pollutants—such as suspended particulates and sulfur compounds. These two compounds are emitted primarily from stationary sources rather than from mobile sources like the automobile. For this reason, these two substances will be considered together under the heading of "Stationary Source Pollutants." More than half of all nitrogen oxides emissions come from stationary sources. However, the major health problem associated with nitrogen oxides is thought to stem from its role as a precursor, with hydrocarbons, of photochemical oxidants. Control policies for these substances have focused on mobile sources. Therefore nitrogen oxides, photochemical oxidants, and carbon monoxide will be considered separately under the heading of "Mobile Source Pollutants."

Stationary Source Pollutants

Table 3.1 shows several measures of concentrations of suspended particulates for the years 1970–76 and sulfur dioxide for the years 1972–77. The table presents both composite national averages and the 90th percentiles of the distributions across sampling sites. The last column of the table shows that, by various measures, suspended particulate pollution has been reduced by between 12 and almost 17% between 1970 and 1976 and sulfur dioxide

TABLE 3.1 Trends in National Suspended Particulates and Sulfur Dioxide Concentrations and Emissions

	1970	1971	1972	1973	1974	1975	1976	1977	Percent Reduction
I. *Total Suspended Particulates (2350 Sampling Sites)*									
A. *Annual Mean*									
1. Composite average ($\mu g/m^3$)	70.4	69.6	67.1	65.4	62.5	60.8	61.8	61	−13.4
2. 90th Percentile ($\mu g/m^3$)	106	104	100	96	92	88	90	86	−18.9
B. *Peak Daily Reading (24 hr. Maximum)*									
1. Composite average ($\mu g/m^3$)	234	230.1	211.6	209.1	198.8	190.3	200.4	—	−14.4
2. 90th Percentile ($\mu g/m^3$)	390	380	345	345	320	310	325	—	−16.7
II. *Sulfur Dioxide (722 Sampling Sites) Annual Mean*									
1. Composite Average ($\mu g/m^3$)	—	—	23.0	21.4	20.7	20.4	19.7	19.4	−15.7
2. 90th Percentile ($\mu g/m^3$)	—	—	52	48	44	42	40	40	−23.0

Source: Environmental Protection Agency (1977) and Environmental Protection Agency (1978).

pollution has been reduced by between 16 and 23% between 1972 and 1977. On a national average basis, pollution levels are within the national primary air quality standards for suspended particulates and sulfur dioxide. But as the 90th percentile rows show, some parts of the country do experience suspended particulate levels above the national primary standards of 260 µg/m^3 for 24-hour readings and 75 µg/m^3 for the annual average.

National Economic Research Associates (NERA, 1980) has used a more comprehensive modeling approach to estimate the differences in emissions in 1978 between the results of the current policy and what would have occurred without the Clean Air Act Amendments of 1970. Their model incorporates economic factors affecting emissions so that the separate effect of this policy can be identified. In order to predict the resulting change in air quality, they regressed national average air quality levels on national emissions estimates. They found that for suspended particulates a 1% reduction in emissions was associated with a 0.22% reduction in ambient concentrations. For sulfur dioxide, a 1% reduction in emissions resulted in a 0.05% reduction in ambient concentrations (NERA, pp. 6-8, 6-9). Using these relationships, NERA concluded that the federal policy was responsible for an 18% reduction in sulfur dioxide concentration and a 27% reduction in suspended particulates.

These aggregate data and models give only a crude picture of changes in the degree of exposure of the American population to air pollutants over time. But as a first approximation based on the EPA monitoring data and the NERA model, I assume that the urban population of the United States experienced a reduction in suspended particulate and sulfur dioxide pollution of approximately 20% between 1970 and 1978. There is some corroboration for this assumption in the report from the Environmental Protection Agency that between 1972 and 1977 there was a 29% reduction in the number of people who were exposed to annual mean suspended particulate levels in excess of the national primary standard. (Environmental Protection Agency, 1978, p. 2-1).

There are two additional factors to consider here in evaluating this assumption. First, if the health effects of concern are due primarily to exposure to sulfate particles, the assumption of a 20% decrease will lead to a substantial overestimate of realized benefits. This is because there has been virtually no decline in sulfate levels over the past 10 years. On the other hand, if, as seems likely, the largest absolute and percentage reductions in pollution have occurred in the dirtiest areas, and if these are areas with larger populations, the *population weighted* average reduction in pollution could be higher than the unweighted average of 20% assumed here. Thus our assumption could also result in an underestimation of realized benefits.

Lave and Seskin (1970, 1977), Waddell (1974), and Crocker et al. (1979), among others, have also published estimates of the national benefits of air pollution control. One important factor in explaining the differences in the magnitude of benefits among these studies is differences in the assumed or postulated improvement in air quality. These studies used the following assumptions:

Lave and Seskin (1970)	50%
Waddell (1974)	26%
Lave and Seskin (1977)	88% for sulfur compounds
	58% for suspended particulates
Crocker et al. (1979)	60%

The Waddell figure was based on an estimate of the required reduction in pollution levels to assure that the primary standard for suspended particulates was met. The first Lave and Seskin figure and that of Crocker et al. are essentially arbitrary. And the second Lave and Seskin figure is based on an EPA estimate of the reduction in pollution emissions expected from the implementation of stationary source control requirements of the Clean Air Act Amendments of 1970. They assumed that ambient pollution levels would decrease proportionately with emissions. However the relationship between national emissions and national average air quality levels is not one of simple proportionality. While particulate levels were being reduced by between 12% and 17% between 1970 and 1977, particulate emissions fell by 44%. And the 15–23% reduction in ambient sulfur dioxide levels between 1972 and 1977 was accompanied by a reduction in national emissions of sulfur compounds of only 8% (Environmental Protection Agency, 1978, p. 5-1).

It would also be useful to know the expected benefits of further improvement in air quality, for example, to full attainment of national primary or national secondary ambient air quality standards. However, the aggregate approach being employed here is not suitable for making such estimates. This approach implies a uniform percentage reduction in pollution levels experienced by all of the affected population. This is surely not precisely true, but it is more reasonable as a representation of the experience between 1970 and 1978 than it would be of the results of moving to obtain compliance in the present nonattainment areas. This is because where national primary standards are not now being met, the appropriate strategy would be selective controls in these areas. This would mean that only that portion of the population presently exposed to violations of the air quality standards would experience improved air quality. EPA estimates that in 1977 only 27% of the metropolitan population of the United States was exposed to suspended particulate levels above the national primary standard (Environmental Protection Agency, 1978, p. 2-1).

Mobil Source Pollutants

The Council on Environmental Quality (1978, pp. 19–26) has reported that, in a sample of 15 monitoring stations in 13 cities across the country, the number of days for which violations of the national primary oxidant standard occurred fell by about 20% between 1973 and 1976. The number of severe violations (over 0.20 ppm.) fell by six percent; and there was a 22% reduction in less severe violations. These data were the basis for the assumption used in my earlier report that oxidant pollution levels declined by 20% between 1970 and 1978 (Freeman, 1979). However, more recent reports from the Council on Environmental Quality (1980, pp. 163–166) and the Environmental Protection Agency (1980, pp. 10–11) show no decline in the annual averages of daily maximum ozone concentrations either for the nation as a whole or for monitoring sites in California.

These data are not necessarily contradictory. The numbers of violations reflect the extremes of air pollution that can occur during adverse meteorological conditions and/or periods of unusually high emissions. Intermittent control programs that reduce emissions during periods of adverse meteorology—for example, programs to discourage automobile use—could result in fewer peak concentrations and violations of air quality standards without having a significant effect on annual average concentrations. The average concentrations are at about 0.06 ppm., while the primary standard in effect during the period in questions was 0.08 ppm.

The question of which set of data to use in estimating benefits hinges on whether damages due to ozone occur only during extreme pollution levels when the standard is violated or are due primarily to the chronic effects of exposures at lower levels. There does not seem to be a consensus on this question. But as there is some evidence supporting the hypothesis of no threshold effects and chronic damages for oxidants and other pollutants, I will assume that there has been no improvement in the relevant measure of ozone pollution during the period 1970–78 (Freeman, 1978, pp. 30–33).[1] The uncertainties about the role of extreme pollution levels in causing damages and the proper measure of changes in air quality will be reflected in the range of the high and low estimates of benefits.

---

[1] The NERA (1980) model of emissions and air quality estimates a 13% decline in ozone concentrations compared with the no-control scenario.

Both the Council on Environmental Quality (1980, pp. 165–167) and the Environmental Protection Agency (1980, pp. 8–9) report substantial downward trends in carbon monoxide concentrations. CEQ estimates a 33% decrease in the annual average of daily maximum concentrations between 1973 and 1978. However, I have not found any empirical basis for attributing significant benefits to reduced carbon monoxide levels.

The data on nitrogen dioxide (NO_2) concentrations apparently do not permit any inferences about trends for this pollutant. Before calculating an average of readings across many monitoring sites, it is necessary to establish some criteria for the adequacy of the data from each site. Sites might be excluded on the basis of the frequency with which readings are taken, gaps in the readings, and so forth. CEQ (1980, p. 169) reports that national averages and estimated trends are very sensitive to the criteria used to determine which sites are included in the averaging process. They concluded, "Because the trend in annual NO_2 concentrations appears to be so sensitive to selection criteria when there are insufficient data, it is not included this year" (Council on Environmental Quality, 1980, p. 169). For this reason, and because EPA (1980, p. 13) reports an 18% increase in emissions of NO_2 from 1970 to 1979, no benefits are attributed to the control of nitrogen oxides in this report.[2]

REFERENCES

Council on Environmental Quality. *Environmental Quality—1978.* Washington, D.C.: U.S. Government Printing Office, 1978.

———. *Environmental Quality—1980.* Washington, D.C.: U.S. Government Printing Office, 1980.

Crocker, Thomas D., William D. Schulze, Shaul Ben-David, and Allen V. Kneese, *Methods Development for Assessing Air Pollution Control Benefits, Vol. 1: Experiments in the Economics of Epidemiology.* Washington, D.C.: Environmental Protection Agency, 1979.

Freeman, A. Myrick, III, "Air and Water Pollution Policy," in Paul R. Portney, ed., *Current Issues in U.S. Environmental Policy.* Baltimore: Johns Hopkins University Press, 1978.

———. *The Benefits of Air and Water Pollution Control: A Review and Synthesis of Recent Estimates.* A report to the U.S. Council on Environmental Quality, 1979.

Lave, Lester B. and Eugene P. Seskin. "Air Pollution and Human Health," *Science,* 169, no. 3947 (August 21, 1970), 723–733.

---

[2]The NERA (1980) emissions and air quality model estimates a 4% decline in nitrogen dioxide concentrations in comparison with the no-control scenario.

References

———. *Air Pollution and Human Health*. Baltimore: Johns Hopkins University Press, 1977.

National Economic Research Associates, Inc. *Cost-Effectiveness and Cost-Benefit Analysis of Air Quality Regulation*. Business Roundtable Air Quality Project, Vol. 4. New York: Business Roundtable, 1980.

U.S. Environmental Protection Agency. *National Air Quality and Emissions Trends Report—1976*. Research Triangle Park, 1977.

———. *National Air Quality and Emissions Trends Report—1977*. Research Triangle Park, 1978.

———. *Trends in the Quality of the Nation's Air—A Report to the People*. Washington, D.C., 1980.

Waddell, Thomas E., *The Economic Damages of Air Pollution*. Washington, D.C.: Environmental Protection Agency, 1974.

4

THE HEALTH BENEFITS OF AIR POLLUTION CONTROL

The procedure used in this study for estimating human health benefits involves three steps. The first is to determine the relationship between exposures to different levels of air quality and human health as measured by mortality and morbidity rates. The second step is to use this relationship to predict the changes in mortality and morbidity associated with some specified change in air quality and exposure to pollutants. The third step is to use monetary measures of willingness to pay to assign values to the predicted changes in mortality and morbidity.

Getting better information on the relationship between air quality and human health is itself a major and difficult research task.[1] A common approach is to use multivariate statistical techniques to test the hypothesis that there is a positive association between air pollution and either mortality or morbidity. These studies typically use data for mortality or morbidity rates for population groups aggregated by, for example, county, city, or Standard Metropolitan Statistical Area (SMSA). Because they are aggregated, these are sometimes termed *macroepidemiology studies.* Microepidemiology studies using individual data are conceptually superior in that it is possible to control for individual characteristics affecting health. But studies based on individuals as the unit of observation are more expensive and time consuming because they require major data gathering efforts.

As an alternative to large-scale statistical studies, analysts might attempt to derive dose–response functions extrapolated from laboratory studies of animals and of clinical effects on humans. Extrapolation from animal studies has been used for estimating the effects of some toxic chemicals and food

---

[1]See Freeman (1982) and references therein for further discussion. This topic is also discussed in Lave and Seskin (1977, Chapters 1 and 2). For reviews of the literature on health effects of air pollution, see Lave and Seskin (1977, Appendix A), and American Lung Association (1977; 1978).

additives but has not been used as a basis for estimating air pollution health effects. Clinical studies of humans usually show only acute health effects and at exposures higher than typical ambient levels. Thus they do not provide a basis for estimating the effects of exposure to ambient pollution concentrations.

Given an empirically or judgmentally derived dose-response function, the next step is to predict the change in mortality or morbidity conditional upon the expected change in air quality, holding all other variables constant. This is a straightforward computation. The third step is to determine the monetary value to be assigned to each death avoided or day of ill health prevented. This step raises some controversial questions. The appropriateness of an economic approach to policy analysis where matters of life and death are involved has been warmly debated.

In the next section I review economic approaches to determining the value of improvements in health. I then review the existing studies of the effects of stationary source pollutants (sulfur compounds and suspended particulates) on mortality and morbidity. On the basis of this review, I select synthesis or best judgment dose–effect relationships to predict the reductions in mortality and morbidity expected from the postulated 20% reduction in stationary source air pollution. Willingness to pay values are used to calculate the monetary benefits of improved air quality. A similar review is then conducted of studies of the health effects of mobile source pollution, and estimates of possible mobile source control benefits are presented.

VALUING HEALTH

A number of approaches to assigning monetary values to ill health or the loss of life have been proposed and used in the literature on the economics of health and safety. These approaches can be broadly categorized as determining values according to either individual preferences (willingness to pay), or resource or opportunity costs. What follows is a brief evaluation of these approaches.[2]

The most common method for valuing the premature loss of life or increased morbidity is the so-called productivity or human capital technique. It is a form of resource or opportunity cost approach to assigning values. This approach values each life lost at the present value of the expected stream of

---

[2]For more extensive discussions of alternative concepts of the value of life or safety, see Schelling (1968), Mishan (1971), Jones-Lee (1976), and Bailey (1980). Raiffa, Schwartz, and Weinstein (1977) present an excellent discussion of concepts and applications in the context of public sector decision making.

future earnings for that individual had that individual's premature death been avoided. Morbidity is valued according to the loss of output as measured by earnings or imputed earnings. This approach is based on the assumption that earnings reflect the individual's marginal productivity, that is, the individual's contribution to total economic output. With the death or illness of the individual, that output is lost.

There are three criticisms of this approach. First, the productivity measure of benefits has no necessary relationship to the theoretically correct measure, individual willingness to pay. Second, the productivity approach allows no role for the probabilistic nature of death and death avoidance in the health and safety areas or for differing individual attitudes or preferences toward risk and risk avoidance. An individual could pay no more than the present value of his or her earnings stream plus accumulated wealth to avoid certain death. But the statistical value of life based upon the person's willingness to pay for small probability changes could be several times this amount. Third, the implicit judgment underlying the productivity–human capital approach is that an individual is worth what he or she does, that is, that output is a measure of worth. According to this approach, preventing the premature death of a retired, unemployed, or disabled person would have no value. This is clearly an unacceptable ethical implication of the productivity concept.

Because of variation in patterns of earnings over the life cycle and differences in labor market experience among individuals, including discrimination, values derived from the productivity approach depend crucially on the age, sex, and race of the individuals involved. For example, using a 6% discount rate and 1972 patterns of earnings, saving the life of a white male between 30 and 34 years of age would prevent the loss of about $180,000 in discounted lifetime earnings (in 1972 dollars), while for a nonwhite woman of the same age, the earnings loss prevented would be only about $70,000 (Cooper and Rice, 1976). Some benefit–cost analyses using productivity values have attempted to adjust for the age, race, and sex composition of the population at risk. Others have used averages for the population as a whole.

Another component of the resource or opportunity cost of illness is expenditures on medical care, that is, doctors, hospitalization, drugs, and so on. Rice (1966) and Cooper and Rice (1976) have estimated the total direct costs of illness in the United States. This total includes those expenditures associated with both temporary illness and illnesses ending in death. Some of the studies discussed below have estimated the fraction of this total that can be attributed to air-pollution-induced illness.

The major alternative to the productivity measure is conceptually more attractive because it is consistent with the basic theory of welfare economics. It is to value increases in life expectancy or reductions in the probability of death due to accident or illness according to what affected individuals are willing to pay to achieve them. Individuals, in a variety of ways, act as if life expectancy were like any other economic good; that is, they are willing to trade off life expectancy for other goods and services that they value more highly or vice versa. They make decisions that involve reductions in life expectancy or increased probability of death in return for increases in income or other goods and services, revealing thereby that they perceive themselves to be better off having made these choices. Some people accept risky or hazardous jobs because of higher wages. Some people make their trips between cities by car or bus rather than by airplane because it is less expensive even though the chance of accidental death is greater.

As these examples make clear, the question is not how much a specific individual would be willing to pay to avoid certain death tomorrow. Rather, it is how much the individual would be willing to pay to achieve a small change in the probability of death during a given period. An individual's willingness to pay for changes in the probability of his death can be translated into a more convenient figure for evaluating strategies, namely, the value of *statistical life* or the value of a *statistical death* avoided. Suppose, in a group of 1,000 similar individuals, each individual has a willingness to pay of $1,000 for a policy that would reduce the probability of his or her death by .01. This policy is a form of collective good for the individuals involved. The benefit to the group is found by adding across all individuals. The aggregate willingness to pay is $1 million (1,000 × $1,000), and the expected number of deaths avoided is 10. The group's aggregate willingness to pay to avoid one death is then $100,000 ($1,000,000 ÷ 10). This we refer to as the statistical value per life.

Two approaches to the empirical measurement of willingness to pay and the statistical value of life have been used in the literature. One is to observe actual behavior and choices where individuals actually exchange or trade off changes in their risk levels for other things that have a monetary value. For example, if wage differentials among occupations are related to differences in occupational risk levels, these differences may be interpreted as reflecting, at the margin, individuals' tradeoffs between certain kinds of risks and money. The other approach is to conduct surveys, asking individuals a series of questions about hypothetical situations involving safety–money trade-offs. If the questions are carefully designed, and if individuals are capable of predicting accurately how they would act if actually placed in these hypothetical situations, their answers may reveal the money values they attach to reductions in risk. Neither approach captures the willingness to pay of relatives or close friends. Needleman (1976) has offered evidence that including others' willingnesses to pay could increase the statistical value of life by 25–100%.

One example of the behavioral approach is Blomquist's (1979) study of individual choice with respect to automobile seat belt use. Individuals can "purchase" decreased probability of death and injury in an automobile accident by taking the time to fasten their seat belts. Using data on seat belt use, effectiveness, and the value (opportunity cost) of time, Blomquist estimated the average value of life for a sample of about 5,000 individuals to be $370,000 in 1978 dollars.

There have been several studies using data on wage rates and various measures of risk to estimate the premiums in wages necessary to compensate workers for greater risk of death.[3] Study results differ because of differences in the data used, model specification, and the other variables used to explain wage differences. Estimates of the value of statistical life range from a low of about $0.3 million (Thaler and Rosen, 1976; Dillingham, 1979) to about $5 million (Smith, 1976; Olson, 1981), all in 1978 dollars. The results of the various studies are summarized in Table 4.1

There are similar differences in the results of two efforts to use the survey approach to obtaining values for statistical life. Acton (1973) obtained 36 responses from a stratified random sample of residents in the Boston area. He asked people to state their willingness to pay for a community program of emergency coronary care that would reduce each individual's probability of death by heart attack. Two different forms of the question implied values for statistical life of $47,000 and $72,000. Jones-Lee (1976) asked a similar small sample of individuals several questions about their willingness to accept higher airplane fares to travel on lines with lower probabilities of experiencing a fatal crash. The value of statistical life implied by the respondents was about $6.1 million.

These disparities among the estimates suggest that substantially more research is required before reliable estimates of the value of life can be obtained by these techniques. But the results do suggest order-of-magnitude bounds on the appropriate figures.

The published estimates of health benefits to be discussed in this chapter have relied primarily on the productivity approach. One exception is Crocker et al. (1979), who use estimates of willingness to pay derived from two of the wage differential studies cited above. In the "synthesis" estimate of health benefits to be derived below, I explicitly reject the productivity approach in

---

[3]See Thaler and Rosen (1976), Smith (1976), Viscusi (1978), Dillingham (1979), Brown (1980), and Olson (1981). For further review and discussion of these empirical results, see Smith (1979), Bailey (1980), and Blomquist (1981).

TABLE 4.1 Values of Life Derived from Wage Rate Studies (in Millions of 1978 Dollars)

Author	Estimate of Value of Life
Thaler and Rosen (1976)	$0.3–0.5 (range)
	$0.4 (most likely value)
Viscusi (1978)	$1.8–2.7
Smith (1976)	$2.2–5.1
Dillingham (1979)	$0.3
Brown (1980)	$0.8
Olson (1981)	$4.7

favor of a value based upon the willingness-to-pay studies cited here. Except for Acton's study of the willingness to pay for emergency coronary care, the estimates cited above range from approximately $0.3 million to $6 million. Although these figures span a range of over one order of magnitude, it seems highly likely that the "true" value for a representative individual in 1978 falls within this range. In the estimates below, I will use a value of $1 million per death avoided. However, the basis for the calculations will be provided so that the reader might easily substitute another value and compute alternative measures of benefits accordingly.

In their analysis of air pollution control benefits, NERA (1980) argue that $1 million per life is too high at least to value air pollution health effects. They offer three reasons for this view. First they argue that the wage rate studies by Dillingham (1979) and Thaler and Rosen (1976), being based on risk data classified by occupations, are superior to those of Smith (1976) and Viscusi (1978), who use risk data by industry. However, Brown (1980) also uses data by occupation and finds a substantially higher risk premium. Olson (1981) also suggests that certain adjustments Thaler and Rosen make to their risk data have the effect of biasing their estimates downward.

NERA also argues that the average age of those affected by air pollution is likely to be higher than that of the workers whose willingness to pay for risk avoidance is measured in wage rate studies. If at least beyond some age, willingness to pay is a decreasing function of age, then estimates of the value of life based on the working-age population would overstate the value of life for the older population at risk to air pollution. Decreasing willingness to pay is an empirical hypothesis that has not been tested against the evidence. And as I have shown elsewhere (Freeman, 1979, pp. 174–181), it is at least possible that willingness to pay could increase with age. Finally, it is not necessarily true that air pollution affects primarily the aged. Lave and Seskin

(1977) found significant associations between air pollution and age-specific mortality rates over all ages, including infants.

The third reason offered by NERA is that unless wage rate studies control explicitly for nonfatal accidents, the wage premium will reflect the willingness to pay to avoid both fatal and nonfatal accidents. In other words, it would be an overestimate of the willingness to pay to reduce the probability of death alone. Bailey (1980) also makes this point. Two of the studies listed in Table 4.1 did control for nonfatal accidents. Dillingham's estimate of the willingness to pay to avoid fatal accidents is one of the lowest values found by the wage differential method. But Olson, who also controls for nonfatal accidents, finds one of the highest values. In summary, it is not clear from this evidence that the appropriate value of life is substantially less than the $1 million used here.

Reductions in morbidity should also be valued according to willingness to pay. However, it is even more difficult to provide a firm empirical basis for the value of morbidity reduction. I will value reductions in morbidity alternatively at $20 and $40 per day of illness or restricted activity. The $40 figure is roughly the average daily earnings for those in the labor force. However, not all instances of morbidity result in lost earnings to individuals. They may work at reduced capacity, or take paid sick leave; and morbidity may occur on other than work days. On the other hand, the earnings measure does not reflect pain, discomfort, and anxiety. Again, the reader may substitute different values in computing the estimate of benefits.

In addition to these imputed values for reduction in mortality and days of morbidity, I will include under morbidity benefits an estimate of the savings in direct medical expenditures. An individual's willingness to pay to avoid the onset of an illness that might lead to death would, in principle, include the willingness to pay to avoid the burden of the direct expenditures on doctors, hospitalization, and the like. Thus adding direct expenditures to estimates of willingness to pay would seem to involve double counting. But there are two reasons why that is probably not the case.

First, the estimates of the willingness to pay to reduce the probability of death are derived primarily from data where accidental injury is the principal cause of death.[4] In such cases, the associated medical costs are likely to be small, and the associated pain, suffering, and anxiety would be of short duration. Thus the willingness to pay to reduce the probability of accidental death may be a substantial underestimate of the willingness to pay to avoid death by some other causes, for example, cancer. In the latter case, both medical expenses and pain and suffering may be substantially greater, as would the willingness to pay to avoid them.

[4]The exception is Thaler and Rosen (1976), who use data on total mortality rates by occupation.

Second, for institutional reasons such as medical insurance, individuals do not directly bear all of the medical costs of their illnesses. These costs would not influence the individual's willingness to pay to reduce the risk of incurring these illnesses. Yet they are opportunity costs to society. For these reasons, direct medical expenditures are added to willingness-to-pay measures in computing overall health benefits due to reduced mortality and morbidity.

STATIONARY SOURCES

There is now a substantial number of aggregate epidemiological studies dealing with the effects of suspended particulates, sulfur compounds, or both on human health. These studies have used a variety of cross-sectional, and in some cases longitudinal, data on mortality and/or morbidity and pollution levels for various population samples, including groupings by SMSA, city, county, and, in one case, census tracts within one urban county. We will first review those studies dealing with mortality and the estimates of health benefits (sometimes including morbidity) that have been based upon them. Then we will turn to the much smaller number of studies examining the relationship between morbidity and air pollution.

It should be noted that there is a good deal of controversy surrounding these studies. The major issues concern: the validity of air quality data from one or a few monitoring sites in each urban area as measures of the current exposures of the individuals residing in that area; the validity of current exposures as a measure of the long-term exposure history relevant to explaining chronic effects and mortality; the correct functional form; the appropriateness of single-equation models where certain kinds of interactions among dependent and explanatory variables are involved; and the adequacy of control for such factors as age, socioeconomic conditions, smoking, diet, and exposure to other environmental health hazards. Also, some researchers have argued that the observed correlations may be spurious and that the true magnitude of the effect is zero.

Studies on Mortality

Lave and Seskin, 1970

In 1970 Lave and Seskin published the first report of their ongoing research on the health effects of air pollution. They presented a thorough review of the existing literature on health effects and reported the results of their own regression analyses of data reported in this literature. They also reported the first results of their own cross-sectional analysis of 1960 mortality and pollution data for 114 SMSAs. This analysis was based on a simple linear regression model of the following form:

$$M = a + bP + cS + e$$

where M is the mortality rate, P is some measure of pollution, and S is a vector of socioeconomic variables such as percent nonwhite, percent over 65 years of age, and percent poor.

It will be most convenient to report their results, and others to follow, in the form of elasticities. An elasticity measure gives the percentage change in mortality associated with a 1% change in a pollution variable. In linear equations, these elasticities are computed at the mean values of the independent and dependent variables. The elasticities for Lave and Seskin's own regressions on U.S. data on mortality from all causes are as follows:

Total Death Rate		
Total suspended particulates		.05
Sulfate particles		.04
	Sum	.09

Infant Death Rate		
Total suspended particulates		.07
Sulfate particles		.03
	Sum	.10

Neo-natal Death Rate		
Total suspended particulates		.06
Sulfate particles		.04
	Sum	.10

Fetal Death Rate		
Total suspended particulates		.09
Sulfate particles		.05
	Sum	.14

These elasticities mean, for example, that a 1% (50%) reduction in pollution would reduce total mortality by 0.09% (4.5%). Lave and Seskin also present judgmental assumptions of elasticities by causes for all pollutants combined derived from their review of the literature and reanalysis of the data:

Bronchitis mortality and morbidity	.5–1.0
Lung cancer mortality	.5
Respiratory disease mortality and Morbidity	.5
Cardiovascular mortality and morbidity	.2
Cancer mortality	.3

Lave and Seskin base their estimate of monetary benefits on the resource or opportunity cost concept of the value of health. They use data by Rice (1966) on the forgone earnings due to mortality and morbidity and direct expenditures on medical care by disease category. Using their best estimates of elasticities by category, and after some unspecified minor adjustment, they estimated the benefits of reducing air pollution by 50% to be approximately $2.1 billion dollars per year in 1963 dollars. Using the Consumer Price Index for a crude adjustment to 1978 dollars would place the figure at approximately $4.5 billion.

There are three comments to be made about this estimate. First, the elasticities from which it is derived are their consensus "best guess" estimates rather than those derived from their regression analysis. Subsequent estimates by Lave and Seskin are based entirely on their own regression equations. Second, the postulated 50% reduction in pollution is not based on any specific policy. Thus it is difficult to draw policy conclusions from this figure. Third, the dollar valuation is based on the inappropriate resource or opportunity cost approach. Using a willingness-to-pay value based on, for example, wage rate differentials would result in a substantially higher figure.

A subsequent report by Lave and Seskin (1973) is the basis for four different estimates of air pollution control, each of which is discussed below. In this study Lave and Seskin expand their sample to 117 SMSAs. All data are for 1960. In their "best" regression equation on total mortality, they control for the percent of the population nonwhite, population density, and the percent of population over age 65. They are not able to control for diet, smoking, exposure to other environmental hazards, or other socioeconomic variables. Pollution values are taken from one, or at best a few, monitoring stations in each urban area. They are not necessarily representative of the current exposure of any one individual or the exposure history of the population. Lave and Seskin are quite aware of the limitations of their data set and the difficulties and pitfalls in the analysis. For a full discussion, see Lave and Seskin (1977).

Lave and Seskin find their best statistical results using the arithmetic mean of suspended particulate readings over the year and the minimum biweekly sulfate reading in the year. Coefficients on both pollution variables are positive and highly significant. The elasticities are .053 for particulates, .037 for sulfates. The combined elasticity for both pollutants is .09.

Waddell

Waddell is the first to use Lave and Seskin's results as the basis for estimating national health benefits from air pollution control. Waddell estimates that total suspended particulate levels in 1970 would have to be reduced by 26% in order to reach the national primary air quality standard. Assuming the same percentage reduction in sulfates, Waddell uses the combined elasticity of .09 to predict a 2.34% reduction in total mortality and associated health costs. The average annual growth rates in private health expenditures and wage and salary incomes are used to inflate the direct and indirect health costs from Rice (1966) from 1963 to 1970 dollars. Rice does not allocate direct medical costs between morbidity and mortality. Therefore a 2.34% reduction in 1970 total health costs must be interpreted as an estimate of mortality and morbidity benefits combined. The resulting estimate is $3.73 billion per year in 1970 dollars. This estimate embodies the assumption that the relationship between direct and indirect morbidity costs and pollution levels is the same as that observed between mortality rates and pollution.

Waddell then uses a separate data set from the EPA CHESS study (Environmental Protection Agency, 1974) to derive a separate estimate of morbidity caused by respiratory diseases. The CHESS data do not lend themselves to regression analysis. Waddell apparently develops subjective estimates of dose–response functions for various types of respiratory diseases, uses them to predict the change in the number of cases of morbidity, and applies imputed values to estimate benefits. The estimates are not well documented in the report. On the basis of the CHESS studies, he estimates respiratory-related morbidity benefits of between $0.9 and $3.2 billion per year, with a midpoint of about $2.0 billion. These cannot be added to the estimate based on Lave and Seskin. Rather, Waddell deducts an estimate of direct and indirect morbidity costs due to respiratory diseases from the Lave-Seskin total and adds his own CHESS-based estimate.

Finally, arguing that the Lave-Seskin regression equation applies only to an urban population exposed to high levels of air pollution while the Rice morbidity and mortality cost data applies to the U.S. population as a whole, Waddell adjusts the Lave-Seskin estimate for the percentage of the total population living in urban areas (73.5%). This gives a revised estimate for

Lave-Seskin of $2.58 billion, which when added to the CHESS morbidity benefits yields a total of $4.6 billion per year as a best estimate of the health benefits of attaining the national primary standards. Waddell places lower and upper bounds on this estimate of $1.6 and $7.6 billion per year.

The main criticisms of this estimate concern the use of the CHESS data for the morbidity component of disease costs and the use of the resource or opportunity cost basis for valuing health benefits. The CHESS study itself has been subjected to a number of criticisms concerning its choice of methodology and data (U.S. House of Representatives, 1976). And as indicated above, Waddell's use of the study to determine the incidence and value of morbidity costs is not well documented.

Small

Kenneth Small (1977) uses Lave and Seskin's 1973 regression equation and estimated elasticity to compute the benefits of a 50% reduction in air pollution, compared to the 26% reduction assumed by Waddell. There are three other principal differences between Small's and Waddell's estimates. Small does not use the CHESS data on respiratory disease morbidity. Rather, he follows Lave and Seskin in assuming proportionality between mortality and morbidity costs. This makes Small's estimate smaller than Waddell's, since the CHESS costs imputed by Waddell were greater than his downward adjustment to Lave and Seskin's total cost figure. Second, Small's estimate is based on 1963 dollars. That is, he does not inflate the mortality and morbidity costs of Rice to 1970 levels. Third, and most substantive, Small uses a different adjustment factor to account for the urban component of total health costs as estimated by Rice.

Small argues that only the portion of the population classified as living in *urbanized* areas was subject to air pollution. This percentage was about 55% in 1963. Small argues that only 55% of the total cost of ill health estimated by Rice could be attributed to people living in areas affected by air pollution. However, it should be recalled that Lave and Seskin's data were drawn from SMSAs. The total SMSA population includes not only those living in urbanized areas but also those in the rural areas within the geographic boundaries of the SMSAs. If the nonurbanized portion of the SMSA population is not affected by air pollution, Lave and Seskin's elasticities underestimate the impact of air pollution on the health of the urbanized portion of those populations. The appropriate counter to this bias would be to apply the Lave and Seskin elasticities to the total SMSA population, not just the urbanized portion. Thus, I conclude that Small's method of adjustment is inappropriate and his estimate is biased downward. His figure if $4.21 billion in 1963 dollars or $7 billion in 1978 dollars.

Heintz, Hershaft, and Horak

The final estimate based on the Lave and Seskin 1973 report was prepared by Heintz, Hershaft, and Horak (1976) for the Enrivonmental Protection Agency. They start with Waddell's estimate in 1970 dollars and use a detailed adjustment to Rice's 1963 total health costs to make them applicable to the 1973 population, prices, and incomes. These adjustments yield an estimate of $5.7 billion (in 1973 dollars) for the benefits of a 26% improvement in particulates and sulfur compounds.

Lave and Seskin 1977

In 1977 Lave and Seskin published the capstone of their long-term research effort (Lave and Seskin, 1977). They use multivariate regression techniques to investigate the relationships between a variety of air quality indicators and mortality rates. They estimate cross-sectional, time series, and combination cross-sectional–time-series models. They investigate the impact of pollution levels on total mortality rates and mortality rates disaggregated by age, sex, race, and disease-specific rates. They examine a variety of functional forms and model specifications and undertake an extensive search for threshold effects. Air quality indicators for each SMSA are used along with other possible explanatory variables in regression equations to explain mortality rates by SMSA. In general, the results of their analysis support the hypothesis that higher exposure to air pollutants leads to higher mortality rates. Moreover, they find no evidence for thresholds for sulfates, particulates, or sulfur dioxide. And they conclude that the linear model gives the best fit to the data. However, for critical reviews of this body of work, see Landau (1978), Viren (1978), and Thibodeau et al. (1980). See also Lave and Seskin (1980), responding to Thibodeau et al.

Table 4.2 provides a summary of their major results in the form of elasticities calculated at the means of the relevant linear regression equations. The estimates of elasticities across different data sets, model specifications, and degrees of disaggregation are substantially similar. These elasticities provide the basis for Lave and Seskin's estimate of the health benefits of controlling air pollution in urban areas.

To be conservative, Lave and Seskin choose the lowest elasticity measure they obtained, that for their original 1960 equation for unadjusted mortality rates. They cite an EPA estimate that successful implementation of the Clean Air Act Amendments of 1970 would reduce sulfur oxide emissions by 88% and particulate emissions by 58% from 1971 levels by 1979. They assume that this would result in an equivalent percentage reduction in air pollution levels. In other words they use a "rollback" model. Using separate elasticities for sulfates and particulates (not reported in Table 4.2), they predict a 7% reduction in mortality rates by 1979.

TABLE 4.2. Estimates of the Elasticity of Mortality with Respect to Air Pollution: from Lave and Seskin

	Combined Elasticity		
Model	Air Pollutants (Combined)	Unadjusted Mortality Rate	Age-sex-race Adjusted Mortality Rate
1960 Annual cross section—117 SMSAs	Sulfates and particulates	.094	.096
1969 Annual cross section— 112 SMSAs	Sulfates and particulates	.116	.100
1969 Annual cross section— 69 SMSAs	Sulfates and particulates	.106	.096
1969 Annual cross section— 69 SMSAs	Sulfur dioxide and particulates	.126	.110
1960–69 Annual cross-sectional– time series— 26 SMSAs	Sulfates and particulates	.094	.102
1962–68 Annual cross-sectional– time series— 15 SMSAs	Sulfates and particulates	.118	.126
1962–68 Annual cross-sectional– time series— 15 SMSAs	Sulfur dioxide and particulates	.106	.114
1963–64 Daily time series— Chicago	Sulfur dioxide	.108	

Source: Adapted with permission from Lave and Seskin (1977, Table 10.1, p. 218).

To assign a monetary value to this reduction in mortality, they use more recent estimates of mortality and morbidity costs developed by Cooper and Rice (1976). These data are for 1972. Lave and Seskin adjust them to apply to a 1979 population with its associated real incomes and relative prices of medical care. The estimates are then presented in 1973 dollars. See Lave and

Seskin (1977, p. 225 and pp. 348–349) for details of the adjustments. On the assumption that the reduction in air pollution has the same percentage impact on morbidity and mortality, they estimate the reduction in total health costs (that is, benefits) of an 88% reduction in sulfur oxide pollution along with a 58% reduction in particulates to be $16.1 billion at the 1973 price level.

This estimate of benefits is substantially higher than any of the previously cited estimates. This difference cannot be attributed to differences in the underlying relationship between pollution and health. The elasticities used in this estimate and the earlier ones by Waddell and others are essentially equal. There are three reasons for the differences. First, Lave and Seskin's estimate applies to a larger 1979 population, with its associated higher real income levels and relative cost of medical care. Second, Lave and Seskin postulate a substantially larger reduction in pollution levels than that used by any previous study. Third, unlike Waddell, they do not include an adjustment to the national health costs to exclude costs associated with the nonurban population. Rather, they assume that control of emissions nationwide would also yield equal percentage decreases in pollution levels in rural areas. Since only about 73% of the national population live in SMSAs, the benefits to the urban population are about $11.8 billion per year. This is still substantially higher than any of the earlier estimates.

Thibodeau et al.

As part of their review of the Lave and Seskin work, Thibodeau et al. (1980) replicate Lave and Seskin's data base and basic cross-sectional equations for total mortality in 1960. They then examine the sensitivity of the results to the treatment of six SMSAs that are outliers in the sense that one or more of their explanatory variables lie quite outside the range of the remaining SMSAs. When the outliers are deleted, there are significant changes in the coefficients of the pollution variables. They conclude that their evidence supports the existence of a positive relationship between air pollution (as measured by particulates and sulfates) and mortality, but that estimates of the relationship's magnitude are quite sensitive to model specification.

Viren

Viren (1978) is more strongly critical of the Lave-Seskin conclusions. He offers a variety of data from other studies and from his own analysis of the 1960 air pollution and mortality data to support his contention that the association between pollution and mortality may well be spurious. For example, he cites studies that show a geographic pattern of cigarette consumption that results in a positive association between smoking and some air pollutant variables, cites the well-established connection between smoking and mortality, and argues that air pollution could be a proxy for smoking.

He also cites evidence of strong regional gradients in mortality and some measures of air pollution and argues that pollution may be a proxy for the true determinants of mortality differences. He also shows that adding variables to the basic Lave-Seskin regressions would sometimes reduce one or both of the pollution variables to statistical insignificance.

Viren's results show both the presence and consequence of multicollinearity among the variables chosen for various regressions. This is one of his major points. However, he does not offer compelling theoretical justifications for some of the variables he chose to include. Nor does he utilize any of the available statistical techniques for coping with multicollinearity. Thus although his study amply illustrates the difficulties and pitfalls in analyzing data in this area and suggests caution in interpreting positive results such as those of Lave and Seskin, it does not disprove the hypothesis that air pollution causes mortality.

Liu and Yu

The next two studies to be reviewed break new ground in two respects. First, they provide separate estimates of mortality and morbidity; and second, they eschew the simple reduced form linear model in favor of more complicated models and estimation techniques. Both studies find smaller mortality effects than do those studies based on the work of Lave and Seskin. One (Liu and Yu, 1976) also finds smaller morbidity benefits. However, the other study (Crocker et al., 1979) finds much larger morbidity benefits. In fact, they are by far the most significant form of health effect according to their results.

Liu and Yu base their analysis of mortality on a sample of 40 SMSAs that have sulfur dioxide readings in excess of 25 $\mu g/m^3$ between 1968 and 1970. To cope with anticipated multicollinearity, they use a forward stepwise regression model with the following structure. First they estimated

$$M_i = a + bS_i + cW_i + u_i \qquad (4.1)$$

where M_i is the observed mortality rate in the ith SMSA, S_i is a vector of socioeconomic variables (percent of population over 65, percent of population with incomes above the poverty level, percent of population white, and percent of population over 25 years of age with four years of college), W_i is a vector of weather variables, and u_i is the error term. They then regress the residual from Equation 4.1 on pollution in a nonlinear specification:

$$M_i - \bar{M}_i = e^{(d-f/P_i)} \qquad (4.2)$$

where $\bar{M}$ is the estimated mortality rate as computed from Equation 4.1 and

P_i is a pollution measure.[5] The coefficient on sulfur dioxide in Equation 4.2 is positive and statistically significant. Liu and Yu also estimate a linear second-stage equation with sulfur dioxide. In this form, the sulfur dioxide coefficient is negative but not significantly different from zero. Finally, Liu and Yu estimate a separate second-stage equation with suspended particulates as the independent variable. The particulate variable is not statistically significant.

I have three comments on the Liu and Yu procedure and results. First, the estimation of separate equations for sulfur dioxide and particulates is inappropriate, especially since the two equations were then used to compute damages for the two pollutants. Most air pollution data show a correlation between sulfur compounds and particulate levels. See, for example, Crocker et al (1979, p. 45), and Lave and Seskin (1977, p. 32). In fact, it is puzzling that Liu and Yu report a partial correlation coefficient between the two pollutants of only .04. To the extent that the two pollutants are positively correlated, the coefficients in the single variable equations will be biased upward—each capturing some of the effect of the omitted variable. The preferred approach is to include all relevant pollution variables in the second equation.

Second, the forward stepwise regression procedure is known to bias the coefficients of the second-stage equation toward zero if the variables in the two equations are correlated with each other. Thus the lack of significance of the pollution variable, except for the nonlinear sulfur dioxide equation, could be attributable to the estimating procedure.

Third, Lave and Seskin (1979, pp. 50–52) also use the forward stepwise procedure but use a linear form for the second stage and include both sulfur compound and particulate variables. Both pollution variables are positive and significant and similar in magnitude to the coefficients in their simple linear model.

These differences in the results between Lave and Seskin and Liu and Yu are puzzling. Thirty-three of the 40 SMSAs in Liu and Yu's sample also appear in the sample of 117 SMSAs used in Lave and Seskin's analysis of 1960 data. Thirty-four of the 40 also appear in Lave and Seskin's 1969 data set. The two studies use similar sets of socioeconomic variables. Lave and Seskin also include population and population density; Liu and Yu include three climate or weather variables in their basic stage equation (Equation

---

[5]Liu and Yu also estimate a third-stage equation they call a *generalized average damage function*. They claim it can be used to estimate damages or benefits for SMSAs outside of their sample. They form a dependent variable consisting of the sum of the computed mortality rate from Equation 4.1 and the *computed* residual given by the estimated form of Equation 4.2. This was regressed on the full set of socioeconomic, weather, and pollution variables. This model has been dismissed as being virtually tautological by Smith (1977).

4.1). Lave and Seskin do not include such variables in their initial analyses reported in Chapters 3 and 4. However, they do devote a chapter to a study of the impact of adding additional climate variables. They find that in general the association between pollution and mortality is maintained. Because of the larger sample size, replication of the results with different data sets, and robustness of the results through various model specifications and functional forms, it seems prudent to place more confidence in the results of Lave and Seskin.

After estimating a pollution–mortality relationship, Liu and Yu employ a version of the productivity approach to assign monetary values to the increase in mortality associated with air pollution. They compute a discounted present-value-of-earnings stream for a representative member of the labor force between the ages of 18 and 64. The earnings stream is adjusted upward to account for the expected increase in productivity over time. Also, their approach to defining the opportunity cost of foregone earnings is less precise than that employed by Rice (1966) and Cooper and Rice (1976) in that it does not take into account the cross-sectional variation in earnings with age nor the differential impact of pollution-induced mortality across the age structure of the population.

Finally, Liu and Yu use their estimated equations and imputed values to calculate the reduction in lost earnings associated with reducing sulfur dioxide from the levels observed between 1968 and 1970 down to a maximum of 25 $\mu g/m^3$ for each SMSA. This disaggregated approach is to be preferred to the aggregated elasticity approach used in the studies described earlier. The benefits of reducing sulfur dioxide to the assumed threshold of 25 $\mu g/m^3$ for the 40 SMSAs in the sample are $0.9 billion per year in 1970 dollars.

Liu and Yu use a similar calculation for mortality benefits due to particulate control, even though the particulate variable is not significant in their second-stage regression. The total particulate control benefits for the 40 SMSAs is $1.0 billion per year. The total for particulates and sulfur compounds combined is $1.9 billion. It should be noted that this estimate does not include the reduction in direct expenditures on health care, nor benefits due to reduced morbidity. This estimate is not directly comparable with any of the other benefit estimates cited here. This is because Liu and Yu have postulated much larger decreases in pollution levels than any of the other studies and estimated benefits for only 40 SMSAs.

Crocker et al.

Crocker et al. (1979) is an interim report on an ongoing research effort being conducted at the University of Wyoming. This study is significant in that it is the first effort to model the impact of individual behavior and choice on epidemiological relationships. Crocker et al. argue that there may be reasons to expect that variables that are exogenous in some structural equations are in fact endogenous to the overall system being modeled. Empirical work on the health effects of environmental pollutants has generally ignored the possibility of such simultaneous equation relationships and their effects on statistical estimation. When single equations containing endogenous variables on the right-hand side are lifted out of the simultaneous system and estimated with ordinary least squares, estimated coefficients may be biased. Where complex processes with simultaneous relationships are involved, the most important of them must be modeled with a set of structural equations reflecting these interrelationships. Then appropriate statistical techniques, such as two-stage least squares, can be employed. Attention must also be given to the identifiability of the relationships to be estimated.

The following example illustrates the potential for simultaneous relationships in the health effects model and the potential problems in estimation. First, suppose that some measure of morbidity (M) for a population is a function of exposure to an enviornmental pollutant (P), access to medical care (D), and other variables. Second, suppose that access to medical care depends upon average income (Y). Finally, income itself may depend upon the health status of the population. For example, higher morbidity means more days lost from work and lower earnings. Specifically,

$$M = a_0 + a_1 D + a_2 P + u_1 \tag{4.3}$$

$$D = b_0 + b_1 Y + u_2 \tag{4.4}$$

$$Y = c_0 + c_1 M + u_3 \tag{4.5}$$

where u_1, u_2, and u_3 are error terms and the coefficients are hypothesized to have the following signs:

$$a_0, a_2, b_1, c_0 > 0$$

$$a_1, c_1 < 0$$

Morbidity, doctors, and income are all endogenous to the system, even though they each appear as an independent variable in one structural equation. If Equation 4.3 were estimated by ordinary least squares, the parameter estimates would be inconsistent. Furthermore, in this specific case, Equation 4.3 cannot be identified.

In their analysis of mortality, Crocker et al. focus on the simultaneous determination of mortality and the availability of medical care as measured by doctors per capita. They do not present a clear statement of the structure of the underlying model. But the structure that is implied by their specification of estimating equations is of the following form:

$$M = a_0 + a_1 D + a_2 P + a_3 S + a_4 B + a_5 F + a_6 E + u_1 \quad (4.6)$$

$$D_d = b_0 + b_1 Y + b_2 P + b_3 S + b_4 B + b_5 F + b_6 E + u_2 \quad (4.7)$$

$$D_d = D_s = D \quad (4.8)$$

where Equation 4.8 implies that the supply of doctors always is adjusted to equal demand, and where: S represents a vector of socioeconomic variables, such as the age structure of the population, racial composition, and educational attainment; B represents a vector of behavioral variables, such as smoking habits and exercise; F represents a vector of dietary variables; and E represents a vector of other environmental variables, such as radiation exposure and climate.

For the first stage, they estimate a reduced form equation for doctors that includes all of the exogenous variables except pollution. For the second stage, they compute a "doctors" variable from the estimated reduced form equation and use it in estimating Equation 4.6, first excluding the pollution variables, and then including pollution for purposes of comparison. The pollution variables included are annual averages for nitrogen dioxide, sulfur dioxide, and suspended particulates. When Equation 4.6 is estimated for total mortality, only two of the three pollution variables have positive signs, and none even approaches conventional levels of statistical significance. The computed elasticity for the three pollution variables combined is about an order of magnitude smaller than those reported by Lave and Seskin (1977).[6]

Crocker et al. also reestimate Equation 4.6 for nine separate disease-specific mortality rates, including those for heart disease, vascular disease, cirrhosis, and cancer. They find statistically significant pollution variables in two of the nine disease-specific mortality rate equations. Suspended particulates are significant in the equation for pneumonia and influenza; and sulfur dioxide is significant in the equation for early infant diseases.

The elasticities of the disease-specific mortality rates with respect to the significant pollution variables are .09 for early infant disease/sulfur dioxide, and .39 for pneumonia/particulates.

Crocker et al. compute benefits for reduced mortality due to pneumonia

---

[6]More recent but similar results from this project were reported in Gerking and Schulze (1981).

and early infant deaths by postulating a 60% reduction in pollution in urban areas. They assume a value of life of $1 million in 1978 dollars. The urban population at risk is estimated to be 150 million. Applying the estimated elasticities to the disease-specific mortality rates leads to a benefit estimate of $15.9 billion per year. Using a lower value of life derived from the work of Thaler and Rosen (1976) of $340,000 in 1978 dollars leads to a benefit estimate of $5.1 billion per year. This estimate of benefits is very close to that provided by Lave and Seskin (1977). But this is primarily because of two offsetting effects: a much higher imputed value of life combined with a much lower estimated impact of pollution reduction on mortality.

Because of the substantial differences between Lave and Seskin and Crocker et al. in their underlying epidemiological relationships, this aspect of these two studies deserves careful scrutiny. In what follows, I will focus first on differences in model structure and the simultaneous equation model presented by Crocker et al. and second on differences in their choice of variables to be included in the mortality equation.

Lave and Seskin and others chose to work with a simple (usually linear) model in which all variables except mortality were taken to be exogenous. The simultaneous equation approach chosen by Crocker et al. is in principle superior, provided that there are in fact significant interdependencies among the variables, and that these interdependencies are correctly modeled. One major form of interdependency is that between the adverse effects of exposure and individual actions undertaken to reduce or avoid exposure. These could include changes in residence or occupation, migration from high pollution to low pollution areas, and a variety of other types of averting behavior (Zeckhauser and Fisher, 1976). Crocker et al. did not choose to investigate this set of interdependencies. If they turn out to be important in practice, then for this reason alone the Crocker et al. model would be misspecified.

Rather, Crocker et al. focus on the role of medical care in mediating the effect of pollution on mortality. This may also be important, but their model does not appear to be capable of disentangling the separate influences of the availability of medical care and the exposure to pollution on mortality.

In the equations they choose to report, they do not include any measures of pollution in the first stage reduced form equation explaining doctors per capita. They eventually report that they included pollution variables in a separate set of estimates and state that for the mortality equations, "the results are consistent for the effect of medical care and for the positive associations between sulfur oxides and infant diseases and for particulates and penumonia" (1979, p. 67). They also report a significant *negative* association between air pollution and doctors in the first stage reduced form equation. They report:

> It appears that doctors may choose *not* to live in polluted cities (perhap for aesthetic reasons). If this is the case, one can easily explain false positive associations between air pollution and mortality where medical care is excluded as an explanatory variable. If doctors avoid polluted cities, and if doctors do reduce mortality rates, then pollution could well be associated with higher mortality rates; but *not* because of any direct health effect of air pollution or mortality. (Crocker et al., 1979, p. 68)

In schematic terms, Crocker et al. are proposing the causal relationship diagramed in Figure 4.1*a*. But the reported evidence is consistent with either of the causal models shown in Figures 4.1*b* and 4.1*c*. In the latter model, the availability of doctors does not influence mortality, a result that Crocker et al. say is consistent with the existing epidemiological literature (1979, p. 25).

There is another question concerning their modeling of the availability of doctors. Equation 4.7 above is implicitly a demand function for doctors. The observed availability of doctors may be the result of some equilibrating process between demand and supply functions. Crocker et al. suggest a supply mechanism in which pollution enters negatively in comparison with a possible positive effect of pollution on the demand for doctors. But the supply side has not been explicitly modeled in deriving the reduced form equations. This aspect of the model has not been given sufficient attention.

There are several differences between the data used in the regressions by Crocker et al. and by Lave and Seskin that might help to explain the differences in the results. First, Lave and Seskin used SMSAs as the unit of observation, while Crocker et al. used cities. Both choices lead to problems because of the nonhomogeneity of populations within the units, spatial variation in actual air pollution levels within the unit, and so on. It is not clear that either should be preferred on a priori grounds. But it is conceivable that the differences in results could arise because of differences in the choice of unit of observation. More experimentation with alternative combinations of units of observation and model specification would be desirable.

There is a major difference in the treatment of the age characteristics of the population. Lave and Seskin use percent over 65 in the total mortality and the disease-, sex-, and race-specific mortality equations. They also investigate age-specific mortality rates. Crocker et al. employ median age in the total and disease-specific mortality equations and do not investigate age-specific mortality rates. It can be argued that percent over 65 is a better

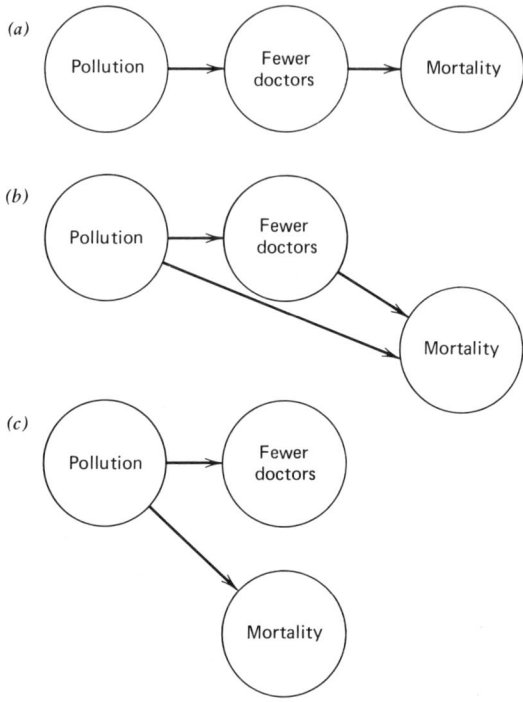

Figure 4.1. Alternative causal models relating pollution, doctors, and mortality.

indicator of the relevant aspects of the age structure of the population than is median age.

Lave and Seskin employ a measure of sulfate particles in most of their equations, while Crocker et al. use sulfur dioxide. Lave and Seskin are able to replicate their results with sulfur dioxide; but they feel that a stronger association is observed when sulfur compounds are measured by sulfate particles.

Lave and Seskin do not control for smoking, while Crocker et al. use a measure of cigarette consumption derived from per capita cigarette tax revenues in the state in which each city is located. One of the most frequent criticisms of the Lave-Seskin work is their failure to control for smoking. But one can question whether the statewide variable employed by Crocker et al. is representative of consumption in the relevant city. Lave and Seskin argue that there is little reason to believe that smoking would be highly correlated with air pollution levels. Thus the exclusion of smoking variables might not bias the estimated coefficients on air pollution variables. In fact, in Crocker et al. the partial correlation coefficients between the smoking variable and the three air pollution variables are only .17, .23, and −.08. Thus it does not seem likely that the addition of the smoking variable can account for the basic differences in their results.

Another difference that may be important is that Crocker et al. attempt to control for diet while Lave and Seskin do not include dietary variables. Controlling for dietary factors (as well as other environmental health hazards, such as contamination of drinking water, occupational exposures to toxic substances, and ionizing radiation) is desirable in principle. But as in the case of smoking, it is difficult to find data on population aggregates that adequately reflect the idiosyncracies of individual behavior. Crocker et al. construct variables for consumption of protein, carbohydrates, and saturated fatty acids for each city on the basis of a U.S. Department of Agriculture survey of food consumption by income level in four regions of the country. Each city's consumption is a weighted average of the consumption by income class in that region, where the weights represent the income distribution of the city.

Protein is significant and positive in the equations for total mortality, cancer, and emphysema/bronchitis; and animal fat is significant in heart disease. This illustrates the importance of trying to control for dietary factors. But one must question whether the variables used by Crocker et al. reasonably reflect differences in diet or differences in income distribution across cities.

Chappie and Lave

Using data for 1974, Chappie and Lave (forthcoming) have replicated the earlier results of Lave and Seskin (1970; 1977) for 1960 and 1969 and have explored several issues raised by critics of this earlier work. In their basic equation for 1974, unadjusted mortality rates by SMSA are regressed on the minimum, mean, and maximum values for both sulfates and total suspended particulates and on percent over 65 years of age, percent nonwhite, percent poor, population density, and the log of SMSA total population. The sulfate variables are significant as a group; but in contrast to the earlier results, none of the particulate variables are significant. However it is not possible to reject the hypothesis that all of the coefficients are identical across years. The sum of the elasticities for the pollution variables is .138.

Chappie and Lave then experiment with alternative model specifications of the following sorts:

alternative socioeconomic variables, for example, education;
the addition of measures of alcohol and tobacco consumption as measured by per capita expenditures by SMSA recorded in the Census of Business of 1967;

the addition of variables to reflect the patterns of industrial activity and occupations;

aggregation by county or city rather than by SMSA;

the simultaneous equation model with doctors, as developed by Crocker et al. (1979).

The results for the alternative specifications are generally similar to the basic model. Particulates are not significant, but sulfates are. The sums of elasticities generally fall in the range of .09–.15. The lowest reported total elasticity is .06.

Schwing and McDonald

Schwing and McDonald (1976) investigated mortality among white males in 46 SMSAs in the years 1959–61. The pollution measures are: hydrocarbon potential, derived from vehicle miles traveled on the assumption that emissions and pollution levels are proportional to vehicle miles; sulfur dioxide potential, derived in a similar manner from estimates of stationary source emissions; annual averages of nitrogen dioxides in 1969; and sulfate and nitrate measures from 1965. The "potential" measures of pollution may be quite poor because of photochemical transformations and dispersion. Also, Schwing and McDonald do not use a measure of total suspended particulates. Schwing and McDonald control for various climate and socio-economic variables and use a proxy for smoking derived from cigarette tax data. They employ ordinary least squares, along with ridge regression and sign-constrained least squares to cope with multicollinearity problems.

One set of regressions investigates disease-specific mortality rates for 15 categories of disease. The results are somewhat mixed but with a tendency for sulfur compound variables to show positive elasticities. A second set of age-specific total mortality rate equations shows a number of positive elasticities for sulfur compound measures. Some representative elasticities are:

	By Ridge Regression	By Constrained Least Squares
White male lung cancer and sulfur compounds	.016	.041
White male arteriosclerotic heart disease and sulfur compounds	.005	.027
White male total mortality and sulfur compounds	.022	.045

To the extent that particulates and sulfates are correlated, these estimates could also be picking up the impact of the omitted particulates variables. Estimates of elasticities for nitrogen compounds vary substantially in sign and magnitude across equations. And the results for hydrocarbons are generally inconclusive. The elasticities for sulfur compounds are the same order of magnitude but somewhat smaller than those reported by Lave and Seskin for sulfur and particulate compounds combined. Thus while there are reservations about this study (the quality of the smoking and air pollution measures), the results are not inconsistent with those of Lave and Seskin.

Jackson et al.

In Jackson et al. (1976) the Schwing-McDonald results provide the basis for an estimate of national air pollution control benefits for controlling sulfur, nitrogen compounds, and hydrocarbons. The age-specific regression equations for white males are assumed to apply to the total urban population. These equations are used to determine the reduction in mortality for the total abatement of pollution. This involves extrapolation beyond the range of the data used in the regression equations and assumes that background levels are zero. Rice's data on cost of illness are used to compute benefits of $12.5 billion per year for total abatement of sulfur compounds and particulates in 1968 dollars.

Mendelsohn and Orcutt

In a recently published study, Mendelsohn and Orcutt (1979) combine data on rates of death due to illness, pollution levels, climate, and socioeconomic variables, all classified by county group. The mortality rates are for illness only. Pollution measures are for 1970 and include sulfates, nitrates, total particulates, carbon monoxide, sulfur dioxide, nitrogen dioxide, and ozone.

Results are reported only for white males and white females. Total mortality and age-specific mortality rates are computed. Sulfates have positive and significant coefficients for all adult whites. Sulfur dioxide and carbon monoxide also have positive coefficients for most adult age and sex groups. However, ozone is typically negative and significant in over half the specifications for total mortality for white males and females. It is also negative but only occasionally significant in age-specific equations. Other pollutants have both positive and negative signs and are generally not statistically significant. Because of incomplete reporting of the data, I am not able to compute any weighted average aggregate elasticities. However, the sum of elasticities for sulfur dioxide and sulfates in the adult male and female age categories range from approximately .10 to .20.

The results for sulfates and sulfur oxides tend to support a conclusion that there are significant health benefits for controlling sulfur emissions. However, the results also provide some support for a conclusion that ozone reduces mortality. Viren (1978) argues that both results may be due to a spurious association of pollution measures with a strong west-to-east gradient in regional mortality rates. But this leaves unanswered the question of what factors, environmental or otherwise, are responsible for the higher mortality rates in the eastern part of the country.

Other Studies

Lipfert (1979a) uses cross-sectional data on annual average levels of sulfur dioxide, total suspended particulates, suspended sulfates, benzo-(a)pyrene, iron, and manganese for over 150 U.S. cities to examine the relationship between air pollution and age-specific mortality rates. Regression equations include percent over 65 years, percent nonwhite, percent in poverty, birth rate, and variables reflecting age of housing stock, smoking, education, and population. In a stepwise regression procedure, sulfur dioxide is excluded as not adding to the explanatory power of the equations. Particulates are significantly positive in the equation for total mortality and for some of the age-specific rates. Generally, the effect of particulates increases with age. The elasticity for particulates in the total mortality equation is .071. Sulfate particles are significant and positive in one equation but significant and negative in several others. In a second paper Lipfert (1979b) uses the same explanatory variables to examine disease-specific mortality rates. Sulfur compound and particulate variables are generally insignificant.

Gregor (1977) examines the variation in sulfur dioxide, suspended particulates, and mortality across census tracts in Allegheny County, which includes Pittsburgh. Control variables include income, race, education, a measure of smoking, access to medical care, population density, and climate variables. The particulate variable is significant, but sulfur dioxide is not. Particulate elasticities in various age-specific equations and for different groupings of cause of death (all causes, pollution related, and nonpollution related) range from .2 to .89. These are much higher than those found in other studies.

Cross-Sectional Time-Series Studies

All of the studies described so far have used observations drawn from a cross section at a single point in time. A major difficulty in these studies is controlling for differences in the relevant population characteristics, such as smoking and diet, across the sample. An alternative method is to use two or more sets of cross-sectional data observed for the same sample at different points in time. Then for each sample unit, the change in mortality rate between two points in time is regressed against the changes in explanatory variables. If personal characteristics such as diet and smoking are constant over the time interval, then they are effectively controlled for by this method.

Lave and Seskin (1977) employ this cross-sectional–time-series approach to examine data on annual changes in mortality and other variables for 26 SMSAs over the period 1960–69. Pollution is measured by sulfates and particulates as in their ordinary cross-sectional analyses. Their results tend to confirm the earlier analyses with the sum of sulfate and particulate elasticities estimated at about .09. Lave and Seskin also examine data for a smaller sample of SMSAs covering 1962–68, with additional data on nitrates, nitrogen dioxide, and sulfur dioxide. The nitrogen compounds are not significant.

Seneca and Asch (1979) also use the cross-sectional–time-series method to examine the effects of changes in air pollution on mortality by county in New Jersey. The pollution variable is the percentage change in the sum of suspended particulates and sulfur dioxide—both as measured by annual changes and by changes over a 6–10 year interval (depending on the availability of monitoring data) ending in 1977. They control for changes in age structure, employment in manufacturing, and other socioeconomic variables. The change in pollution is statistically significant in the 16-county sample. The implied elasticity is .137. Seneca and Asch estimate that annual mortality in New Jersey has been reduced by over 2,000 because of air quality improvements during the time period analyzed.

Two points must be kept in mind when interpreting results of cross-sectional–time-series studies such as these. First, to the extent that mortality is caused by the cumulative effect of long-term exposures, improvements in air quality would affect mortality only with a lag. Very little is known about the lag structure involved. But it seems likely that results based on changes over one-year intervals would understate the true long-term impact of air quality changes on mortality.

On the other hand, if the omitted life style variables, such as smoking, diet, and exercise, are themselves changing over time, the coefficients on the change in pollution will be biased. If we are experiencing a secular trend toward more healthy life styles, the Seneca-Asch results could be biased upward.

A Comparison of Existing Benefit Estimates

It may be difficult to discern a pattern from this lengthy and detailed review and evaluation of existing estimates of the mortality benefits from stationary source air pollution control. Table 4.3 organizes and summarizes the

TABLE 4.3. Summary of Estimates of Health Benefits from Stationary Source Air Pollution Control

Source	Basis of Response Function	Implied or Computed Elasticity	Basis for Values	Percent Reduction in Pollution	Year	Benefits (Billion)	Adjusted to 1978 and 20% Reduction in Pollution[a]
Lave and Seskin (1970)	Subjective judgment based on literature review and own regressions	.09	Resource–opportunity cost, Rice (1966)	50%	1963	$2.1	$1.8[b]
Waddell (1974)	Lave-Seskin (1973) regressions on 1960–61 data by SMSA; CHESS–EPA (1974) for respiratory morbidity	.09	Resource–opportunity cost, Rice (1966) adjusted	26%	1970	$4.6[b]	$5.9[b]
Small (1977)	Lave-Seskin (1973)	.09	Resource–opportunity cost, Rice (1966)	50%	1963	$4.2	$3.6
Heintz, Hershaft, and Horak (1976)	(Same as Waddell)	.09	(Same as Waddell)	26%	1973	$5.7	$6.4

Lave and Seskin (1977)	Lave-Seskin (1977) regressions on 1960–61 data by SMSA	.09	Resource–opportunity cost, Cooper and Rice (1976)	88% (for sulfur) 58% (for particulates)	1973	$16.1	$4.7[c]
Liu and Yu	Liu and Yu (1976) two-stage regressions by SMSA	—	Resource–opportunity cost	Varies[d]	1970	$2.2[e]	$3.7[f]
Crocker et al. (1979)	Crocker et al. (1979) regressions by city	.01	Willingness to pay $1 million per life	60%	1978	$15.9	$5.3

[a]Original estimates were inflated to 1978 by the Consumer Price Index. For comparison purposes, estimates were then adjusted to an assumed 20% reduction in pollution by assuming proportionality—or constant elasticity.

[b]Of this total, 43% is attributed to morbidity, and 57% is due to mortality.

[c]Reduced by .2[(.88 + .58)/2] for assumed change in pollution and by .73 to cover only urban population.

[d]Varies for each city in sample—in order to achieve assumed threshold levels.

[e]Morbidity and mortality combined—for 40 SMSAs.

[f]Not adjusted for assumed reduction in pollution. See also Note *e*.

information reviewed above on eight different studies. The first five columns of the table present information that may make it possible to identify the major sources of differences among the estimates. The next-to-last column presents the aggregate benefit figure as stated in the original study. These figures are not directly comparable because the studies use different bases for imputing values; they assume different percentage reductions in pollution; and they are for different years with different prices, incomes, and so on. The last column represents an effort to correct for these latter two sources of differences. The Consumer Price Index has been used as a crude means of adjusting all estimates to 1978 dollars. Also, on the assumption that the elasticity of the damage function is constant over the relevant range, a proportionality factor has been used to compute the benefits (in 1978 dollars) of a 20% reduction in pollution based on each study's underlying elasticity of mortality with respect to pollution. The major sources of difference remaining among the figures in the right-hand column are differences in the dose–response function and in the basis of imputing values.

The adjusted figures lie within the range of $1.8–6.4 billion per year with the median estimate being about $4.7 billion. These figures will serve to place in perspective the best judgment estimates presented in the next section.

Synthesis Estimate of Mortality Benefits

In this section I draw upon the information and analyses already summarized and reviewed here to derive a synthesis or "best judgment" estimate of the mortality benefits of stationary source air pollution control. This will be an estimate of the benefits actually realized in 1978 by the U.S. urban population due to the reduction in air pollution from 1970 levels associated with the Clean Air Act Amendments of 1970. In order to calculate these benefits, we need three major pieces of information: the reduction in air pollution levels actually experienced, the resulting decrease in morbidity and mortality, and the values to be assigned to avoiding illness and premature death. I postulate a 20% reduction in ambient concentrations of suspended particulates and sulfur compounds.

The next step is to use a dose–response relationship to predict the change in mortality. Several of the analyses of the health effects of stationary source air pollution have reported their results in elasticity form. This dimensionless coefficient is a useful device for simplifying computations. I will assume an elasticity and use it to predict the percentage change in mortality associated with the postulated percentage change in pollution.

This approach does have several limitations. First, it assumes that the elasticity coefficient computed for the mean values of the sample applies to all members of the relevant population. Actually, if the dose–response relationship is linear (and most of the research reviewed here used a linear specification), the point values of the elasticity vary with the position on the dose–response curve. Population units with higher pollution levels will have higher point values for their elasticities.[7] Second, this approach assumes that all of the population units experience the same percentage reduction in pollution. This ignores variation around the mean values for pollution and other factors influencing mortality. The most dirty urban areas in the United States probably have experienced larger percentage reductions in pollution. It is certainly true that they must experience larger percentage reductions to meet existing standards. Third, this approach assumes that the elasticity is constant over the relevant range; but the actual point value of the elasticity varies with movements along a linear function.

The conceptually preferred approach to computing the change in mortality is to utilize directly the dose–response function underlying the elasticity estimate to compute the change in mortality for each urban area with its own specified change in pollution levels, conditional on the values for all other control variables for that particular urban area. This is the approach utilized by Liu and Yu (1976). However, neither the resources available for this study nor the published data permit us to use this approach.

What is our best estimate of the elasticity of mortality with respect to stationary source air pollution? The results of Lave and Seskin and Chappie and Lave suggest an elasticity of .1. The Seneca-Asch estimated elasticity is higher (.14). On the other hand, Crocker et al. found a computed elasticity with respect to total mortality of only .01, and this was not significantly different from zero. Lipfert (1979a; 1979b) and Schwing and McDonald (1976) also found elasticities smaller than those of Lave and Seskin but above those of Crocker et al. It seems likely that these values will bracket the

---

[7] The formula for the elasticity is:

$$E = \frac{\Delta M/M}{\Delta P/P}$$

$$= \left(\frac{\Delta M}{\Delta P}\right)\left(\frac{P}{M}\right)$$

where P is pollution and M is mortality. The term $\Delta M/\Delta P$ is the (constant) slope of linear dose–response function. The elasticity must vary with pollution unless the ratio P/M is constant. This ratio would be constant only if the dose–response function went through the origin, that is, if mortality fell to zero when pollution was zero. Since mortality would be positive with zero pollution, the ratio P/M, and therefore the elasticity, must rise with higher pollution.

true elasticity. Therefore, I will assume that the true value lies in the range of .01 to .10, and that the most reasonable point estimate is .05.

Recalling that stationary source air pollution is primarily an urban problem and that most of the epidemiological studies on which our estimates are based used urban units (SMSAs) as units of observation, the expected reduction in U.S. urban mortality can be computed. These computations are detailed on facing page.

It is estimated that the experienced reductions in sulfur oxide and particulate pollution have reduced annual mortality by between 2,780 and 27,800 per year, with a most reasonable point estimate of 13,900 per year. Mortality reductions for the nation as a whole may be somewhat greater to the extent that rural areas also experience air quality improvements. Ignoring possible rural mortality effects lends a conservative bias to the estimates of benefits.

In order to compute a monetary measure of benefits, it is necessary to specify some value for death avoided. As indicated above, I choose the value of $1 million per death avoided as being representative of those individuals' willingness to pay for reduced mortality based upon observations of individual behavior with respect to risk of death. This value of statistical life is substantially higher than the values based on productivity that were utilized in most of the studies summarized in Table 4.3. This difference in the value of life helps to account for the higher benefit figures estimated here. Using this value leads to an estimate of mortality related benefits of between $2.78–27.8 billion per year, with a most reasonable point estimate of $13.9 billion per year. The reader is free to apply alternative values of life in computing alternative benefit measures. An illustrative calculation based upon a value of life of $500,000 is included in the preceding list of computations.

Morbidity

I turn now to morbidity and consider the results of five separate studies of the morbidity effects of stationary source pollution. The first is by Liu and Yu (1976). Their estimate of morbidity benefits was derived from the CHESS study (Environmental Protection Agency, 1974). As indicated above, the CHESS data are not in a form amenable to regression analysis. However, Liu and Yu employ an imaginative technique to try to overcome this difficulty. The CHESS study covers four geographic areas. In each, sulfur dioxide and suspended particulate levels are recorded for each of several subareas categorized as low, intermediate, or high pollution areas. Liu and Yu regress the bronchitis prevalence rate against pollution readings. Separate regressions are run for sulfur dioxide and particulates. There are no other control variables in either set of equations. The number of observations for

Mortality Benefits for Stationary Source Air Pollution Control

Assumptions	a. Reduction in pollution	=	20%	
	b. Elasticity of mortality with respect to pollution	=	.01–.1	(most reasonable point estimate = .05)
Initial data	a. U.S. mortality in 1978	=	1,900,000	
	b. Percent of U.S. population living in metropolitan areas	=	73% in 1977	
Computations	a. U.S. urban mortality (73% of 1,900,000)	=	1,390,000	
	b. Percentage reduction in urban mortality with 20% reduction in pollution (20% times .01–.1)	=	0.2%–2%	(most reasonable point estimate = 1%)
	c. Reduction in mortality (.2–2% times 1,390,000)	=	2,780–27,800 deaths	(most reasonable point estimate = 13,900
Benefits	a. At $1 million per death avoided ($1 million times 2,780–27,800)	=	$2.8–$27.8 billion/year	(most reasonable point estimate = $13.9 billion)
	b. At $500,000, per death avoided ($500,000 times 2,790–27,900)	=	$1.4–$13.9 billion/year	(most reasonable point estimate = $7.0 billion

each equation ranges from three to five. Significant coefficients for a pollution variable are to be found in two of the eight regressions.

All eight regression equations were then used to generate a larger sample of pollution and morbidity data through Monte Carlo techniques. This sample is used to regress morbidity on sulfur dioxide and particulates in separate nonlinear regression equations. Liu and Yu then apply their own estimates of direct (physicians, hospitalization, drugs, and so on) and indirect (lost earnings) morbidity costs. Applying these imputed cost figures to the reduction in morbidity predicted by their Monte Carlo regression technique produces estimates of morbidity benefits of $99 million for sulfur dioxide and $141 million for particulates.[8]

The major weakness with the Monte Carlo technique is the weak empirical foundation on which the Monte Carlo data generator is based. Liu and Yu do not investigate the errors of the estimates of the means and standard deviations employed in the Monte Carlo mechanism to generate the sample data for their regressions. Thus one cannot estimate the impact of these initial errors on the error properties of the dose–response functions used to generate the benefit estimates.

Crocker et al. use a University of Michigan longitudinal survey of approximately 5,000 households (the Panel Study of Income Dynamics) to estimate the morbidity effects of air pollution. The survey consists of annual interviews from 1968 through 1976. The survey questions apply to the work and health experience of the head of household. The data include socioeconomic variables, work experience, and place of residence. Thus it is possible to determine residential air pollution levels for a substantial part of the survey group and to control for migration and its effect on the exposure histories of the members of the sample.

The research consists of two stages. In the first, the authors seek to determine the association between measures of acute and chronic health effects and annual averages of nitrogen dioxide, sulfur dioxide, and total suspended particulates in the counties in which the sample resides. Acute illness is measured by number of work days lost as reported in each annual interview.

In nine different linear regressions on seven samples drawn randomly from the total survey group, a pollution measure is statistically significant, with a positive sign in explaining acute illness. Elasticities computed at the mean range from about .3 to .6. Partitioned samples were also drawn. Pollution is significantly positive for those households always living in one state and for those with real incomes equal to or less than $7,500, but not significant for

---

[8]There are errors in the tabular presentation of the data. The figures here include corrections provided by Liu.

households with heavy cigarette consumption or chronically disabled households.

Chronic illness is defined in terms of disability, that is, some limitation on ability to work. The variable analyzed is the length of the disability period. This variable is scaled as follows: Equal to or less than 2 years = 1; 2–4 years = 2; 5–7 years = 3; 8 years or more = 4; and otherwise = 0. These are two questions to be raised about this measure of chronic illness. First, there are many forms of disability that are entirely unrelated to air pollution, for example, those due to war injury, occupational or other forms of accidental injury, and congenital defects. Second, it is not clear from biomedical considerations why the length of the disability, or more precisely, the interval from the onset of the disability to the time of the survey, should be a function of air pollution levels at the time of the administration of the survey. These questions about the definition and measure of chronic illness take on considerable significance in the following discussion when it is seen that according to Crocker et al., chronic illness accounts for about 95% of the total economic impact of the morbidity associated with stationary source air pollution.

In the unpartitioned samples, a pollution variable is significant and positive in four of the seven equations to explain length of disability. Pollution is significantly positive in all four of the partitioned samples. Reported elasticities range from .25 to .95. These figures are offered for illustrative purposes only. True elasticities cannot be computed because of the open-ended class interval for the dependent variable.

In the second stage of analysis, Crocker et al. use a recursive model to assess the impact of air pollution on both acute and chronic illness, and through them on hours worked and wages. This model has the following structure:

$$\text{Length of disability} \equiv L = f(P, D, S, B, M, E)$$
$$\text{Acute illness} \equiv A = g(L, P, S, B, M, E)$$
$$\text{Wage} \equiv W = h(L, D, A, S, B, C)$$
$$\text{Hours worked} \equiv H = k(W, L, A, G)$$

where M represents access to medical care, D is severity of disability, C represents a vector of human capital and related variables influencing productivity, F represents other conventional determinants of labor supply, and other variables are as defined in the discussion of the Crocker et al. mortality study above.

The value of reduced morbidity due to air pollution control is based on a resource–opportunity cost concept measured by foregone earnings, but it does not include direct medical expenses. Benefits are defined as

$$\text{Benefit} = -\frac{\Delta \text{ Income}}{\Delta P} = -\left[\left(\frac{\Delta H}{\Delta P}\right)(W) + \left(\frac{\Delta W}{\Delta P}\right)(H)\right]$$

where H and W are hours worked and the wage rate respectively.

They calculate the per household benefit for a one $\mu g/m^3$ reduction in pollution as measured by suspended particulates to be $4.80 per year in 1978 prices or $288 per year for a 60% reduction in particulate pollution. Remembering that the $288 benefit figure is derived from the responses from heads of households and is not necessarily a per capita benefit figure, one can use this number in several ways to estimate national aggregate benefits for controlling air-pollution-induced morbidity. At one extreme, Crocker et al. assume that every member of the urban population of the United States is or will be a head of household and therefore experiences (on average) the same annual benefit. Given this, a 60% reduction of pollution (as measured by particulates) results in annual benefits of between $28.4 billion and $58.1 billion, with a most reasonable point estimate of $43.2 billion. To provide a more conservative estimate, Crocker et al. assume that the earnings of working wives are 60% of their husbands', and that there are additional benefits due to improved productivity in household activities. They compute benefits to the 1970 urban population of $25 billion per year (Crocker et al., 1979, p. 160). The lower and upper bounds are $16 billion and $34 billion. Finally, as an alternative to these assumptions, one could asume that the individual figure applies only to heads of households in urban areas and that no other members of the household experienced pollution-induced morbidity losses. Then if 68% of the 63.4 million households in 1970 lived in urban areas, annual benefits would be $12.4 billion.

These estimates, if valid, suggest that air-pollution induced morbidity may be more significant in welfare terms than mortality. This is an important conclusion. But there are several problems in the study that should make one cautious about placing great weight on the precise figure. We have already mentioned the large role played by the length of disability in the benefit measures and the questions about the use of this as a measure of the prevalence of chronic illness. The second issue is possible biases in the subsample selected for each regression run. For both acute and chronic illness, only those households residing in counties with air pollution data were included. This probably biases the sample toward urban and more polluted areas. The sample for the chronic illness equations was also restricted to include only those who had lived within the same state throughout their lives.

In several instances, Crocker et al. have used integer values rather than dummy variables to represent different possibilities. For example, for education attainment, grades zero to five are assigned a value of one, grades six to eight a value of two, etc. In one case (degree of disability) the integer values assigned do not correspond to a monotonic ranking. And last, the study did not control for occupational exposures to toxic substances.

Cropper (1981) also has examined the data from the Michigan Panel Study of Income Dynamics. She finds that annual average sulfur dioxide levels are positively associated with numbers of work days lost per year. The level of statistical significance is .9 or better in the equations estimated for each of three different years. Cropper also develops a model of personal choice with respect to what she calls "health care capital." In the model individuals could choose to spend money on improvements in health subject to the constraints of limited income and the impairment of health associated with factors such as age and air pollution. A decrease in pollution would lower the cost of attaining any given level of health. The reduction in the cost of health could be taken as a measure of the willingness to pay for cleaner air. Work days lost are taken as a measure of health impairment. Willingness to pay could be calculated from the parameters of the regression equation for work days lost. Cropper estimates that in 1976 a worker earning $6.00 per hour would pay $7.20 per year for a 10% reduction in mean SO_2 levels. This is equivalent to a willingness to pay of $16.50 per year for a 20% reduction in air pollution in 1978 dollars.

Two morbidity studies limited their attention to hospitalization rates. Carpenter et al. use data on hospital admissions in Allegheny County, Pennsylvania and sulfur dioxide and particulate levels at the patient's residence. They find significant associations between pollution levels and respiratory and circulatory system diseases. It is not possible to compute the elasticity from the data reported. Hospital costs per day are used as a measure of the benefits of achieving air quality standards. Benefits are estimated to be $9.8 million per year in 1972—or $6.13 per capita. This is an underestimate of the total cost of pollution-related morbidity. In contrast to these results, in a similar study of Portland, Oregon, Bhagia and Stoevener (1978) did not find a significant association between daily suspended particulate levels and utilization of in-patient medical services by already hospitalized patients. Both of the studies can be criticized for not treating the decision to seek hospitalization as in part an economic one that would be influenced by price and income.

The calculation of the benefits of reduced morbidity can be carried out in a fashion similar to that for mortality benefits. Again the key questions are the choice of an elasticity of morbidity with respect to pollution and the choice of a basis for valuing morbidity reductions. The morbidity studies reviewed here can provide some guidance as to the appropriate elasticity. Lave and Seskin assume that the morbidity elasticity is the same as that estimated for mortality, about .09. Crocker et al. estimates elasticities for acute morbidity ranging from .3 to .6, with an average of over .4. I think that it is unlikely that the true elasticity would be as high as the highest elasticity estimated by Crocker et al. from one partitioned subsample. Rather, I take the average of their elasticities, about .4, to be an upper-bound estimate of the true value. Somewhat arbitrarily, I take .01 to be the lower bound, the same as for mortality. The most reasonable point estimate is .1.

There are two approaches to estimating the value of changes in morbidity. The first, employed by Lave and Seskin (1977), is to compute the proportionate reduction in the direct and indirect costs of morbidity as estimated by Cooper and Rice (1976). Cooper and Rice estimate the direct costs, that is, expenditures on doctors, drugs, hospitalization, and the like, to be $75.2 billion in 1972. This figure is inflated by the population growth and growth in the medical care cost component of the Consumer Price Index between 1972 and 1978. The component of this cost accruing to the urban population (73% of the total) is $95.2 billion. Indirect morbidity costs are measured by lost productivity and wages. Cooper and Rice estimate this to be $42.3 billion in 1972. This figure is adjusted to account for the sex and age composition of the labor force and to include imputations for household productivity and an imputed value for the institutionalized component of a population. This figure is inflated to 1978 by a factor representing the growth in average gross weekly earnings in the private nonagricultural sector. The urban component of indirect costs was $48.0 billion in 1978.

If the morbidity elasticity lies between .01 and .4, a 20% reduction in pollution will reduce morbidity costs by between 0.2% and 8% (with a most reasonable point estimate of 2%). This would lead to the following estimates of benefits:

	Low	High	Most Reasonable
Direct costs	$190 million	$7,613 million	$1,900 million
Indirect costs	96 million	3,842 million	960 million
Total	$286 million	$11,455 million	$2,860 million

The alternative approach to computing values involves a direct estimate of the reduction in some physical measure of morbidity and the application of some imputed value per day of morbidity avoided. To this figure should be added some measure of direct medical cost, such as that estimated by Cooper and Rice. Morbidity can be measured either by work days lost or restricted activity days. The work days lost measure applies only to people in the labor force. Restricted activity days apply to all people of all ages and include degrees of illness and incapacitation that are not severe enough to result in absence from work. Given data on total morbidity and urban morbidity (by either measure), the reduction in morbidity expected to accompany a 20% reduction in air pollution can be calculated by applying the assumed elasticity. The details of these calculations are:

Most Likely Values of Morbidity Benefits Under Alternative Assumptions

I. Workdays lost
   A. Workdays lost due to acute illness in 1977[9]   314.8 million days
   B. Workdays lost to the urban population (73% of A)   229.8 million days
   C. Reduction in lost work days with 20% reduction in pollution (elasticity of .1) (2% of B)   4.6 million days
   D. Benefits:
      1. a. Lost work days, valued at $20 per day $ 92 million
         b. Reduction in direct medical costs (2% of $95,161 million) $1,900 million

                          TOTAL BENEFITS *$1.99 billion*

      2. a. Lost work days, valued at $40 per day[10] $184 million
         b. Reduction in direct medical costs (2% of $95,161 million) $1,900 million

                          TOTAL BENEFITS *$2.08 billion*

(continued next page)

[9] U.S. Department of Health, Education, and Welfare (1978).

[10] This approximates average gross daily earnings in the private nonagricultural sector in 1978.

II. Restricted Activity Days
- A. Restricted activity days due to acute illness in 1977[11] — 1,996 million days
- B. Restricted activity days for the urban population (73% of A) — 1,457 million days
- C. Reduction in restricted activity days with 20% reduction in pollution (elasticity of .1) (2% of B) — 29 million days
- D. Benefits:
  1. a. Restricted activity days, valued at $20 per day $ 580 million
     b. Reduction in direct medical costs (2% of $95,161 million) $1,900 million

     TOTAL BENEFITS *$2.48 billion*

  2. a. Restricted activity days, valued at $40 per day $1,160 million
     b. Reduction in direct medical costs (2% of $95,161 million) $1,900 million

     TOTAL BENEFITS *$3.06 billion*

Work days lost and restricted activity days are alternatively valued at $20 per day and $40 per day. The latter figure represents average gross daily earnings in the total private nonagricultural sector of the economy. Thus it is an approximation of lost productivity (but without adjustments for household services and such). The $20-per-day figure is used to take account of the fact that many restricted activity days are not severe enough to result in a full loss of earnings. In any event, as the preceding list of computations shows, the results are relatively insensitive to alternative approaches to valuation. This is

[11]U.S. Department of Health, Education, and Welfare (1978).

because in this approach to estimating benefits the major component of morbidity benefits is reduced medical expenditures.

Using the more comprehensive measure of morbidity (restricted activity days) and the $40 per day value of reduced morbidity, I estimate the morbidity benefits of reduced particulates and sulfur compounds to lie in the range of $.3–12.4 billion per year. The most reasonable point estimate is $3.1 billion. This amounts to just under $20 per year per capita for the urban population of the United States.

Summary

Combining the estimates of morbidity and mortality benefits, I find the total health benefits associated with reducing sulfur oxide and particulate pollution levels to those of 1978 to lie within the range of $3.1 billion to $40.2 billion per year. The most reasonable point estimate is $17.0 billion per year. As the range indicates, there is a good deal of uncertainty about both the epidemiological basis for this estimate and the imputed values for health and mortality reduction. Over 80% of the benefits estimated here are attributed to the reduction in mortality. However, it should be noted that the direct health expenditure component of morbidity benefits includes expenditures associated with chronic morbidity, including morbidity ending in pollution-related death.

MOBILE SOURCES

Those pollutants coming primarily from mobile sources and for which ambient air quality standards have been set are carbon monoxide, nitrogen dioxide, and photochemical oxidants. In comparison with stationary source pollutants, there have been substantially fewer published estimates of the health benefits of controlling mobile source pollutants. And the weight of the existing evidence suggests that the magnitude of such benefits is small.

Babcock and Nagda (1973) estimate total damages due to mobile source air pollutants to be $2.3 billion in 1968 dollars. But this figure is not derived from an independent estimate of the effects of these pollutants. Rather, it is derived by extrapolation from an earlier estimate of the health benefits associated with suspended particulates and sulfates. Babcock and Nagda take as their starting point a preliminary estimate of health damages developed by Barrett and Waddell (1973). This in turn is derived from the first study of Lave and Seskin (1970) discussed above combined with a crude approach to inflating health costs from the 1963 Rice data. Babcock and Nagda estimate "severity factors" for the five major criteria pollutants based on the national primary ambient air quality standards and their implied threshold or no-effect levels. They then apply these severity factors to estimates of the emissions of nitrogen oxides, hydrocarbons, and carbon monoxide to impute additional dollar damages to these substances. The imputed damages due to these mobile source pollutants is about 35% of the basic health damages attributed to particulates and sulfur compounds.

This imputation is based on two assumptions. The first is that the national primary ambient air quality standards accurately reflect the relative health effects of various substances. The second is that the Lave-Seskin mortality equation captures *only* health effects due to sulfur compounds and particulates, so that the additional imputations are fully additive.

Small (1977) also uses severity factors to impute damages to mobile source air pollutants. The basis for his imputation is the 1973 mortality study by Lave and Seskin. However, Small chooses to assume that the Lave-Seskin estimate reflects damages due to all forms of pollutants, not just suspended particulates and sulfur compounds. Small also uses a revised set of severity factors to reallocate the Lave-Seskin total among the five criteria pollutants. However, since neither Babcock and Nagda nor Small base their estimates on an independent measure of mobile source pollution levels or assessment of their separate effects, their estimates will not play a further role in the analysis here.

Schwing and McDonald's (1976) epidemiological study of 46 SMSAs includes observations on ambient nitrate levels for the year 1965 and a measure of potential hydrocarbon pollution based on gasoline consumption. There is no particulates variable. Given the complex photochemistry and transport processes involved in the transformation of hydrocarbons into photochemical oxidants, the hydrocarbon potential variable is not a good proxy for ambient concentrations. However, Schwing and McDonald did find a positive association between some age-adjusted mortality rates for white males and their hydrocarbon and nitrate variables. Using Rice's data on cost of illness and assuming zero background levels, they estimate the benefits of total abatement to be $1.3 billion per year for nitrogen compounds and $1.6 billion per year for oxidants.

Lave and Seskin (1977) include an investigation of the role of nitrates, nitrogen dioxide, and nitric oxide (NO) in their comprehensive study of air pollution and human health. They conclude:

The results across SMSAs indicated that nitrates were unimportant in explaining the variation in either the total mortality rates (unadjusted and adjusted) or race (adjusted) mortality rates for infants under one year of age. There was however some indication of an association between levels of nitrogen dioxide and the variation in total (unadjusted and adjusted) mortality rates. No association was exhibited between nitrogen dioxide levels and infant mortality.

In our cross sectional time series analysis, involving 15 SMSAs over the period 1962–68 (see Chapter 8), we failed to isolate a consistent significant association between either nitrates or nitrogen dioxide and either the total mortality rates (unadjusted and adjusted) or the race (adjusted) mortality rate for infants under one year of age.

Regarding analysis of daily mortality (see Chapter 9): although we found an association between levels of nitric oxide (NO) and daily mortality in Chicago, the relationship between sulfur dioxide and daily mortality was even more significant. We found no strong relationships between daily mortality and the observed levels of other mobile source air pollutants (including carbon monoxide, nitrogen dioxide, and hydrocarbons) in any of the cities examined. (Lave and Seskin, 1977, pp. 221–222)

On the other hand, Crocker et al. do find some evidence of an association between illness and nitrogen dioxide levels in their longitudinal morbidity study. NO_2 is significant in some subsamples for both acute and chronic illness. When NO_2 is significant, elasticities are generally in the range of .3– .6, with one exceeding 1.0.

Negative or inconclusive results generally have characterized efforts to find an association between photochemical oxidants and human health effects. Seskin (1979) examines data on unscheduled visits to a group health practice and photochemical oxidant levels in Washington, D.C. There are some significant positive associations. But with the exception of the results for unscheduled visits to the opthalmology department, results are inconclusive. While acknowledging the weak empirical basis for extrapolation, Seskin estimates benefits for the Washington metropolitan area that would be associated with the roughly 45–55% reduction in oxidant levels required to meet the old national primary standard (0.08 ppm.) in Washington. Seskin estimates direct and indirect medical costs per visit and suggests metropolitan area benefits of roughly $90,000 (in 1973 dollars). To put this figure in perspective, if the same per capita benefit figure applied to all of the urban population of the United States, national benefits would not exceed $5 million per year.

The next two estimates to be reviewed are based upon dose–response functions derived from the judgment of experts. Aherne's (1973) primary purpose is to establish a framework for the analysis of data. The accuracy of the data is apparently of a secondary concern. Aherne employs a panel of three experts to provide estimates of the incidence of chronic and acute health conditions at different levels of carbon monoxide and oxidant concentrations. The three experts display sharp differences in their estimates of effects.

Aherne uses data on the frequency distribution of carbon monoxide and oxidant readings, relationships between emissions and ambient levels, and the spatial distribution of pollution and population in urban areas to estimate the hours of exposure at various emission levels. This is combined with dose–response information and weighting factors to compute estimates of equivalent days of restricted activity. Finally, these are combined with assumed willingnesses to pay to avoid days of restricted activity to compute damages associated with 1967 levels of emissions and benefits associated with 50% and 75% emissions reductions. Because of the variety of alternative assumptions that are built into the final estimates of total damages, they range over two orders of magnitude from a low of $120 million to $20.75 billion per year. Because of the imprecision of these estimates, and because of the lack of a firm empirical basis in epidemiological data, this study should best be considered as a demonstration of the feasibility of developing a consistent framework for data analysis; but the specific figures cannot be considered very accurate.

A similar but less elaborate approach is taken by Gillette (1974). The dose–response function is derived from a panel of medical and air pollution experts compiled by the California Air Resources Board. Frequency distribution data are used to estimate the population at risk for different patterns of ambient concentrations of photochemical oxidants. Assumed values for different degrees of discomfort or disability are used to compute damages associated with oxidant levels above an assumed threshold of 100 $\mu g/m^3$. Gillette estimates that damages due to oxidant levels in 1973 are $183 million per year. He also estimates the benefits associated with a 20% reduction in ambient oxidant levels. The estimated benefits are $131 million per year.

Finally, the National Academy of Sciences (1974) estimates health damages associated with mobile source air pollution to be between $360 million and $3 billion per year. There are two sources for this estimate. The first is a study of self-reported symptoms of eye discomfort, chest discomfort, cough, and headache conducted with a panel of student nurses in Los Angeles. On the assumption that the student nurses are representative of the urban population of the United States, the data on incidence of the symptom at various oxidant levels are used to compute the incidence of symptoms for the U.S. population given 1973 ambient levels of oxidants. The total oxidant related "person days" of symptoms are estimated to be 195 million for the United States as a whole. Total person days due to all symptoms are estimated to be 26.8 billion. This seems high compared with the estimate of a total of less than two billion restricted activity days reported in the *Vital and Health Statistics* (Department of Health, Education and Welfare, 1978). If avoiding a symptom day is valued at between $1 and $10, oxidant-related health damages are estimated at between $200 million and $2 billion per year.

The National Academy of Sciences (1974) also added an estimate of the benefits of reduced mortality due to nitrogen dioxide pollution. This is derived from an extrapolation from data presented in a preliminary, unpublished version of Lave and Seskin (1977). The National Academy of Sciences estimates that the elasticity of mortality with respect to nitrogen dioxide is .025.[12] Then based on alternative assumptions concerning the population at risk and the reduction in nitrogen dioxide levels, they estimate a reduction in mortality of between 800 and 4,400 per year. But there is a puzzling aspect of this estimate. The published version of Lave and Seskin (1977) states that there is not a significant association between nitrogen dioxide and mortality in the cross-sectional–time-series analysis used by the National Academy of Sciences.[13] And the cited elasticity estimate cannot be found in any of the published regression equations. Hence we must discount this aspect of the National Academy of Sciences' estimate.

In a study that does not deal directly with the epidemiology of mobile source air pollution, Brookshire et al. (1979) asked households in the Los Angeles area their willingness to pay for a 30% reduction in air pollution. An analysis of responses suggests that about 70% of the total willingness to pay is attributable to a desire to avoid perceived health effects. This amounts to almost $0.5 billion per year in 1978 for the South Coast Air Basin of Los Angeles.

After this review of existing estimates of the effects of mobile source air pollution on health, we find little hard data to support a hypothesis of significant mortality effects. There is virtually no sound epidemiological data on a national level on which to base any firm estimate of morbidity effects. Based on the available data, it appears that morbidity effects on a national level due to existing ambient concentrations might be as high as $2 billion per year; but this is an upper-bound estimate. I take zero to be the lower bound and $1.0 billion, the midpoint, to be the most reasonable point estimate.

What data we have found refers to the *potential* benefits to be associated with significant reductions in ambient concentrations of mobile source pollutants. The magnitude of national benefits realized by actual reductions in mobile source pollution between 1970 and 1978 depends on how much ambient concentrations of mobile source pollutants have actually been reduced since 1970. As reported in Chapter 3, there has been no decrease in average levels of oxidants or nitrogen oxides over the period 1970 to 1978.

---

[12]See National Academy of Sciences (1974, pp. 356–358). In a personal communication Seskin states that although the printed percentage reduction in mortality is incorrect (a typographical error), the predicted reductions in mortality are correct, given the data.

[13]See Chapter 8 of Lave and Seskin (1977), especially page 185.

Therefore my most reasonable point estimate of benefits is zero. The upper bound is $.04 billion per year.

It should be noted that in the absence of the Clean Air Act Amendments of 1970, ambient levels of oxidants, carbon monoxide, and nitrogen dioxide probably would have risen significantly over 1970 levels due to increases in vehicle utilization. It is possible that there might be evidence of more serious health effects at higher ambient levels of mobile source pollutants. Therefore, it seems likely that the Clean Air Act Amendments have yielded significant benefits in preventing a rise in mobile source pollution levels and associated health effects. It is not possible to quantify those benefits here, both because of the difficulty in estimating potential vehicle use and emissions in the absence of the Clean Air Act Amendments and because of the lack of data on the dose–response functions for these three pollutants in the relevant range.

REFERENCES

Acton, Jan P. *Evaluating Public Programs to Save Lives: The Case of Heart Attacks.* Santa Monica: Rand Corporation, 1973.

Ahearne, William R. "Measuring the Value of Emissions Reductions," in Henry D. Jacoby, and John D. Steinbruner, *Clearing the Air.* Cambridge: Ballinger, 1973.

American Lung Association. *The Health Costs of Air Pollution.* New York, 1977.

———. *The Health Effects of Air Pollution.* New York, 1978.

Babcock, Lyndon R., and Miren L. Nagda. "Cost Effectiveness of Emission Control," *Journal of the Air Pollution Control Association*, 23, no. 3 (March, 1973), 173–179.

Bailey, Martin J. *Reducing Risks to Life: Measurement of the Benefits.* Washington: American Enterprise Institute, 1980.

Barrett, Larry B., and Thomas E. Waddell. *The Cost of Air Pollution Damages: A Status Report.* Research Triangle Park: Environmental Protection Agency, 1973.

Bhagia, Gobind S., and Herbert Stoevener. *Impact of Air Pollution on the Consumption of Medical Services.* Corvallis: Environmental Protection Agency, 1978.

Blomquist, Glenn. "Value of Life Saving: Implications of Consumption Activity," *Journal of Political Economy*, 87, no. 3 (May/June, 1979) 540–558.

———. "The Value of Human Life: An Empirical Perspective," *Economic Inquiry*, 19, no. 1 (January, 1981), 157–164.

Brookshire, David S., Ralph C. d'Arge, William Schulze, and Mark A. Thayer. *Methods Development for Assessing Air Pollution Control Benefits, Vol. 2: Experiments in Valuing Nonmarket Goods.* Washington, D.C.: Environmental Protection Agency, 1979.

References

Brown, Charles. "Equalizing Differences in the Labor Market," *Quarterly Journal of Economics*, 94, no. 1 (February, 1980), 113–134.

Carpenter, Ben H., D. A. LeSourd, James R. Chromy, and Walter D. Bach. *Health Costs of Air Pollution Damages: A Study of Hospitalization Costs.* Research Triangle Park: Environmental Protection Agency, 1977.

Chappie, Mike, and Lester Lave. "The Health Effects of Air Pollution: A Reanalysis," *Journal of Urban Economics* (forthcoming).

Cooper, Barbara S., and Dorothy P. Rice. "The Economic Cost of Illness Revisited," *Social Security Bulletin.* 39, no. 2 (1976) 21–36.

Crocker, Thomas D., William Schulze, Shaul Ben-David, and Allen V. Kneese. *Methods Development for Assessing Air Pollution Control Benefits, Vol. 1: Experiments in the Economics of Epidemiology.* Washington D.C.: Environmental Protection Agency, 1979.

Cropper, Maureen L. "Measuring the Benefits From Reduced Morbidity," *American Economic Review,* 71, no. 2 (May, 1981), 235–240.

Dillingham, Alan E. *The Injury Risk Structure of Occupations and Wages.* Doctoral dissertation, Cornell University, 1979.

Freeman, A. Myrick, III. *The Benefits of Environmental Improvement: Theory and Practice.* Baltimore: Johns Hopkins University Press, 1979.

_____. "The Health Implications of Residuals Discharges: A Methodological Overview," V. Kerry Smith and John V. Krutilla, eds., *Explorations in Natural Resource Economics.* Baltimore: Johns Hopkins University Press, 1982.

Gerking, Shelby, and William Schulz. "What Do We Know About Benefits of Reduced Mortality from Air Pollution Control?" *American Economic Review,* 71, no. 2 (May 1981) 228–234.

Gillette, Donald G. "Ambient Oxidant Exposure and Health Costs in the United States—1973," *Journal of the Air Pollution Control Association,* 27, No. 4 (April 1977), 329–331.

Gregor, John J. *Intra-Urban Mortality and Air Quality: An Economic Analysis of the Costs of Pollution Induced Mortality.* Corvallis: Environmental Protection Agency, 1977.

Heintz, H. T., A. Hershaft, and G. C. Horak. *National Damages of Air and Water Pollution.* A report submitted to the Environmental Protection Agency, 1976.

Jackson, Clement J., Calvin R. von Buseck, Richard C. Schwing, and Bradford Southworth. "Benefit-Cost Analysis of Automotive Emission Reductions," *GMR-2265*, Warren, Michigan: General Motors Research Laboratories, 1976.

Jones-Lee, Michael W. *The Value of Life: An Economic Analysis.* Chicago: University of Chicago Press, 1976.

Landau, Emanuel. "The Danger in Statistics," *The Nation's Health,* (March 1978), p. 3.

Lave, Lester B., and Eugene P. Seskin. "Air Pollution and Human Health," *Science*, 169, no. 3947 (August 21, 1970), 723–733.

_____. "An Analysis of the Association Between U.S. Mortality and Air Pollution," *Journal of the American Statistical Association*, 68, no. 342, (June 1973), 284–290.

──────. *Air Pollution and Human Health.* Baltimore: Johns Hopkins University Press, 1977.

──────. "Comments on 'Air Pollution and Human Health: A Reanalysis,'" *Environmental Health Perspectives,* 34 (February, 1980), 181–183.

Lipfert, Frederick W. "Statistical Studies of Mortality and Air Pollution: Multiple Regression Analyses Stratified by Age Group" (processed), 1979a.

──────. "Statistical Studies of Mortality and Air Pollution: Multiple Regression Analyses by Cause of Death" (processed), 1979b.

Liu, Ben-Chieh, and Eden S. Yu. *Physical and Economic Damage Functions for Air Pollutants by Receptor.* Corvallis: Environmental Protection Agency, 1976.

Mendelsohn, Robert, and Guy Orcutt. "An Empirical Analysis of Air Pollution Dose–Response Curves," *Journal of Environmental Economics and Management,* 6, no. 2 (1979), 85–106.

Mishan, E. J. "Evaluation of Life and Limb: A Theoretical Approach," *Journal of Political Economy,* 79, no.4 (July/August, 1971), 687–705.

National Academy of Sciences, Coordinating Committee on Air Quality Studies. *Air Quality and Automobile Emissions Control, Vol. 4. The Costs and Benefits of Automobile Emissions Control.* Washington, D.C., 1974.

National Economic Research Associates, Inc. *Cost-Effectiveness and Cost-Benefit Analysis of Air Quality Regulation. The Business Roundtable Air Quality Project,* Vol. 4. New York: Business Roundtable, 1980.

Needleman, L. "Valuing Other People's Lives," *Manchester School of Economic and Social Studies,* 44, no. 4 (December, 1976), 309–342.

Olson, Craig A. "An Analysis of Wage Differentials Received by Workers on Dangerous Jobs," *Journal of Human Resources,* 16, no. 2 (Spring, 1981), 167–185.

Raiffa, Howard, William B. Schwartz, and Milton C. Weinstein. "Evaluating Health Effects of Societal Decisions and Programs," in *Decision Making in the Environmental Protection Agency, Vol. 2b: Selected Working Papers* Washington, D.C.: National Academy of Sciences, 1977.

Rice, Dorothy. *Estimating the Cost of Illness.* Publication 947–6. Washington, D.C.: U.S. Department of Health, Education and Welfare, Public Health Service, 1966.

Schelling, Thomas C. "The Life You Save may Be Your Own," in Samuel B. Chase, ed., *Problems in Public Expenditure Analysis.* Washington, D.C.: Brookings Institution, 1968.

Schwing, Richard C., and Gary C. McDonald. "Measures of Association of Some Air Pollutants, Natural Ionizing Radiation, and Cigarette Smoking with Mortality Rates," *The Science of the Total Environment,* 5 (1976), 139–169.

Seneca, Joseph, and Peter Asch. *The Benefits of Air Pollution Control in New Jersey.* Center for Coastal and Environmental Studies, Rutgers University, April, 1979.

Seskin, Eugene P. "An Analysis of Some Short Term Health Effects of Air Pollution in the Washington, D.C. Metropolitan Area," *Journal of Urban Economics,* 63 (July, 1979), 275–291.

Small, Kenneth A. "Estimating Air Pollution Costs of Transport Modes," *Journal of Transportation Economics,* 11, no. 2 (May, 1977), 109–132.

Smith, Robert S. *The Occupational Safety and Health Act: Its Goals and Its Achievements.* Washington, D.C.: American Enterprise Institute for Public Policy Research, 1976.

———. "Compensating Wage Differentials and Public Policy: A Review," *Industrial and Labor Relations Review,* 32, no. 3 (April, 1979), 339–352.

Smith, V. Kerry. "Comment on 'Mortality and Air Pollution: Revisited'." *Journal of the Air Pollution Control Association,* 27, no. 7 (July, 1977), 667–669.

Thaler, Robert H., and Sherwin Rosen. "The Value of Saving a Life: Evidence from the Labor Market," in N. E. Terleckyj, ed., *Household Production and Consumption.* New York: Columbia University Press, 1976.

Thibodeau, L. A., et al. "Air Pollution and Human Health: A Review and Reanalysis," *Environmental Health Perspectives,* 34 (February, 1980), 165–181.

U.S. Department of Health, Education and Welfare. *Vital and Health Statistics, Current Estimates from the Health Interview Survey—United States, 1977.* Series 10, no. 126, 1978.

U.S. Environmental Protection Agency. *Health Consequences of Sulfur Oxides: A Report from CHESS, 1970–1971.* Research Triangle Park, 1974.

U.S. House of Representatives, Committee on Science and Technology. *Community Health and Environmental Surveillance System (CHESS): An Investigative Report.* 94th Congress, 2nd Session, 1976.

Viren, John R. *Cross-Sectional Estimates of Mortality Due to Fossil Fuel Pollutants: A Case for Spurious Association.* prepared for U.S. Department of Energy, Washington, D.C. 1978.

Viscusi, W. Kip. "Labor Market Valuations of Life and Limb: Empirical Evidence and Policy Implications," *Public Policy,* 26, no. 3 (Summer, 1976), 359–386.

Waddell, Thomas E. *The Economic Damages of Air Pollution.* Washington, D.C.: Environmental Protection Agency, 1974.

Zeckhauser, Richard, and Anthony Fisher. "Averting Behavior and External Diseconomies" (processed), 1976.

5

VEGETATION, MATERIALS, AND CLEANING

Some forms of air pollution can impair the growth of ornamental and commercial plants and trees. The benefits of avoiding this impairment are estimated in the first section of this chapter. I then turn to estimates of the benefits to producers and households of reduced damages to materials and structures. Benefits to households due to reduced soiling and lower cleaning costs are assessed in the third section. Finally, in the fourth section I briefly review the current state of knowledge regarding the monetary damages due to acid rain.

VEGETATION

Ecological systems are of direct economic significance because they are the source of agricultural, fishery, and forestry products that are allocated through markets. Basically, there are two types of techniques for estimating the value of changes in the productivity of these systems associated with improvements in air quality. They both use the market approach to benefit estimation.

The first technique is to identify dose–response functions in order to predict changes in outputs of the system and to use market-derived prices to assign values to the changes in output. For example, changes in the yields of spinach could be related to changes in ozone levels. If it can be assumed that the changes in productivity are so small that they do not affect market price, then this market price can be used to value the change in physical productivity. The constant price assumption may be valid if the product is sold on a national market and the improvement in air quality affects only a small locality or region.

For example, if an improvement in air quality would increase agricultural output by two tons per acre per year, and the constant market price of the product is $10 per ton, then benefits are equal to $20 per acre per year. This figure must be adjusted, however, if the productivity changes also require adjustments in the levels of other inputs. This is because it is the *net* increase in productivity that measures benefits. For example, greater productivity may require more effort at harvest time. If the marginal cost of harvesting is, say, $2 per ton, then the gross benefit must be reduced by the extra harvesting costs. Benefits are $16 per acre. It should be noted that measures of value— for example, retail sales—that include value added after the product leaves the farm do not constitute valid measures of benefits. A farm product worth $5 at the time of harvest may after processing, transportation, and distribution be worth $20 on the supermarket shelf. But the extra $15 of value added in subsequent stages of production is not a benefit; rather, it is a measure of the opportunity cost of the other resources consumed in the activities of processing, distribution, and transportation.

This simple technique is the most common approach to estimating agricultural productivity benefits. It is the basis of the estimates provided by Waddell (1974), Heintz, Hershaft, and Horak (1976), and Ryan et al. (1981). However, there are two problems with this approach. First, changes in air quality may induce farmers to change their cropping patterns. For example, a reduction in ozone levels may lead farmers to shift from crops more resistant to ozone to higher valued crops like spinach that are less resistant to ozone. Second, changes in agricultural productivity stemming from air quality changes may lead to price adjustments in product and factor markets. For example, if an increase in crop output leads to a decrease in its market price, this decrease must be taken into account in computing benefits.

Where producer adjustments and price changes are lifely to be significant, it is necessary to use a more sophisticated approach in which models of the production processes and the markets where the products are sold are constructed. Then it may be possible to predict changes in both product and factor prices and costs. Where product prices are constant, benefits can be measured by estimating changes in the returns to the fixed factor—land, in the case of agriculture. When product price changes, a more comprehensive analysis is required. Figure 5.1 shows the demand curve for the agricultural output and two supply functions (S_1 and S_2). S_1 represents the supply curve under the polluted conditions; S_2 represents the supply curve after the improvement in air quality. The improvement in productivity results in both a decrease in product price and an increase in total output. The benefit of the change is the area *ABCD*. In order to estimate this area, the analyst requires a complete model of both the supply and demand sides of the market.

Damages to ornamental and commercial crops may be caused by ambient concentrations of oxidants, sulfur compounds, and fluorides. However, fluoride pollution is a localized problem and will be given no further attention

88   Vegetation, Materials, and Cleaning

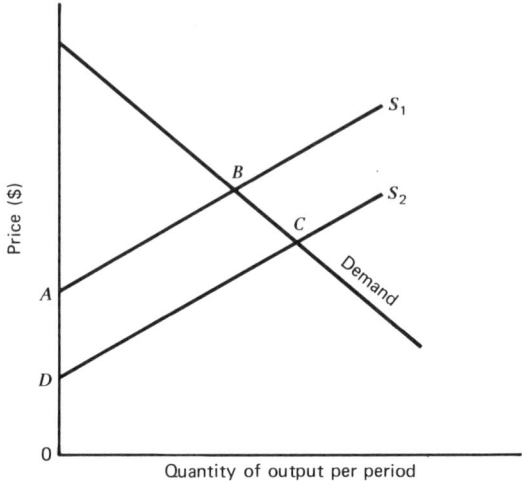

Figure 5.1. Benefits from improvement in air quality when the price of the product changes.

in this report. The first effort to estimate national damages to vegetation due to oxidant pollution was made by Benedict, Miller, and Smith (1973). Their estimate is based on pollution levels and cropping patterns in 1964. Photochemical oxidant pollution potential is estimated by county based upon fuel consumption data. Coefficients of crop loss or plant sensitivity are estimated based on a review of the literature. Crop loss factors are apparently derived for the most part from visual inspection of such evidence as leaf damage. More subtle effects on plant vigor and yield are probably underestimated by Benedict, Miller, and Smith. The crop loss factors are applied to estimates of the values of crop production and ornamental plants in counties with high pollution potential.[1]

Benedict, Miller, and Smith estimate crop damages of $78 million and the replacement of damaged ornamental plantings at $43 million per year. The total oxidant-related damages add up to $131 million per year in 1964 dollars. Damages in 1978 dollars would be about twice this figure. Total estimates of vegetation damages by Waddell (1974), National Academy of Sciences (1974), Babcock and Nagda (1973), Jackson et al. (1976), and Liu and Yu (1976) are also based on the Benedict, Miller, and Smith data and methodology.

There are several limitations to this somewhat crude method. First,

---

[1] For a further description of the Benedict, Miller, and Smith method, see Waddell (1974) and National Academy of Sciences (1974). These studies also include reviews and discussion of other efforts to quantify vegetation losses on a local level.

emissions and fuel consumption are likely to be poor proxies for oxidant levels. Oxidant formation depends not only on emissions of both hydrocarbons and nitrogen oxides, but also on meterological conditions and the movement of air masses. In many parts of the country, because of air pollutant transport patterns, peak photochemical oxidant readings occur tens of miles down wind from the major sources of emissions. The degree to which emissions are converted into photochemical oxidants depends strongly upon local climate and weather conditions. Benedict, Miller, and Smith did adjust emissions estimates by local dispersion factors. But these adjustments are not likely to reflect adequately the complexities and spatial and temporal variability of the processes involved.

Second, the method does not take into account the possible effect of reduced crop output on food product prices. If reduced output leads to higher prices, consumer welfare losses may be magnified, especially for products with inelastic demands. And third, producers may respond to high pollution levels by choosing to grow more resistant types of crops, or by changing locations. Where these adjustments occur, applying crop loss factors to observed crop patterns will underestimate true economic losses since it will fail to capture the costs associated with these adjustments.

The damage estimate by Heintz, Hershaft, and Horak (1976) is a marked improvement over that of Benedict, Miller, and Smith in that it employs data on actual oxidant levels rather than oxidant potential, and it was based on more recent studies of dose–response relationships for crops at ambient pollution levels. Heintz, Hershaft, and Horak review and summarize a number of controlled field experiments dealing with actual yield reductions observed with ambient concentrations of oxidants in the range of 0.05 ppm. to 0.08 ppm. To put this range of concentrations in perspective, the national primary standard for oxidants was 0.08 ppm. until 1979, when it was raised to 0.12 ppm; and the annual average of daily maximums for the nation was approximately 0.06 ppm. in 1978.

On the basis of their review of these field studies, Heintz, Hershaft, and Horak conclude that the best estimate for the average yield loss to crops exposed to that level of photochemical oxidants is about 15% with a low–high range of 5–25%. Some corroboration for this loss factor is found in Hamilton (1979). He uses a theoretical loss function derived by Larsen and Heck (1976) to derive estimates of percent of leaf injury to be expected at different ozone concentrations for 10 different crops. The averages of these figures for different ozone levels fall within the range assumed by Heintz, Hershaft, and Horak. On the other hand, Adams, Thanavibulchai, and Crocker (1979), using a more comprehensive economic methodology that also takes into account input and output substitution and price effects, estimates losses due to oxidant pollution for 14 vegetable and field crops in

90   Vegetation, Materials, and Cleaning

southern California. Their estimate of losses amounts to only 1.48% of the total value of crop production in the study area.

To compute damages, Heintz, Hershaft, and Horak identify those counties within 100 miles of major urban centers for which on the basis of existing measurement of oxidant levels and/or knowledge of oxidant transport patterns there is reason to expect high oxidant readings. They then determine that the total value of agricultural crops raised in these counties in 1973 was $18.7 billion. Applying the expected loss factor to this total production gives an estimate of 1973 damages due to oxidants of between $0.9 and $9.5 billion per year in 1973 dollars. Their most reasonable point estimate is $2.8 billion. Losses to ornamental plants are estimated at $0.1 billion per year by adjusting the estimate of Benedict, Miller, and Smith to take account of changes in the price level.

Adjusting this figure to 1978 levels by the growth in gross farm income leads to an estimate of damages of between $1.2 billion and $12.2 billion per year. The most reasonable point estimate is $3.6 billion per year. This estimate may still be too low since it fails to account for producers' changes in cropping patterns in response to pollution levels and possible changes in product price (Freeman 1979, pp. 238–240). It also probably underestimates the welfare losses associated with damaged ornamental plants. Finally, Hamilton (1979) suggests that more recent data on the impact of oxidants on western forests, especially in southern California, give reason to believe that forestry damages have also been substantially underestimated.

In a report to the National Commission on Air Quality, Ryan et al. (1981) use unpublished damage functions from EPA and air quality data by county to estimate the benefits of achieving the national secondary standards for ozone and sulfur dioxide in 1980. The damage functions are used to predict the change in yield per acre and total production for each of 18 crops in those counties where pollution levels exceeded the secondary standards in 1980. Market prices are used to calculate monetary benefits. Benefits of attaining the ozone standard in the 531 counties now in nonattainment status are estimated to be $1.3 billion per year in 1978 prices. Of this total $0.7 billion are benefits of reducing chronic damages and $0.6 billion are for reducing acute damages associated with pollution episodes. The benefits of SO_2 control are only $26 million per year.

Since the national data show little or no improvement in ozone concentrations, at least through 1978, the Ryan et al. figure of $1.3 billion can also be interpreted as the damages associated with failure to achieve the ozone standard. The damage functions on which this estimate is based do not incorporate thresholds at the level of the standards. Thus total ozone damages are greater than $1.3 billion. It is not possible to compute total damages on the basis of the information published by Ryan et al. But considering that some damages could be occurring in counties that are presently in compliance with the standard, total damages might be 50–100% higher than the estimated benefits of attaining the standard.

On the basis of Heintz, Hershaft, and Horak, and Ryan et al., I estimate the damages to agriculture of ozone pollution to be in the range of $1 billion to $4 billion per year. The most reasonable point estimate is $2.5 billion. Damages to ornamentals are not included here. It seems likely that this category of damage, if significant, would be captured in property value differentials. Studies of property values are discussed in Chapter 6.

Given this level of damages, what can be said about the benefits that have been realized by control programs since 1970? If there has in fact been no improvement in oxidant levels, then the benefits of the control of oxidants since 1970 must be zero. But if oxidant damages to crops are due to short-term exposures to very high levels of oxidants, then the 20% reduction in the number of violations of the national primary standard may have led to pollution control benefits. If the 20% reduction in violations is the relevant measure of improved air quality between 1970 and 1978, if about half the damages are due to acute exposures as the Ryan et al. data suggest, and if the relationship between the number of violations and damages is linear, then the benefits in 1978 are $0.3 billion per year. The lower and upper bounds are $0.1 billion and $0.4 billion. These benefits are attributed to the control of mobile sources of pollution.

MATERIALS

Estimating the impacts of air pollution on materials, productivity, and costs of production can be a complex task. Most of the practical empirical techniques for benefit estimation involve some degree of simplification. Simplifying assumptions must be made to deal with the variety of possible effects, producers' responses, and impacts on market prices and quantities.

To elaborate: First assume that the pollutant in question produces a well-defined effect and that the dose–damage function is known. If it is possible to assume that market prices are unchanged as a consequence of the impact of the pollutant on yield, output, and/or product quality, then the relevant market prices may be used to value the impacts of the pollution damage. Impacts can be either cost increasing or input decreasing. Where production costs are increased, the cost increase itself can be taken as a first approximation of the magnitude of damages. The benefits resulting from pollution control policy are the damages avoided. Similarly, where output is decreased, damages can be approximated by the value (price times quantity) of the reduced output.

The damage functions that underlie this technique are typically derived from laboratory and engineering studies. They typically describe readily identifiable and quantifiable impacts. But they may neglect more subtle but significant forms of damage. Also, materials dose–damage functions may be derived from test procedures that do not accurately correspond to actual conditons of use. Another problem with measurement of physical effects is determining the marginal impact of pollutants from human activities when both human and natural sources contribute to ambient levels of the pollutant. Even if the proportion of total discharges that are caused by humans is known, estimation of human-caused damages is difficult if the dose–damage function or economic cost function is nonlinear.

Another problem is that these physical effect functions are typically defined in per unit terms, for example, corrosion rates per square foot of steel. The estimation of economic effects then requires some knowledge of the quantities of materials actually exposed to air pollution. Where materials such as steel are used in many kinds of production activities, the empirical problem is compounded by the likelihood that producers' responses to a given level of the pollutant and potential physical damage may be quite different for different production activities.

Perhaps the most difficult problem for the empirical estimation of materials damages is determining the size of the inventory of materials being exposed to pollutants. Even well-defined categories such as nonferrous metals or painted surfaces embody a heterogeneous mix of specific materials in a wide variety of uses exposed to a range of air pollution levels. Dose–damage functions derived for a particular set of circumstances will reflect only imperfectly at best the actual damages of a class of materials in a variety of uses. Much ingenuity must be used in deriving an estimate of the inventory of materials actually exposed to different levels of air pollution.

Where the simple dose–damage/constant price assumptions are inappropriate, it is necessary to model the production processes and related markets in an attempt to capture behavioral responses to potential or actual physical damages and related effects on prices and outputs. It is difficult to model fully the economics of production so that producers' responses can be analyzed. For many forms of physical damage, there is a variety of potential responses; and producers may undertake several types of adjustments simultaneously. Corrosion of materials can be countered by painting the material, switching to a substitute material that is corrosion resistant, or simply replacing the material more frequently. On the other hand, if the economic life of the material is shorter than its physical life, for example, because of obsolescence, the economic impact of physical deterioration may be negligible.

If materials deterioration increases the probability of the failure of a component in a system, at least part of the economic cost must be measured in terms of the cost of systems failure. Producers can reduce the impact of component failure on the functioning of the system by system design. In this case the analysis must identify the extra cost of system redundancy.

Producers may respond by accepting a reduction in product quality without raising production costs, reducing the quantity of output, or changing product price. Because lower quality products typically are sold at lower prices, the imputed price differential may be taken as a measure of the loss to consumers due to the reduced product quality. The benefits of preventing this loss could be approximated by multiplying the price differential by the output.

In addition to producers' responses, market responses may also have to be modeled. For a given class of production activity, the physical damages, producers' responses, and their impacts on cost must be aggregated across producers in order to determine the effect, if any, on product price. If supply is less than perfectly elastic, the effect on product price will be less than the effect on marginal cost. Thus predicting price effects requires analysis of both supply and demand conditions. The analysis is similar to that of price effects in agricultural markets. (See Figure 5.1.)

The early 1970s saw the publication of a number of estimates of damages to various types of materials and equipment due to air pollution. Waddell (1974) and National Academy of Sciences (1974) provide useful descriptions, summaries, and critiques of many of these studies. Table 5.1 summarizes these studies and includes an allocation of monetary damages by type of material and pollutant most responsible. Many of the studies do not specify the reference year and price level. In what follows, it will be assumed that all studies are based on 1970 prices.

Most of these studies used technical, engineering, or best judgment damage functions, made some estimate of the quantity of materials to risk to pollution exposure and damage based on data on aggregate production or inventories, and estimated monetary values on the basis of the costs of more frequent repair, maintenance, painting, or replacement. This basis for valuation may not capture the more subtle or indirect costs, such as those due to down time or reduced performance. On the other hand, producers and households may respond to materials damages by other less costly adaptations and adjustments than those on which these estimates are based, for example, material substitutions. These factors would tend to cause estimates of damages to be biased upward. It is difficult to judge the net effect of these offsetting biases.

The weakest link in most of these studies is the estimation of quantities of materials at risk and exposure levels. Gillette's (1975) study is noteworthy in its utilization of actual ambient air quality data for sulfur dioxide to estimate degrees of exposure of materials. Other studies use more crude approaches, such as dichotomous variables, that is, polluted versus nonpolluted. The

TABLE 5.1. Estimates of Types of Materials Damages (in millions of 1970 Dollars)

	Attributed To		
Class of Materials Source of Study[a]	Sulfur Compounds and Particulates	Oxidants and Nitrogen Oxides	Total
1. Electrical switches (Robbins, 1970)	$ 65		$ 65
2. Electrical components (ITT, 1970)	$ 16		$ 16
3. Paints (Salmon, 1970)	$1,195		$1,195
4. Paints (Spence and Haynie, 1972)	$ 704		$ 704
5. Zinc corrosion (Salmon, 1970)	$ 778		$ 778
6. Corrosion (Fink et al., 1971)			
Zinc	$1,353		$1,353
Other	$ 97		97
7. Corrosion and paint (Gillette, 1975)	$ 400		$ 400
8. Textiles and dyes (Salvin, 1970)[b]	$ 636	$ 300	$ 936
9. Fibers (Salmon, 1970)		$ 358	$ 358
10. Rubber and elastomers (Mueller and Stickney, 1970)		$ 355[c]	$ 355
11. Rubber (Salmon, 1970)		$ 194	$ 194
12. All other materials (Salmon, 1970)	$1,272[d]		$1,272
13. All other materials not covered by other studies (Salmon, 1970)	$ 400[e]		$ 400

[a]Information on these studies is based on Waddell's (1974) survey and review, except where otherwise noted.

[b]These totals and allocations are based on the review of Salvin (1970) in National Academy of Sciences (1974, pp. 384–388). Soiling of fabrics is excluded.

[c]This is adjusted to exclude retail markups on higher manufacturing costs. See Waddell (1974, pp. 80–81) or National Academy of Sciences (1974, pp. 379–383).

[d]Salmon does not allocate this total to pollutants. But since the vast bulk of the materials are metal or masonry, they have been allocated to sulfur compounds and suspended particulates.

[e]This estimate is due to Waddell (1974). See also Note d.

National Academy of Sciences (1975, pp. 695–699) argues that these estimates are biased downward due to omitted categories of damages (corrosion and paint damage to automobiles and deterioration of art works and historic buildings) and underestimation of materials at risk.

After evaluating the conceptual and empirical bases of the various studies and considering problems of overlaps and gaps in coverage, Waddell compiled estimates of national damages by category. These are shown in Table 5.2.

The studies used by Waddell are also the basis for estimates by Liu and Yu (1976), Heintz, Hershaft, and Horak (1976), and Small (1977). These authors make various adjustments for inflation and other factors.

I have chosen to make some minor revisions in Waddell's treatment of these various studies and to attempt to allocate them by class of pollutant. The results are shown in Table 5.3. First, I have included estimates of damages to electrical switches and electrical components. Second, I have used the National Academy of Sciences (1974) description of the Salvin study of textiles and dyes. Finally, I have used the lower figure for elastomers, that is, excluding retail markups on production costs. The total damages in 1970 dollars due to suspended particulates and sulfur compounds comes to $2.2 billion. If we use the Consumer Price Index, the 1978 dollar figure is $3.7 billion. The total for oxidants and nitrogen oxides is $655 million in 1970 or $1.1 billion in 1978. The total for all classes of damages is

TABLE 5.2. Waddell's Estimates of National Materials Damages (in Millions of 1970 Dollars)

Category	Basis	Amount
Elastomers	Line 10 of Table 5.1	$ 500
Corrosion	Line 7 of Table 5.1	$ 400
Textiles[a]	Line 8 of Table 5.1	$ 200
Paints[b]	Line 4 of Table 5.1	$ 700
Other	Line 13 of Table 5.1	$ 400
	Total	$2,200

Source: Waddell (1974).

[a]Waddell's description of the Salvin study differs substantially from that in National Academy of Sciences (1974). This figure is based on the latter; the figure in the text comes from Waddell.

[b]Waddell included the allowance for retail markup on increased production costs. The markup has been deducted to arrive at the figure included in Table 5.3.

96 Vegetation, Materials, and Cleaning

TABLE 5.3. Materials Damage Estimates (in Millions of 1970 Dollars)

	Attributed To	
Category	Sulfur Compounds and Particulates	Oxidants and Nitrogen Oxides
1. Electrical switches (line 1 of Table 5.1)	$ 65	
2. Electrical components (line 2 of Table 5.1)	$ 16	
3. Textiles and dyes (line 8 of Table 5.1)	$ 636	$300
4. Paints (line 4 of Table 5.1)	$ 704	
5. Elastomers (line 10 of Table 5.1)		$355
6. Corrosion (line 7 of Table 5.1)	$ 400	
7. Other (line 13 of Table 5.1)	$ 400	
Total	$2,221	$655
		2.9 billion

$4.8 billion. Lacking a better basis for doing so, I assume a low–high range of ± 50%, or $2.4–7.2 billion per year.

To estimate benefits realized by actual improvements in air quality since 1970, I assume a 20% improvement in suspended particulates and sulfur compound pollution since 1970. Assuming that the damage function is linear in this range, realized benefits due to stationary source control are estimated to lie in the range of $.4–$1.1 billion per year. The most reasonable point estimate is $0.7 billion. On the assumption that materials damages are associated with longer term exposures as measured by annual averages, the most reasonable point estimate of the benefits of mobile source control is zero. I take $0.3 billion per year as an estimate of the upper bound.

Two sets of estimates of the benefits to materials of attaining the national secondary air quality standards were released in 1981. The first, by Ryan et al. (1981), uses variations of the damage function approach to estimate benefits in 1980 dollars for air pollution changes by county. The results after conversion to 1978 dollars are shown in Table 5.4. For those materials estimated by the damage function approach, the total stocks of materials in 1980 are assumed to be equal to cumulative production plus net imports since 1968. That is, economic life is assumed to be 12 years. Exposure indexes developed by Salmon (1970) are used to compute the percentages of total stocks potentially subject to air pollution. Exposed stocks are allocated

TABLE 5.4. Materials Benefits for Attaining Secondary Standards—by Ryan et al. (in Millions of 1978 Dollars)

	Suspended Particulates	Sulfur Dioxide	Ozone
By Damage Function Approach			
Concrete	$96		
Paint		$ 356	
Steel		$ 10	
Zinc		$ 3	
By Extrapolation			
Aluminum		$ 267	
Copper		$ 111	
Fibers			$ 523
Nickel		$ 352	
Plasters			$ 284
Tin		$ 452	
Direct Estimation			
Rubber			$ 890
Totals	$96	$1,551	$1,697

Source: Ryan et al. (1981).

to countries according to population, numbers of households, or manufacturing employment in each county as appropriate. Damage functions are drawn from the literature. Values are equal to producers' prices plus an estimate of labor cost for installation. Extrapolations are based on earlier damage estimates by Salmon (1970) adjusted for changes in air quality by county and for changes in the stocks of materials. The benefit estimate for rubber is based on a direct estimate of preventive costs and costs of failures.

The total benefits of controlling stationary sources to meet the secondary standards for suspended particulates and sulfur dioxide are $1.6 billion in 1978 dollars. Mobile source control benefits are estimated to be $1.7 billion.

It is not possible on the basis of the published data to use the benefit figures of Ryan et al. to estimate the benefits of air quality changes between 1970 and 1978. However some illustrative calculations show that except for the category of rubber–elastomers, Ryan et al.'s and my own estimates are not seriously out of line. My most likely estimate of total damages from stationary sources is $3.7 billion per year. Assuming a 20% improvement in air quality and associated benefits of $0.7 billion leaves damages remaining in 1978 of $3.0 billion. Ryan et al. estimate the stationary source benefits of moving from 1980 air pollution levels to the secondary standard to be an additional $1.6 billion per year. The difference ($1.4 billion) could be accounted for, at least in part, by two factors: a possible reduction in air pollution levels between 1978 and 1980 that would reduce damages in 1980 to less than $3.0 billion per year; and damages remaining even after secondary standards are met. The apparent differences in the data on mobile source pollutants has no bearing on my estimate of benefits since the change in air quality is estimated to be zero.

The second new study is an estimate of the benefits of achieving the secondary standards for suspended particulates and sulfur dioxide prepared by Mathtech, Inc. for EPA (Mathtech, Inc., 1980).[2] Mathtech developed what they called an "economic sector" approach to benefit estimation to avoid some of the conceptual limitations and empirical problems with the damage function approach. Basically, if the cost function or supply curve of a firm is known and it can be determined how the resulting supply curve shifts with changes in pollution, the benefits of a reduction in pollution can be estimated as shown in Figure 5.1. Mathtech uses regression analysis to estimate cost functions for six three-digit Standard Industrial Classification (SIC) industries: meat products, dairy products, paperboard containers and boxes, fabricated structural metal products, metal forgings and stampings, and metalworking machinery. A separate estimate is done of the electric utility industry. The selection of industries is based primarily on availability of data.

The cost function gives the total cost of production of a firm as a function of the level of output, input prices (for capital, labor, materials, fuels, and so forth), and environmental variables, including air pollution. If air pollution causes materials damages to producers, costs will be higher for those firms operating in high pollution areas, other things being equal. There are several advantages of the cost function approach:

it is not necessary to determine damage functions for specific materials;
it is not necessary to estimate the stock of each material actually exposed to pollution;
it is not necessary to determine specific producers' responses to air pollution—such as materials substitution and preventive actions.

Either sulfur dioxide or suspended particulates is found to be significantly and positively associated with total cost in four of the six industry categories examined. Lower pollution levels could be expected to lower production costs for firms in these industries. Mathtech calculates benefits on

[2] I was a consultant to Mathtech on this project.

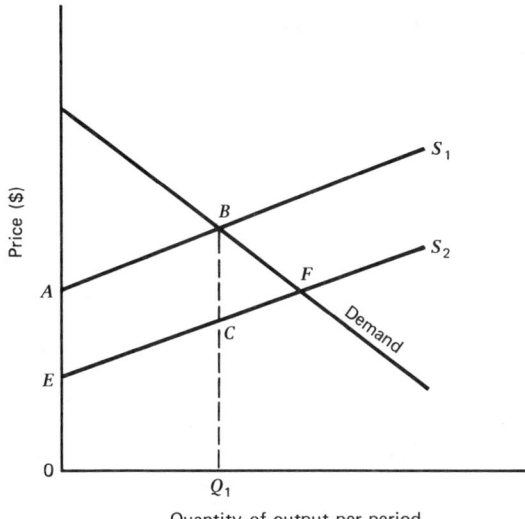

Figure 5.2. Producers' benefits as estimated in the Mathtech Model.

the simplifying assumption that the lower costs would not result in an increase in output. This is equivalent to estimating the area *ABCE* in Figure 5.2, where S_I is the supply curve before pollution control. Unless firms face perfectly inelastic (vertical) demand curves, lower costs will lead to higher outputs. True benefits will include the area *BCF*. Thus conceptually Mathtech's calculations lead to underestimates of true benefits.

Mathtech estimates benefits not only for specific industry categories for which regressions are estimated, but also for closely related industry categories by extrapolation. Their estimates of the annual benefits (converted to 1978 dollars) of meeting the secondary standards for the electric utility sector and those manufacturing categories covered by the extrapolation are[3]

Sulfur dioxide	$0.3 billion per year
Suspended particulates	$2.6 billion per year

They estimate that their extrapolated benefits cover between 15 and 30% of all manufacturing and utilities. But because of the high variability of pollution impacts across industries and the nonrandomness of their sample, it is not possible to infer that total benefits are 3⅓ times their estimate.

---

[3] As this was written, the Mathtech study had been made available by EPA for peer review and public comment. The specific figures must be considered to be preliminary and subject to possible revision.

Vegetation, Materials, and Cleaning

Since Mathtech and Ryan et al. are basically asking the same question but using quite different methods and data to obtain answers, it is interesting to compare their results:

	Ryan et at.	Mathtech
Suspended particulates	$0.1 billion per year	$2.6 billion per year
Sulfur dioxide	$1.6 billion per year	$0.3 billion per year
	$1.7 billion per year	$2.9 billion per year

First, comparisons of absolute levels is not meaningful because while Ryan et al. purport to estimate total benefits to all affected producers the Mathtech study covers only part of the manufacturing and utility sectors and omits completely the commercial, transportation, and government sectors. What is striking is the difference in the relative importance accorded to the two pollutants. That the estimates of Ryan et al. seem to be consistent with earlier estimates is not surprising and should not be considered a strong point in their favor. Their estimates are based on the same methodology and to a large extent the same data as the earlier studies. The Mathtech study represents a conceptual and methodological breakthrough. It is "state-of-the-art" in its use of economic theory and econometric technique. But there are severe problems in obtaining data of the proper form for this approach. At this point it would be premature to pass judgment. What is required is additional work to obtain better data and to refine and extend the economic sector approach.

CLEANING AND SOILING

Air pollution can affect households directly through increased soiling and cleaning costs and by reducing the life of paints, curtains, and other materials. One approach to estimating the benefits of reduced soiling and materials damage is to determine the reduction in cleaning costs and expenditures for materials replacement and repair. This approach assumes, in effect, that households will always alter cleaning and repair activity and expenditures so as to maintain an average level of cleanliness or materials quality no matter what the level of air pollution. An alternative approach is to assume that the level of cleanliness and materials repair and the expenditure necessary to attain them are variables that are determined by supply and demand.

Assume that cleanliness matters to people and that they will want more of it when its price is lower. A demand curve for cleanliness can then be derived as a function of its price or cost and other variables, such as income. This demand curve is shown in Figure 5.3. The price of cleanliness depends in part on the prices of goods and inputs, such as soap and labor time, that are used to produce cleanliness, and in part on the effectiveness of these goods in producing cleanliness, that is, their productivity. Pollution may mean that more soap must be used or that washings must be more frequent in order to produce a given level of cleanliness averaged over time.

Suppose that initially, with pollution, the cost of cleanliness is P_1 in Figure 5.3. Now let air quality be improved. The price of cleanliness falls to P_2, and the quantity of cleanliness increases to C_2. The benefits of improved cleanliness are the increase in consumer surplus, that is, the area P_1ABP_2. Total expenditure on cleaning will increase, remain the same, or decrease depending upon whether the elasticity of demand for cleanliness is greater than, equal to, or less than one. Changes in cleaning expenditure would measure benefits accurately only if the elasticity of demand for cleanliness were zero. What is required in order to implement this market approach to benefit estimation is knowledge of the demand curve for cleanliness. Two efforts to implement this model will be described.

In some cases households can defend against or avoid the adverse effects

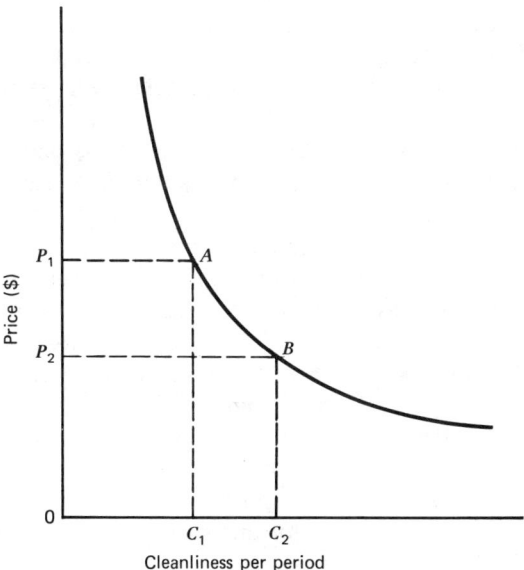

Figure 5.3. The demand for cleanliness, cleaning expenditures, and the benefits of controlling air pollution.

102 Vegetation, Materials, and Cleaning

of low air quality by "defensive expenditures." These are expenditures made to prevent or counteract the adverse effects of low air quality. For example, suppose that purchasing an air filter system is a perfect defense against interior soiling due to suspended particulate pollution. Then an individual can effectively purchase interior cleanliness through the purchase of the air filter. The reductions in these outlays that accompany improvements in air quality can be taken as a measure of the benefits of air pollution control.

In practice, defensive outlays that would be perfect substitutes for improved air quality are rare. There is no such thing as a perfect defense. There are some disutilities associated with low air quality that cannot be prevented by further spending. Hence, changes in defensive outlays are likely to give underestimates of the true benefits of reductions in air pollution. Nevertheless, recognizing this limitation, analysis of changes in defensive outlays related to air quality changes could substantially narrow the range of ignorance about benefits.

There is an alternative approach to estimating some types of household benefits. This approach relies on an explicit model of behavior in the market for housing. Increased cleaning costs, for example, and the disutility of higher dirt levels both reduce the value of the stream of services flowing from a house. If housing markets function well, the disutility of air pollution should be reflected in housing prices. The same argument applies to other types of effects that are location specific, for example, aesthetics and health effects associated with lower air quality at home. A market approach to measuring benefits by examining differences in housing prices will be described in the next chapter.

I turn now to a review of several estimates of the national benefits to households due to decreased soiling and cleaning costs associated with the abatement of suspended particulates. The first, by Jackson et al. (1976), is an extrapolation to 65 SMSAs from an earlier survey by Michelson and Tourin (1966).[4] Michelson and Tourin examine differences in cleaning frequencies for households in Steubenville, Ohio and Uniontown, Pennsylvania. They identify an additional $84 per capita in cleaning costs for households in the higher pollution town. The respective suspended particulate levels in the two towns are 235 $\mu g/m^3$ and 115 $\mu g/m^3$ annual average, both well above the national primary ambient air quality standard. Jackson et al. reduce this figure to $42 per capita to account for the lower particulate levels typical of urban areas and apply this to an unspecified sample of 65 SMSAs. They estimate additional cleaning costs for this group of $2.077 billion per year, apparently in 1967 dollars. This sample covers only about a third of the urban population. Adjusting for this and for increases in the Consumer Price

---

[4]For a review and discussion of Michelson and Tourin, see Waddell (1974, pp. 109–111).

Index produces a revised estimate of damages for the total urban population of $12.2 billion in 1978.

There are three qualifications that must be attached to this estimate. First, the single comparison of cleaning costs in two cities is a weak empirical foundation on which to build an estimate of national benefits. Second, the extrapolation technique is crude at best. In particular, the extrapolation does not involve a precise specification of the change in pollution levels over which benefits are presumably being measured. And third, as was discussed above, changes in cleaning costs are not the most appropriate measure of benefits. Reliance on changes in cleaning costs may lead to a substantial underestimate of the benefits to households of reduced soiling due to particulate pollution.

The second study, by Liu and Yu (1976), utilizes a survey of the cleaning practices of households in Philadelphia conducted by Booz, Allen, and Hamilton (1970).[5] Liu and Yu apply a Monte Carlo technique to the survey data to create a sample of data pairs, cleaning frequency, and total suspended particulate levels, for each of nine household cleaning tasks. They then regress cleaning frequency on total suspended particulate levels without controlling for other social and economic factors. Each regression takes the form

$$F = a + bP$$

where F is cleaning frequency and P is the annual average particulate level at the household location.

Unit costs for each cleaning task are used to compute the change in total cleaning costs due to the predicted change in cleaning frequency as the level of suspended particulates is reduced from its observed value to 45 $\mu g/m^3$. Predictions are made for each of 168 SMSAs based upon the average suspended particulate reading for each SMSA. The total benefits for reducing suspended particulates from 1970 levels to 45 $\mu g/m^3$ summed for all of the 168 SMSAs are $5.0 billion per year. Liu and Yu do not specify the year for which unit costs and prices apply. But I infer from their discussion (p. 69) that they used current dollar values at the time the research was carried out, that is, 1974–75. If so, then benefits in 1978 dollars would be $6.3 billion per year.

Ryan et al. (1981) also use the Booz, Allen, and Hamilton data and the damage function approach to estimate the benefits of achieving the secondary standards for total suspended particulates. They revise the Booz, Allen, and Hamilton cleaning frequency data to take account of demographic and

---

[5]See Waddell (1974, pp. 112–115) for a discussion of this survey.

104 Vegetation, Materials, and Cleaning

environmental changes that had occurred between the date of the original survey and 1978. They also take explicit account of the opportunity cost of time devoted to household tasks. They then estimate that the monetary damage per household per $\mu g/m^3$ annual average is $6.63 in 1980 dollars. Finally, they estimate benefits county by county for those counties not in compliance with the secondary standard in 1980. Their estimate in 1978 dollars is $0.4 billion per year.

A recent study by Watson and Jaksch (forthcoming) is an effort to employ a model based on the theory of household behavior to derive a measure of willingness to pay as distinct from a measure of changes in expenditure. They use the Booz, Allen, and Hamilton (1970) survey data on frequency of cleaning and pollution levels in Philadelphia. They regress frequency of cleaning on total suspended particulates and include variables reflecting socioeconomic characteristics and responses to questions concerning attitudes toward household cleanliness. The latter are intended to characterize differences in preferences or utility functions across households. They report finding generally low R^2 ($<$ .2) in all cases. They conclude that "frequency of cleaning is not significantly different across households with different socioeconomic characteristics, attitudes, and exposure to pollution." They do not present their regression results and tests of significance.

There are at least three possible explanations for this lack of association between cleaning frequency and pollution level. The first is that pollution of the outdoor air has no effect on cleanliness levels indoors or on the cost or price of cleanliness. Thus decreases in pollution will have no effect on cleanliness and produce no benefits. The second explanation is that the economic model of behavior is not relevant to cleaning, but rather cleaning frequency is governed by habit and custom. Then an increase in pollution will not lead to alterations in cleaning habits. People "put up" with the dirt. There may be a loss of utility, but there is no manifestation of that loss in market behavior. The third alternative is that the economic model is relevant and that the demand curve of Figure 5.3 has an elasticity of one. Thus changes in the price of cleanliness associated with changes in pollution lead to changes in the amount of cleanliness, but total expenditure on cleanliness is unchanged. The demand curve of Figure 5.3 has an elasticity of one. The rectangles representing total expenditure, $P_1 A C_1 O$ and $P_2 B C_2 O$, have the same area.

If the prices of cleaning products and the times required for cleaning operations are invariant to cleaning frequency, then expenditure on cleaning can change only if cleaning frequency changes. Watson and Jaksch infer constant expenditure from the constancy of frequency, and therefore they argue that the demand curve for cleanliness has an elasticity of one. This assumption, along with information on the original frequency and price

(Point A of Figure 5.3), are sufficient to define the demand curve. Watson and Jaksch use a function relating pollution to degree of physical soiling and data on cleaning costs to estimate changes in the price of cleanliness associated with changes in suspended particulate levels. Benefits of reduced pollution are measured from changes in consumer surplus as shown in Figure 5.3.

Using data on the spatial distribution of pollution in the Philadelphia SMSA in 1970, Watson and Jaksch estimate the benefits of reducing suspended particulate levels to the national primary and secondary standards at all monitoring points. Benefits for the Philadelphia SMSA for moving from existing levels of air quality to the primary standards are calculated to be between $37 and $137 million in 1978 dollars. To go from existing levels to the secondary standards would yield benefits of between $71 million and $266 million. Gains per household are $26–91 and $48–180 for the moves to the primary and secondary standards respectively.

Assuming the spatial distribution around the SMSA mean is the same for all SMSAs, Watson and Jaksch also compute benefit measures for each of an additional 122 SMSAs. The aggregate for all SMSAs, including Philadelphia, is between $1.6 and $5.2 billion for the national primary standard and between $2.4 and $9.1 billion for the secondary standard. The most likely values are $2.5 billion for the primary standard and $4.3 billion for the secondary standard.

Hamilton (1979) uses the Watson-Jaksch framework to estimate soiling benefits for six California SMSAs. He also assumes a unitary elasticity of demand for cleanliness. Per household soiling benefits for a 25% reduction in particulates of about $40 are comparable to those estimated by Watson and Jaksch. Aggregate benefits for a 25% reduction in particulates for the six California SMSAs (including San Francisco–Oakland and Los Angeles–Long Beach) are $223 million in 1978 dollars. Applying the per household figure of $40 to the approximately 50 million households in metropolitan areas yields a crude estimate of national benefits of $2 billion per year.

Mathtech, Inc. (1981) employs a market approach based on a model somewhat similar to that of Watson and Jaksch to estimate the cleaning and soiling benefits to households of attaining the secondary standards for suspended particulates and sulfur dioxide. The basis of their estimate is a sophisticated model of consumer behavior that invokes the concept of household production. Assume that households have demands for a limited number of basic goods, such as nutrition, shelter, cleanliness, and transportation. These goods are "produced" by households by combining commodities purchased in markets, for example, meat, vegetables, houses, soap, and automobiles.

It is hypothesized that pollution affects the productivity of market commodities used to produce some basic goods. If this is true, then pollution will affect the demand curves for market commodities and through them the costs or implicit prices of the basic goods. It is possible to use a two-stage procedure to estimate first the derived demands for market commodities as functions of their prices, income, and pollution, and then the demands for basic goods such as cleanliness. In effect, this model is a generalization of the model of Watson and Jaksch to encompass a number of basic goods in addition to pollution. It also has the advantage of allowing direct estimation of the demand curves for basic goods rather than requiring assumptions about their elasticity as in Watson and Jaksch.

The Mathtech empirical model is estimated using data from the U.S. Survey of Consumer Expenditures. Some measure of pollution is found to affect demands for market commodities used in the production of shelter, cleanliness (home operations), furnishings, and transportation. The benefits of meeting the secondary standard for suspended particulates in 1987 are estimated to be $0.9 billion per year in 1978 dollars. In addition, Mathtech finds the benefits of meeting the sulfur dioxide secondary standard to be about $0.2 billion per year.[6]

The damage function estimated by Ryan et al. can be used to estimate the benefits of the postulated 20% reduction in suspended particulates. In 1978 there were about 76 million households in the U.S. About 73% of them lived in metropolitan areas, that is, areas presumably affected by air pollution. As Table 3.1 shows, the reduction in particulates from 1970 to 1977 was 9.4 $\mu g/m^3$ annual average, or 13.3%.[7] If this trend had continued through 1978, the total decrease would have been 10.4 $\mu g/m^3$. Multiplying this change in pollution by the damage per $\mu g/m^3$ from Ryan et al., applying it to all urban households, and converting to 1978 dollars gives benefits of $3.1 billion per year.

The Watson-Jaksch estimates of the benefits of attaining primary and secondary standards also provide a basis for estimating the realized benefits of particulate control. As Table 3.1 indicates, the composite annual average of particulates has been reduced almost to the secondary standard of 60 $\mu g/m^3$, while the 90th percentile has closed almost half of the gap between the 1970 level and the secondary standard. On this basis I infer that approximately one half of the Watson-Jaksch estimate of the benefits of attaining the secondary standard had been realized by 1978. This works out to a range of between $1.2 and $4.6 billion per year. The most reasonable point estimate is $2.2 billion per year.

[6]In the Mathtech scenario, the ambient standards are met in 1987. The figures reported here are based on the assumption that the standards were met in 1978; that is, they are undiscounted annual benefits.

[7]A 20% reduction from 1970 levels would be 14.1 $\mu g/m^3$.

It is not possible without additional information to use the Mathtech data to calculate the realized benefits of pollution control. This is because the Mathtech study is based on a different way of expressing air quality standards (the second-highest 24 hour average rather than the annual mean). However, since the Mathtech estimate of the benefits of achieving the secondary standards for TSP is over twice that of Ryan et al., one can infer that an estimate of realized benefits based on the Mathtech data would also be higher than the $3.1 billion per year figure derived from Ryan et al.

Giving relatively more weight to the estimates of Mathtech than to those of Ryan et al., Watson and Jaksch, and Liu and Yu (all of which are based on the old data of Booz, Allen and Hamilton), I estimate that the benefits of the 20% reduction in particulates lie in the range of $1.0 billion to $6.0 billion per year. The most reasonable point estimate is $3.0 billion per year.

ACID RAIN

There has been increasing concern with the effect of acid rain from sulfur and nitrogen compound pollution on agricultural and forest productivity and aquatic ecosystems. The National Academy of Sciences (1975, pp. 181–182) suggests that sulfur dioxide damages to vegetation may have been underestimated in the past and that the potential for damages from acid rain is serious. They also suggest $0.5 billion per year as a best guess for acid rain damages in the northeastern United States (p. 624). This figure may be too low because of the potential for long-term, cumulative impacts on soil fertility and because of ecological impacts to fish, wild life, and so on.

More recently, Crocker et al., (1980) reviewed the literature on the effects of acid rain and concluded that the damages are "unlikely to exceed $5 billion per year" in 1978 dollars for the eastern part of the United States (east of the Mississippi River, plus Minnesota). This total upper-bound estimate is apportioned as follows:

Materials	$2.00 billion
Forest ecosystems	1.75 billion
Agriculture	1.00 billion
Aquatic ecosystems	0.25 billion
Other (health, water supply)	0.10 billion
Total	$5.10 billion

This is a draft report, and the results must be considered preliminary. I take the range of possible benefits to controlling sulfur compounds to be $0–5 billion per year. The most reasonable point estimate is $2.5 billion per year.

Since there has been virtually no downward trend in sulfur particulate levels in the eastern part of the country, it seems prudent to conclude that *realized* benefits as of 1978 are zero.

REFERENCES

Adams, Richard M., Narongsakdi Thanavibulchai, and Thomas D. Crocker. *Methods Development for Assessing air Pollution Damages for Selected Crops Within Southern California.* Washington D.C.: Environmental Protection Agency, 1979.

Babcock, Lyndon R., and Miren L. Nagda. "Cost Effectiveness of Emission Control," *Journal of the Air Pollution Control Association,* 23, no. 3 (March, 1973), 173–179.

Benedict, H. M., C. J. Miller, and J. S. Smith. *Assessment of Economic Impact of Air Pollutants on Vegetation in the United States: 1969 and 1971.* Palo Alto: Stanford Research Institute, 1973.

Booz, Allen and Hamilton Inc. *Study to Determine Residential Society Costs of Particulate Air Pollution.* Research Triangle Park: National Air Pollution Control Administration, 1970.

Crocker, Thomas D., John T. Tschirhart, Richard M. Adams, and Bruce Forster. *Methods Development for Assessing Acid Precipitation Control Benefits.* A draft report to the U.S. Environmental Protection Agency (no date).

Fink, F. W., F. H. Buttner, and W. K. Boyd. *Technical Economic Evaluation of Air Pollution Corrosion Costs in Metals in the United States.* Research Triangle Park: Environmental Protection Agency, 1971.

Freeman, A. Myrick, III. *The Benefits of Environmental Improvement: Theory and Practice.* Baltimore: Johns Hopkins University Press, 1979.

Gillette, Donald G. "Sulfur Dioxide and Material Damage," *Journal of the Air Pollution Control Association,* 25, no. 12 (December, 1975), 1238–1243.

Hamilton, James D. "A Synthesis and Critical Review of Methods for Estimating the Economic Damage of Air Pollution." Presented at the meeting of the Air Pollution Control Association, June 1979.

Heintz, H. T., A. Hershaft, and G. C. Horak. *National Damages of Air and Water Pollution.* A report submitted to the Environmental Protection Agency, 1976.

ITT Electro-physics Laboratories, Inc. *A Survey and Economic Assessment of the Effects of Air Pollutants on Electrical-Components.* Research Triangle Park: Environmental Protection Agency, 1971.

Jackson, Clement J., Calvin R. von Buseck, Richard C. Schwing, and Bradford Southworth. "Benefit-Cost Analysis of Automotive Emission Reductions, *GMR-2265,* Warren, Michigan: General Motors Research Laboratories, 1976.

Larsen, Ralph I., and W. W. Heck. "An Air Quality Data Analysis System for Interrelating Effects, Standards, and Needed Source Reduction, Part 3, Vegetation," *Journal of the Air Pollution Control Association*, 26, no. 4 (April, 1976), 325–333.

References

Liu, Ben-Chieh, and Eden S. Yu. *Physical and Economic Damage Functions for Air Pollutants by Receptor.* Corvallis: Environmental Protection Agency, 1976.

Mathtech, Inc. *Benefits Analysis of Alternative Secondary National Ambient Air Quality Standards for Sulfur Dioxide and Total Suspended Particulates.* A report submitted to the U.S. Environmental Protection Agency, 1981.

Michelson, Irving, and B. Tourin. "Comparative Method for Studying Costs of Air Pollution," *Public Health Reports,* 81, no. 6 (1966), 505–511.

Mueller, W. J. and P. B. Stickney. *A Survey and Economic Assessment of the Effects of Air Pollution on Elastomers.* Raleigh, North Carolina: National Air Pollution Control Administration, 1970.

National Academy of Sciences, Coordinating Committee on Air Quality Studies, *Air Quality and Automobile Emissions Control, Vol. 4, The Costs and Benefits of Automobile Emissions Control.* Washington, D.C., 1974.

Robbins, R. C. *Inquiry Into the Economic Effects of Air Pollution on Electrical Contacts.* Raleigh, North Carolina: National Air Pollution Control Administration, 1970.

National Academy of Sciences, Commission on Natural Resources, *Air Quality and Stationary Source Emission Control.* Committee Print, Senate Committee on Public Works, 94 Congressional Session, March, 1975.

Ryan, John W., et al. *An Estimate of the Nonhealth Benefits of Meeting the Secondary National Ambient Air Quality Standards.* A report to the National Commission on Air Quality, 1981.

Salmon, R. L. *Systems Analysis of the Effects of Air Pollution on Materials.* Raleigh, North Carolina: National Air Pollution Control Administration, 1970.

Salvin, V. S. *Survey and Economic Assessment of the Effects of Air Pollution on Textile Fibers and Dyes.* Raleigh, North Carolina: National Air Pollution Control Administration, 1970.

Small, Kenneth A. "Estimating Air Pollution Costs of Transport Modes," *Journal of Transportation Economics,* 11, no. 2 (May 1977), 109–132.

Spence, J. W., and F. H. Haynie *Paint Technology and Air Pollution: A Survey and Economic Assessment.* Research Triangle Park: Environmental Protection Agency, 1972.

Waddell, Thomas E. *The Economic Damages of Air Pollution,* Washington D.C.: Environmental Protection Agency, 1974.

Watson, William and John Jaksch. "Household Cleaning Costs and Air Pollution," *Journal of Environmental Economics and Management* (forthcoming).

6

AESTHETICS

People may experience disutility or welfare losses when exposed to reduced air quality even when there are no significant effects on health, materials, soiling, or agriculture. Air pollution can cause odors that affect people's utility and welfare. When smog impairs the view of a nearby mountain range, this could result in a loss of amenity values. Aesthetic effects of this sort are not easily quantifiable and usually are not associated with the production or consumption of market goods and services. For these reasons, they pose difficult measurement and valuation problems for the benefit–cost analyst. But they may nevertheless make up a significant portion of total benefits.

Those aesthetic and visibility effects that impinge on the residential sites of households are likely to be reflected in housing prices or property values. We discuss benefit estimates based on property value studies in the next section. An alternative approach to estimating aesthetic and visibility benefits is to ask people what they would be willing to pay rather than do without the aesthetic and visibility improvements. There have been several studies designed to determine willingness to pay for air quality and related aesthetic improvements through survey questionnaires and bidding games with respondents.[1]

The first study (Randall, Ives, and Eastman, 1974) deals with the aesthetic impact of the Four Corners Power plant complex in the Southwest. Aesthetic impacts covered by the study include both those directly associated with air pollution (haze, visible smoke plume, and so forth) and effects on the landscape due to unreclaimed soil banks from mining and electric power transmission lines. Respondents indicated an average bid per household of $50 per year to move to a somewhat improved aesthetic state and an additional $85 per year to go beyond that to a substantially improved state (both figures in 1972 dollars). On the basis of their sample, Randall, et al.

---

[1] For discussions of some of the methodological and empirical aspects of estimating benefits from survey data, see Freeman (1979a) and the three studies cited later in this chapter.

estimate that the aggregate bids for the region are $15.5 million and $24.6 million for the two stages of improvement.

The second study also examines the aesthetic impacts of power plants in rural environments. Brookshire, Ives, and Schulze (1976) asked local residents and recreationists their willingness to pay to prevent the scenic and aesthetic degradation associated with a proposed power plant siting near Lake Powell. Responses were in the range of $2–4 per recreation day in 1975 dollars. Aggregate bids are estimated to be $0.4 million and $0.7 million per year, respectively.

In the third study (Brookshire et al., 1979), households in the Los Angeles area were asked their willingness to pay for improvements in air quality as portrayed by photographs showing different degrees of visibility impairment. Respondents were also given information on the health effects of air pollution. Household bids for a 30% improvement in air quality averaged about $29 per month in 1978 dollars. Average annual benefits for the South Coast Air Basin are estimated to be $0.65 billion. A breakdown of the responses indicates that about 30% of this total is attributable to aesthetics, with the remainder due to acute and chronic health effects.

None of these studies lends itself to an estimate of national aesthetic and visibility benefits. However, the results do indicate the potential for significant benefits in this category.

BENEFITS TO RESIDENTIAL PROPERTY VALUES

Aesthetic effects that are specific to housing locations may be reflected in housing price differentials. To the extent that this is so, aesthetic benefits can be measured by estimating the demand for the aesthetic creating characteristics of the house. Such characteristics might include ambient air quality, ambient noise levels, or proximity to a lake or recreational water body. Estimating the demand for such characteristics of housing involves a two-step procedure in which first the implicit price of the characteristic is estimated by examining the relationship between the prices of housing units and their characteristics and then the implicit price is regressed against observed quantities to estimate the demand function itself. This procedure is known in the economics literature as the hedonic price technique. See Rosen (1974) for an elaboration of the theoretical basis of the technique. A number of theoretical and empirical issues regarding the application of the technique to air and water quality are discussed in Freeman (1979a, Chapter 6) and Freeman (1979b).

Houses constitute a product class differentiated by characteristics such as number of rooms and size of lot. Any large urban area has in it a wide variety of sizes and types of housing with different locational or neighborhood characteristics and, if air quality varies across the urban area, different levels of air quality. An important assumption of the technique is that the urban area as a whole can be treated as a single market for housing services. Individuals must have information on all alternatives and must be free to choose a housing location anywhere in the urban market. It is as if the urban area were one huge supermarket offering a wide selection of varieties of housing. Of course, households cannot move their shopping carts through the supermarket. Rather, their selection of a residential location fixes for them the whole bundle of housing services. It is much as if shoppers were forced to make their choice from an array of already-filled shopping carts. Households can alter the level of any characteristic by finding an alternative location that is alike in every respect but offers more of the desired characteristic. It must be assumed that the housing market is in equilibrium, that is, that all households have made their utility maximizing residential choices, given the prices of alternative housing locations, and that these prices just clear the market given the existing stock of housing and its characteristics.

In principle, if there are enough houses with different combinations of rooms and lot size, it is possible to estimate an implicit price relationship that gives the price of any type of housing as a function of the quantities of these two characteristics. Where P_h is the price of housing, this function can be represented as

$$P_{h_i} = f(S_i, N_i, Q_i) \tag{6.1}$$

where S_i represents a set of structural characteristics for the ith housing unit, such as size, number of rooms, age, and type of construction; N_i represents a set of characteristics of the neighborhood in which the ith house is located, for example, quality of local schools, accessibility to parks, stores, and work place, and crime rates; and Q_i is the level of air quality at the ith site.

Assume that Equation 6.1 has been estimated for an urban area. The partial derivative with respect to any of its arguments, for example, Q, gives the implicit marginal price of that characteristic, that is, the additional amount that must be paid by any household to move to a bundle with a higher level of that characteristic. For example, the difference in price between a one-bedroom and a two-bedroom house identical in all other respects can be interpreted as the implicit price of an additional bedroom.

If Equation 6.1 is nonlinear, the marginal implicit price of a characteristic is not constant, but depends on the level of the characteristic and perhaps on the levels of other characteristics as well. Thus, a household can be viewed as facing an array of implicit marginal price schedules for various characteristics. A household maximizes its satisfaction by simultaneously moving along each marginal price schedule until it reaches a point where its marginal willingness to pay for an additional unit of that characteristic just equals the marginal implicit price of the characteristic. If a household is in equilibrium, the marginal implicit prices associated with the housing bundle actually chosen must be equal to the corresponding marginal willingness to pay for those characteristics.

Now let us consider only the implicit price of Q. Figure 6.1(a) shows the partial relationship between P_h and Q as estimated from Equation 6.1. Figure 6.1(b) shows the marginal implicit prices of Q as a function of Q. Denote this as $P'(Q)$. The figure also shows the inverse demand or marginal willingness to pay functions for two households, $w_i(Q)$ and $w_j(Q)$, and the equilibrium positions for these two households. Each household chooses a location where its marginal willingness to pay for Q, $w_i(Q)$, is equated with the marginal implicit price of Q, $P'(Q)$.

This first stage of the analysis yields a measure of the price Q and each household's equilibrium marginal willingness to pay for Q. But it does not directly reveal or identify the inverse demand function for Q. The second stage of the technique is to combine the quantity and implicit price information in an effort to identify the inverse demand function for Q. It is hypothesized that w_i, the household's demand price or willingness to pay for

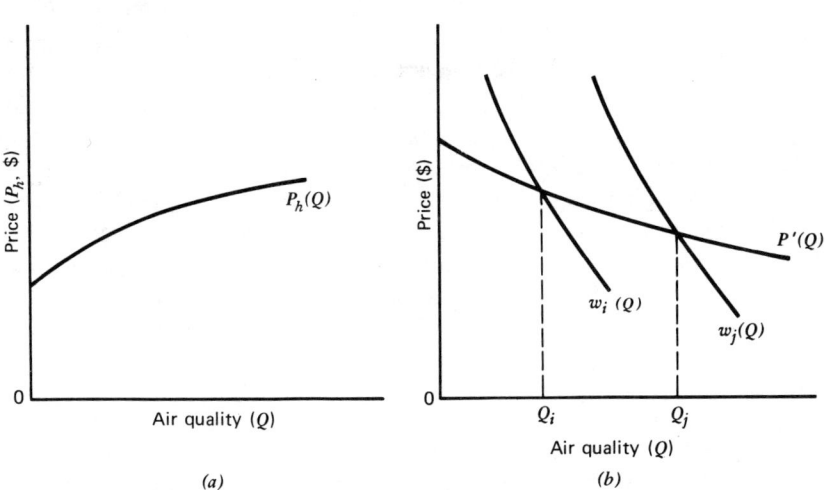

Figure 6.1. Housing prices, the marginal implicit price of Q, and individuals' willingness to pay—all as functions of air quality.

Q_i, is a function of the level of Q, household income (M_i), and other household variables that influence tastes and preferences. In other words,

$$w_i = f(Q, M_i, \ldots)$$

Each household's observed $P'(Q)$ is taken to be a measure of w_i.

Can this demand function be identified with the information at hand? There are two special cases. First, if the price function Equation 6.1 is linear in Q, identification of the inverse demand function (willingness to pay) is not possible. This is because the implicit marginal price is constant when the hedonic price function is linear. With no variation in price across the data set, nothing is revealed about the relationship between the implicit price and Q. However, most of the empirical studies have found that nonlinear forms fit the data better than linear functions.

The second special case arises when all households have identical incomes and utility functions. In this case, Equation 6.1 is the inverse demand function. Recall that the marginal implicit price curve is a locus of points on households' marginal willingness-to-pay curves. With identical incomes and utility functions, these points all fall on the same marginal willingness-to-pay curve.

If neither special case applies, then the supply side of the implicit market for the characteristic must be examined. There are three possibilities. First, if the supply of houses with given bundles of characteristics is perfectly elastic at the observed prices, then the implicit price function of a characteristic can be taken as exogenous to households. A regression of observed levels of the characteristic against the observed implicit prices as defined by Equation 6.1, incomes, and other socioeconomic characteristics of households should identify the demand function. Second, if the available quantity of each type of housing is fixed, households can be viewed as bidding for fixed quantities of housing with desired bundles of characteritics. A regression of each household's marginal willingness to pay for a characteristic, as measured by its implicit price, against the quantity of the characteristic actually taken, income, and other variables should identify the inverse demand function. Finally, if both the quantities demanded and quantities supplied of characteristics are functions of prices, a simultaneous equation approach can be used.

Once the households' marginal-willingness-to-pay functions have been identified, they can be used to estimate the benefits of pollution control strategies, for example, meeting the national primary air quality standards. Each household's benefit is the area under the marginal willingness to pay function between the old and new levels of Q at that site. Aggregate benefits are obtained by summing over all households. If the housing price is measured as an annual rental rate, aggregate benefits are also in annual terms. But if the price of housing is represented by the price of a house as a capital asset, the result of this calculation is the present value of the stream of future benefits. A discount rate must be used to calculate annual benefits.

A number of studies have used this technique to estimate the marginal implicit price of air quality. Harrison and Rubinfeld (1978a), Nelson (1978a), and Brookshire et al. (1979) have used implicit price data to estimate the demand for air quality and benefits of air quality improvement for specific urban areas. This technique has also been applied to the analysis of the implicit prices of quiet (Nelson, 1978b) and to the value of proximity to water bodies (Brown and Pollakowski, 1977).

There are two important limitations to the use of property values in benefit estimation. First, because they are based on the consequences of households' choices of residence, they do not capture households' willingness to pay for improvements in air quality away from their residence, for example, at the work place, in shopping areas, and in parks and recreation areas. Second, because the property value approach is based on observing behavioral responses to the effects of pollution, it is limited to estimating willingness to pay for perceived effects of improved air quality. It is important to be clear about what is being assumed. For example, if one residential site has better air quality and as a consequence individuals there experience less respiratory disease, what is required is that individuals know that they will feel better if they choose to live at this site. They need not know why they feel better; that is, they need not know the cause of the perceived effects on health and mortality. It is unlikely that property value measures capture those subtle and chronic effects on health associated with long-term exposures.

In summary, it is clear that property values do not capture all of the components of benefits from improved air quality. But it is not clear to what extent benefits from other sources can be added to property values without leading to double counting. However, one should not conclude from this that property values are not useful. For broad policy decisions, order-of-magnitude or lower-bound estimates may be quite valuable to decision makers.

Stationary Source Benefits

Waddell (1974) was the first to attempt an estimate of national benefits of controlling air pollution through the use of property value information. His estimate was derived from six different studies involving eight separate cities, including St. Louis, Kansas City, Washington, and Chicago.[2]

---

[2]for a more comprehensive and up-to-date review of existing studies, see Freeman (1979a, Appendix to Chapter 6).

116 Aesthetics

The conceptually correct approach to deriving a national estimate of benefits from property value studies would involve four steps: (1) estimating the implicit price function for all major urban areas; (2) estimating the inverse demand functions for air quality for each major urban area; (3) using each city's set of demand functions to estimate the benefits of the specified improvement in air quality; and (4) summing these estimates for each city to arrive at a national aggregate measure.

None of the property value studies available at the time of Waddell's work included sufficient information to enable an appropriate computation of benefits. Waddell was forced to use a less than ideal approach to extrapolation from the limited number of imperfect studies in his effort to obtain an aggregate national benefit measure. He proceeded in the following manner: After reviewing the existing studies, he picked a value for a representative household's marginal willingness to pay for air quality improvements (as measured by sulfation rates) that lay in the middle of the range found by those studies. He estimated marginal willingness to pay for a 0.1 μg/100cm^2/day reduction in sulfation to lie in the range $20–50 per year, with a best estimate of $35. Waddell assumed that this marginal willingness to pay would be the same for all households in all urban areas independent of their existing air pollution levels, income, and other socioeconomic characteristics. He also assumed that this marginal willingness to pay would be constant for each household for nonmarginal changes in air quality. This is equivalent to assuming that the demand curve for air quality improvements is horizontal. It can be shown that this results in an overestimate of benefits.[3]

Then for each SMSA (the actual number of SMSAs is not stated), benefits were computed according to the following formula:

$$B = - \sum_{i=1}^{n} W \cdot h_i \cdot \Delta P_i$$

where n is the number of SMSAs, W is the marginal willingness to pay per household (assumed the same and constant for all SMSAs), h_i is the number of households in the ith SMSA, and ΔP_i is the change in sulfation levels realized by reducing pollution from 1970 levels to a desired background level of 0.1 μg/100cm^2/day annual arithmetic mean. Note that this assumes that the estimated marginal willingness to pay of single family dwelling homeowners is representative of the marginal willingness to pay of all households. On the basis of these assumptions, Waddell estimated national benefits to be $5.9 billion per year in 1970 with a low–high range of $3.4–8.4 billion.

[3] See Freeman (1974).

Waddell's estimate will be the basis of our revised and updated estimate of realized benefits to residential property values. The first adjustment is to take account of the upward bias due to the assumption of constant marginal willingness to pay for households. Harrison and Rubinfeld (1978b) provide quantitative estimates of the magnitude of upward bias due to this and other elements of model misspecification. They show that the magnitude of upward bias due to the assumptions employed by Waddell is itself an increasing function of the size of the postulated change in pollution levels. Their estimates of upward bias are as follows:

Δ Pollution	Upward Bias
10%	45.9%
25%	56.7%
50%	79.5%

Waddell's benefit estimate is probably based on observations on cities with a wide range of required air pollution improvements. Some may have been as small as 10%, and others may have been well over 50%. To be conservative, we assume that Waddell's estimates are biased upward by 50%. Therefore adjusting to take account of diminishing marginal willingness to pay as air quality improves, the revised estimates for 1970 are $3.9 billion, with a low–high range of $2.3–5.6 billion.[4]

This revised figure is updated to 1978 values through the use of the Consumer Price Index and adjusted to take account of the growth in housing stock between 1970 and 1978. These adjustments in Waddell's figures lead to an estimate of benefits to the 1978 population of improving sulfation levels from 1970 values to the background level in the range of $4.7 to $11.5 billion per year. The most reasonable point estimate is $8.0 billion per year. Since sulfation and suspended particulate readings tend to be highly correlated, we take this to be an estimate of the potential benefit for controlling all sulfur compound and particulate pollution.

With the assumption of a realized 20% reduction in sulfur compound and particulate pollution levels between 1970 and 1978, this adjustment to Waddell's figures leads to an estimate of realized benefits of between $0.9 to $2.3 billion per year. The most reasonable point estimate is $1.6 billion. Note, however, that this computation assumes that the relationship between national benefits and pollution levels is linear. If people have higher marginal willingness to pay for improved air quality at high pollution levels, then the realized benefits of the first 20% reduction in air pollution will be larger than

---

[4]If B_t represents the true benefit figure, we have $B_t \times 1.5 = B_w$, or $B_t = B_w \div 1.5$.

20% of the total estimated above. Thus the estimate of $1.6 billion realized benefits may be too low.

The only other estimate of the national benefits of controlling stationary source pollution based on property values was prepared by Polinsky and Rubinfeld in conjunction with the National Academy of Sciences' study of automotive air pollution control policy (National Academy of Sciences, 1974). Polinsky and Rubinfeld use three different models to provide alternative estimates of the benefits of a 45% control of suspended particulates and sulfur compounds in St. Louis. Property value data are for 1960. Pollution readings are from 1963. According to the preferred model, benefits in 1960 dollars are $81 million per year. Polinsky and Rubinfeld assume that the St. Louis SMSA contains about 2% of the national urban population. Thus they estimate national benefits at $4.1 billion.

This figure can be made comparable to the revision of Waddell's estimate in a similar manner. Thus after inflating for the growth in the Consumer Price Index and the change in the housing stock between 1960 and 1978, and assuming only a 20% reduction in pollution, realized national benefits would be $6.9 billion per year in 1978 dollars. It should be noted that this extrapolation to national benefits from an estimate based on a single SMSA is dangerous since St Louis may not be representative of other cities either in terms of demand for air quality or pollution levels. Specifically, if pollution levels in St. Louis in 1960 were higher than the average of all urban areas, this figure would be an over estimate of national benefits.

Taking account of the Polinsky and Rubinfeld estimate and the fact that revision of the Waddell estimate is likely to be biased downward, we estimate realized benefits to residential property values from the control of stationary source air pollution to be in the range of $0.9 to $6.9 billion per year in 1978. The most reasonable point estimate is taken to be one-third of the upper bound, or $2.3 billion per year. It should be noted that property value benefits almost certainly reflect such factors as reduced soiling and cleaning requirements and reduced materials damages to household paints. Thus this estimate is not fully additive with all of those other estimates given for other categories above. The question of double counting will be taken up in the next chapter.

Mobile Source Benefits

There are three studies relating property values to mobile source pollutants that lend themselves to the estimation of national air pollution control benefits. The first was conducted by Harrison and McDonald in conjunction with the National Academy of Sciences' study of automotive air pollution control policy (National Academy of Sciences, 1974). Harrison and McDonald estimate housing price equations for both the Los Angeles and Boston SMSAs. They estimate separate equations using nitrogen oxides, hydrocarbons, and oxidants as alternative pollution variables; and they estimate all equations in both linear and log form. Pollutant and housing value data are for 1970.

To estimate benefits, they assume full compliance with the national automotive emission standards and use an air quality model to predict air quality levels as of 1990. They assume that the average willingness to pay estimated from the housing value equations is constant and the same for all households. On the assumption that 30 million households across the country would be affected by auto pollution control, they compute national benefits for each possible combination of city, functional form, and pollutant. The results are shown in Table 6.1. Because of measurement problems, and because hydrocarbons are not themselves a pollutant of major concern, the hydrocarbon equation results are probably the least reliable. Omitting them, national benefits are estimated to lie in the range 2.0–7.2 billion per year. Harrison and McDonald note that suspended particulates and nitrogen oxides and oxidants are correlated in their sample. Thus some part of this total may be attributable to particulates and stationary source pollutants rather than mobile source pollutants. After examining the results of two-stage least squares regressions, they estimated that two-thirds of this total is due to mobile source pollutants, roughly $1.5–5 billion per year.

This estimate can be made comparable with others in this section by inflating to 1978 dollars with the Consumer Price Index. Also, their assumption of constant marginal willingness to pay leads to an overestimate of benefits of perhaps 50%. Taking this into account leads to an adjusted measure of the benefits of meeting the standards of $1.7–5.6 billion dollars per year in 1978 dollars. The midpoint of the range, $3.7 billion, is taken as the best estimate.

Nelson (1975) employs a similar methodology to estimate national benefits extrapolated from his study of property values and pollution levels in the Washington SMSA. Assuming a 45% reduction in mobile source pollution levels, he estimates benefits in 1970 of $810 million. Adjusting this for the growth in the Consumer Price Index and taking account of the overestimation due to the assumption of constant willingness to pay leads to an estimate of national benefits of $0.9 billion in 1978 dollars.

The third study is an extensive analysis of property values and nitrogen oxide levels in Los Angeles. Brookshire et al. (1979) estimate the benefits of mobile source control for Los Angeles both with property value data and with a survey or bidding game approach. Data were collected for the years 1977 and 1978. A 30% reduction in pollution is postulated. Using the

TABLE 6.1. National Benefits of Mobile Source Air Pollution Control (Based on Property Values in 1970; in Billions)

	Extrapolated From[a]	
Regression Based On	Los Angeles	Boston
NO_x	$ 2.4– 5.7	$3.0–7.2
Hydrocarbons	$12.3–10.0	$2.6–0.3
Oxidants	$ 4.2– 3.2	$3.1–2.0

Source: National Academy of Sciences (1974, pp. 237–238).

[a]In each entry the first number is based on a linear housing price equation while the second is derived from a log–linear specification.

housing value equation to estimate a marginal-willingness-to-pay function, and using the latter to compute the benefits of nonmarginal changes, they obtained an estimate of average annual benefits per household of $511 and annual benefits for the Los Angeles area of $0.95 billion per year. At the same time, Brookshire et al. conducted a survey of willingness to pay to obtain improved air quality. Average annual bids amount to $316–353 per household, and annual benefits for the Los Angeles area are $0.58–0.65 billion per year.

This figure can be used to extrapolate to a national estimate of benefits following assumptions similar to those used by Harrison and McDonald and Nelson. If the range of average annual benefits per household is $350–500, and 30 million households are affected by mobile source air pollution, national benefits could be $10.5–15 billion per year. This figure can only be a realistic estimate of national benefits if Los Angeles is representative of other cities with respect to both the demand for clean air and typical pollution levels. But since in fact Los Angeles has one of the worst mobile source air pollution problems in the country, extrapolation from the Los Angeles per household benefit to the nation as a whole is likely to lead to a substantial overestimate.

I have reviewed national estimates of mobile source pollution control benefits based on property values that range from $0.9–$15 billion per year, with the latter being clearly an overestimate. The Harrison-McDonald best estimate of $3.7 billion per year may also be on the high side because the estimate is partly based on data from Los Angeles. I assume that the potential benefits attributable to the control of mobile source pollutants lie in the range of $1 to $10 billion per year. The most reasonable point estimate is $2.0 billion per year. Since there has not been a reduction in ozone or nitrogen oxide levels, the most reasonable point estimate of realized benefits is zero. I take the upper bound to be 2.0 billion per year. Again, there is likely double counting involved if this number is simply added to estimates derived through other categories of benefits. This question will be taken up in the next chapter.

WAGE DIFFERENTIALS

From a worker's perspective, a job can be viewed as a differentiated product—a good with a bundle of characteristics such as working conditions, prestige, training and enhancement of skills, and degree of risk of accidental injury or exposure to toxic substances. If workers are free to move from one urban area to another, then jobs are differentiated in part by the environmental and other characteristics of the urban area in which the job is located. If workers can be assumed to be free to choose from a menu of differentiated jobs in different areas, then the hedonic price technique can be applied to the data on wages, job characteristics, and worker characteristics in an effort to estimate the marginal implicit prices of job characteristics.

In a pioneering study conducted in conjunction with the National Academy of Sciences' analysis of automotive air pollution control policies (National Academy of Sciences, 1974, pp. 243–255), Meyer and Leone interpret differences in wages among cities as reflecting workers' willingness to pay (in the form of lower wages) to work and live in cities with higher levels of environmental and other amenities. After seeking to relate wage differentials to differences in a variety of urban amenities and disamenities, Meyer and Leone estimate the benefits associated with a 45% reduction in particulate, sulfur dioxide, and nitrogen dioxide levels.

First considering only the two stationary source pollutants, benefits are estimated at $6.1 billion and $2.1 billion respectively. Adjusting these figures for the growth in the consumer price index, growth in the labor force, and for an assumed 20% realized reduction in pollution leads to an estimate of $4.9 billion in 1978 dollars for suspended particulates and $1.7 billion for sulfur dioxide. This is a total of $6.6 billion for both stationary source pollutants. The Meyer-Leone estimate for nitrogen dioxide is $5.1 billion. Adjusting this for the growth in the Consumer Price Index and the labor force since 1972 results in an estimate of $9.1 billion for 1978.

These estimates must be considered tentative. First, at the empirical level, the estimated coefficients for the air pollution variables under different model specifications, while usually of the correct sign, are not statistically significant. Thus a lower-bound estimate would have to be zero. Second, there is the question of whether other influences on urban wage differentials have been adequately controlled. For example, there are no variables other than scale (population) to reflect differences in productivity that might be attributable to differences in industrial mix or natural resource endowments. Finally, there are questions of how estimates of benefits should be computed from observations on wage differences across cities. For example, can benefits computed from wage differences be added to benefit measures derived by other means, such as property values, or are they alternative ways of measuring the same phenomenon? It can be shown that under certain conditions wage differential benefits should be added to property value benefits in computing an aggregate benefit measure (Freeman, 1979a, pp. 118–121). However, it is not known whether these conditions hold in practice or are applicable to the type of study carried out by Meyer and Leone.

Cropper (1979) has developed a labor supply model which takes into account interurban amenity differences, housing site location within the urban area, and wages. Under certain assumptions, knowledge of the labor supply function makes it possible to estimate the coefficients of the utility function and to compute willingness to pay for changes in the level of urban amenities. Cropper estimates the model using 1969 wage data. SO_2 is one of the amenity variables. She estimates that a laborer with income of $9,000 per year would be willing to pay $55–65 per year for a 20% decrease in SO_2 levels. She does not estimate aggregate or national benefits. However, it appears that an appropriate extrapolation to the national labor force could yield estimates of willingness to pay of the same order of magnitude as those of Meyer and Leone.

Finally, as part of their project to determine the benefits of achieving the secondary standards for suspended particulates and sulfur dioxide, Mathtech (1981) estimates a hedonic wage equation from data in the University of Michigan Panel Study of Income Dynamics. Suspended particulate levels are significantly positively associated with wages.[5]

Rather than estimate the marginal willingness to pay functions directly, Mathtech assumes a particular functional form for these curves in order to estimate the benefits of achieving the standards. They estimate benefits for two SMSAs, Cleveland and Denver. Achieving the standard for suspended particulates is predicted to lower the equilibrium wages in these two cities by approximately 10¢ per hour. For one who works 2,000 hours per year, this means that about $200 per year in extra salary is required in order to compensate the worker for enduring pollution levels above the secondary standard. Mathtech does not estimate national benefits.

These three studies demonstrate the potential usefulness of the wage

---

[5]Rosen (1979) also finds a positive association between wages and particulates in his analysis of the influence of urban quality of life factors on interurban wage differences. He does not use his data to estimate the benefits of pollution control.

differential approach to benefit estimation. But the method requires more theoretical examination to clarify the relationships between wage differentials and other measures of benefits, such as those derived from property values. And there needs to be more empirical work to determine whether there is in fact a significant association between wages and air pollution in a properly specified model. For these reasons, wage benefit estimates will not be included in the aggregate estimate developed in the next chapter.

REFERENCES

Brookshire, David S., Ralph C. d'Arge, William Schulze, and Mark A. Thayer. *Methods Development for Assessing Air Pollution Control Benefits, Vol. 2: Experiments in Valuing Nonmarket Goods.* Washington, D.C.: Environmental Protection Agency, 1979.

Brookshire, David S., Berry C. Ives, and William D. Schulze. "The Valuation of Aesthetic Preferences," *Journal of Environmental Economics and Management*, 3, no. 4 (December, 1976), 325–346.

Brown, Gardner M. and Henry O. Pollakowski. "Economic Valuation of Shoreline," *Review of Economics and Statistics*, 59 (August, 1977), 272–278.

Cropper, Maureen L. "The Valuation of Locational Amenities: An Alternative to the Hedonic Price Approach," in Maureen L. Cropper et al., *Methods Development for Assessing Air Pollution Control Benefits, Vol. 4: Studies on Partial Equilibrium Approaches to Valuation of Environmental Amenities.* Washington, D.C.: Environmental Protection Agency, 1979.

Freeman, A. Myrick, III. "On Estimating Air Pollution Control Benefits from Land Value Studies," *Journal of Environmental Economics and Management*, 1, no. 1 (May, 1974), 74–83.

_____. *The Benefits of Environmental Improvement: Theory and Practice.* Baltimore: Johns Hopkins University Press, 1979a.

_____. "Hedonic Prices, Property Values, and Measuring Environmental Benefits: A Survey of the Issues," *Scandinavian Journal of Economics*, 81, no. 2 (1979b), 154–173.

Harrison, David, and Daniel L. Rubinfeld. "Hedonic Housing Prices and the Demand for Clean Air," *Journal of Environmental Economics and Management*, 5, no. 2 (1978a), 81–102.

_____. "The Air Pollution and Property Value Debate," *Review of Economics and Statistics*, 60, no. 4 (November, 1978b), 635–638.

National Academy of Sciences, Coordinating Committee on Air Quality Studies. *Air Quality and Automobile Emission Control, Vol. 4. The Costs and Benefits of Automobile Emission Control*, Washington, D.C., 1974.

Nelson, Jon P. *The Effects of Mobile Source Air and Noise Pollution on Residential Property Values.* Washington, D.C.: U.S. Department of Transportation, 1975.

_____. "Residential Choice, Hedonic Prices, and the Demand for Urban Air Quality," *Journal of Urban Economics*, 5 no. 3 (1978a), 357–369.

――. *Economic Analysis of Transportation Noise Abatement.* Cambridge: Ballinger, 1978.

Polinsky, A. Mitchell, and Daniel L. Rubinfeld. "Property Values and the Benefits of Environmental Improvements: Theory and Measurement," in Lowdon Wingo and Alan Evans, eds., *Public Economics in the Quality of Life.* Baltimore: Johns Hopkins University Press, 1977.

Randall, Alan, Berry Ives, and Clyde Eastman. "Bidding Games for Evaluation of Aesthetic Environmental Improvement," *Journal of Environmental Economics and Management*, 1, no. 2 (August, 1974), 132–149.

Rosen, Sherwin. "Hedonic Prices and Implicit Markets: Product Differentiation in Perfect Competition," *Journal of Political Economy*, 82, no. 1 (January/February, 1974), 34–55.

――. "Wage-based Indexes of Urban Quality of Life," in Peter Mieszkowski and Mahlon Straszheim, eds., *Current Issues in Urban Economics.* Baltimore: Johns Hopkins University Press, 1979.

Waddell, Thomas E. *The Economic Damages of Air Pollution.* Washington, D.C.: Environmental Protection Agency, 1974.

7

AIR POLLUTION CONTROL BENEFITS: A SUMMARY

Table 7.1 shows for each category of benefits the realized benefits associated with the change in pollution levels between 1970 and 1978—in all cases, in 1978 dollars per year. It is probably not valid simply to add the property value benefits to other categories in Table 7.1 because tangible impacts on households due to soiling, damage to household paints, and perhaps morbidity are also likely to affect property values. It is also possible that some forms of benefits have not been captured by any of the measures reviewed here. An example is benefits associated with amenity and aesthetic values away from the residence. We must consider, therefore, the question of gaps and overlaps in our measures of benefits.

OVERLAPS AND GAPS IN ESTIMATING BENEFITS

One major problem in estimating benefits is the possibility of either overlap among or gaps between categories of benefits as estimated by presently used techniques. This problem can arise where two types of effects associated with the same pollutant are estimated separately. For example, do estimates of health effects and property value differences associated with suspended particulates involve some double counting of the benefits of reducing concentrations of suspended particulates, or are there additional effects not captured by either measure? Although definitive answers to this question cannot be given here, the discussion will show that it should be possible to determine when such gaps and overlaps exist. It should also be possible to make some judgment as to the significance and likely direction of any biases in the estimated total benefit figures. This should be useful in deriving confidence limits or high and low bounds surrounding best estimates of total benefits.

Consider the case where health benefits are measured by mortality rate studies, and aesthetic, soiling, and materials benefits are measured through property value differentials. The justification for measuring the two classes of benefits separately and adding them to obtain aggregate benefits is that only those effects of air pollution that are perceived by individuals can influence property values, and that people have for the most part been ignorant of the effects of air pollution on their health and life expectancy. However, this simple resolution of the problem should leave one uneasy. Some kinds of short-term health problems, such as eye irritation and shortness of breath, may be directly perceived as being caused by poor air quality. In addition, there has been a substantial increase in the information available to the general public about long-term health effects and related air quality levels around urban areas. Thus, perceptions of health effects may be influencing property value differentials and leading to the possibility of double counting. To gain a better understanding of the problem, it is necessary to consider in more detail exactly what is captured by each of the two approaches to measurement.

It will be helpful to develop a system of classification for different types of effects associated with poor air quality. Two broad classes of effects are aesthetic and health. The former includes effects such as odor, taste, reduced visibility, soiling, and damage to external paints, all of which are perceived by individuals. With respect to health effects, no distinction need be made between morbidity effects and mortality effects for purposes of this discussion. At the conceptual level a distinction can be made between those health effects that are perceived by individuals and those of which they are ignorant. The former are likely to be primarily clinical manifestations of short-term exposures to relatively high concentrations. Finally, it is necessary to distinguish between those effects that are caused by the individual's exposure at home and those due to exposure as she travels around the urban air shed, to work, for shopping, for recreation. These "away-from-home" effects are independent of the individual's place of residence.

This classification approach is displayed schematically in Figure 7.1. There are six subsets of effects classified by aesthetics, health perceived, and health unperceived, and in all cases further divided between home and away. Property value studies can only capture those effects associated with the home that are perceived. Health benefits derived from mortality and morbidity studies capture both home and away effects and both perceived and unperceived health effects.

The figure illustrates both an overlap and a gap. Perceived effects to health, materials, and so forth, at home are captured by both property value and damage function approaches. But aesthetics associated with away-from-home exposures are not captured by either approach. Whether the addition of

Overlaps and Gaps in Estimating Benefits 127

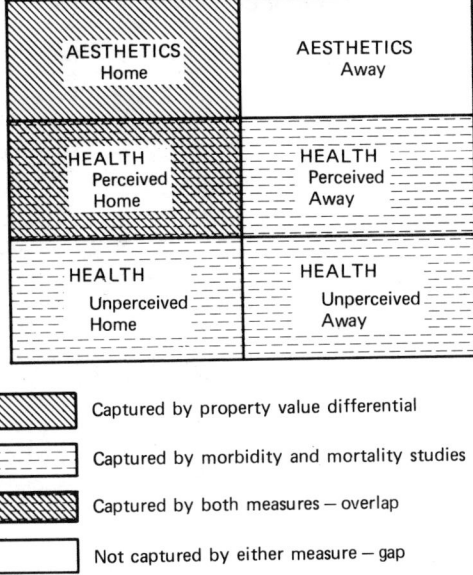

Figure 7.1. Overlaps and gaps in property value and health benefit estimates in relation to air quality.

property value and health effect benefits results in an overestimate or an underestimate depends upon the relative size of the double-counted and omitted categories. Nothing can be said about this question on a priori grounds.

It is interesting to compare the property value total with those portions of the other four categories in Table 7.1 that one might plausibly assume would affect property values. Most of the soiling and cleaning benefits of $3.0 billion should be reflected in property values. The estimate of vegetation damages is derived primarily from commercial agriculture. So this figure would not be captured by residential property value measures. A large portion of materials benefits is related to commerce and industry. But some portion, perhaps $0.2 billion, is related to household paints and coatings and would be capitalized in property values.

The health effects are more difficult to allocate. But for illustrative purposes, I assume that all the mortality effects involve such subtle biomedical processes that people are unaware of the connection between mortality and air pollution. Then none of this category would be reflected in property values. I also assume that morbidity effects are perceived to be due to air pollution, and that half of the total, or $1.6 billion, is associated with

TABLE 7.1. Air Pollution Control Benefits Being Enjoyed in 1978 (In Billions of 1978 Dollars)

Category	Realized Benefits Range	Most Reasonable Point Estimate
1. Health		
Stationary Source		
Mortality	$2.8–27.8	$13.9
Morbidity	$0.3–12.4	$ 3.1
Total	$3.1–40.2	$17.0
Mobile Source	$0.0– 0.4	$ 0.0
Total Health	$3.1–40.6	$17.0
2. Soiling and Cleaning	$1.0– 6.0	$ 3.0
3. Vegetation		
Stationary Source	0	0
Mobile Source	$0.1– 0.4	$ 0.3
Total Vegetation	$0.1– 0.4	$ 0.3
4. Materials		
Stationary Source	$0.4– 1.1	$ 0.7
Mobile Source	$0.0– 0.3	$ 0.0
Total Materials	$0.4– 1.4	$ 0.7
5. Property Values		
Stationary Source	$0.9– 6.9	$ 2.3
Mobile	$0.0– 2.0	$ 0.0
Total Property Value	$0.9– 8.9	$ 2.3

exposures at home. This means that a total of $4.8 billion of benefits measured by other means should also be reflected in property values. This is more than double the estimated property value benefits. This indicates that we cannot completely reconcile our accounting of benefits in different categories. However, the orders of magnitude are similar. And this lends some plausibility to these estimates.

The most conservative approach to treating property value benefits is to assume that those beneficial effects reflected in property values are also fully captured by our estimates of benefits in the other four categories. This means that amenity and aesthetic effects, both at home and away, are assumed to be zero. This is very conservative. However, there is very little evidence on the possible magnitude of aesthetic effects at the national level. In their survey or bidding game approach to measuring benefits in Los Angeles, Brookshire et al. (1979) asked people to allocate their total bid between aesthetics and health effects. An examination of their reported results suggests that perhaps 30% of respondents' willingness to pay is attributable to aesthetic rather than health benefits. Brookshire et al. also found that the survey approach yielded estimates comparable in magnitude to their property value estimates. If this proportion is representative of the urban population as a whole, the $0.7 billion of property value benefits can be added to the total in categories 1–4. Given these assumptions, total national benefits that have been realized due to reductions in pollution since 1970 lie in the range of $4.9 to $51.1 billion per year. The most likely value is $21.7 billion per year.

It is important to bear in mind the major qualifications attached to the estimates presented here. The first, of course, is that these estimates are not based on new data or research but rather are derived from a review of other studies. Many of those studies can be, and have been, criticized on methodological or empirical grounds. The estimates presented here reflect my own judgments as to the quality and reliability of the results of the studies reviewed. Others may differ with the judgments made and the weights given here to various pieces of evidence.

Second, it is important to emphasize the range of uncertainty reflected in my estimates. The low and high values differ by more than a factor of 10. I believe that the probability is .9 that the true value of realized benefits lies within this range. But the true value could lie either substantially above or below the most likely point estimate of $21.7 billion.

About three-quarters of the total benefits are estimated to be in the health category. This estimate is subject to uncertainty about both the air pollution–health relationship and the value of health and reduced mortality. Only the former uncertainty is reflected in the range between low and high values. If the reader believes that $500,000 per death avoided is more reasonable than the $1 million used here, the estimated total benefits would be reduced by about 35%.

There is much controversy regarding estimates of the air pollution–mortality relationship. This is reflected in the wide range of the estimates of mortality benefits. Additional research now being done in several places may help to resolve the uncertainty. But it is also possible that the interactions among socioeconomic, environmental, and health variables are so complex and the degree of correlation among independent variables so severe that existing statistical techniques may be incapable of resolving the questions of whether and to what extent ambient concentrations of air pollution cause mortality. If this turns out to be the case, we will be left with a substantial uncertainty about a major question affecting environmental policy.

Finally, I must reemphasize that the benefits estimated here are only those associated with my estimate of realized improvements in air quality since 1970. To the extent that the Clean Air Act has prevented further degradation of air quality, additional benefits in the form of damages prevented can be attributed to the Act.

BENEFITS AND COSTS COMPARED

A comparison of information on benefits and costs would be potentially useful to the extent that it could shed light on two questions: Have the air and water pollution control programs been worth it (are benefits greater than costs)? And do the programs maximize net benefits?

This latter question is especially important when changes in standards and possible new requirements are being considered. What is required is estimates of incremental or marginal benefits and costs for each substance for small changes from existing levels of control. Unfortunately, the benefit estimates presented here are neither precise enough nor in a form that permits incremental policy analysis. However, the estimates of the total benefits of a 20% improvement in air quality can be compared with estimates of total air pollution control costs.

The Council on Environmental Quality (1979) has published estimates of the total annual costs attributable to the air pollution control programs in 1978 and expected in 1987—both in 1978 dollars. As in the case of benefits, there is substantial uncertainty in the estimation of costs. Yet the CEQ presents only point estimates as if they were certain. Air pollution control costs are estimated at $16.6 billion per year in 1978. This compares with air pollution control benefits of between $4.9 and $51.1 billion, with a most likely point estimate of $21.7 billion. In aggregate it appears that the air pollution control program has been worth the cost. But taking account of uncertainty in the estimates of both benefits and costs, the possibility that realized benefits are substantially less than costs cannot be ruled out.

These aggregate figures obscure significant differences in the benefit–cost relationship for stationary and mobile source air pollution. The CEQ estimates stationary source control costs at $9.0 billion per year. Benefits of controlling stationary sources are estimated to be between $4.8 and $49.4 billion, with a most likely point estimate of $21.4 billion per year. Thus a fair degree of confidence can be attached to a statement that the control of stationary sources has been worthwhile on benefit–cost grounds.

On the other hand, the CEQ estimates mobile source control costs to be $7.6 billion per year. But benefits of controlling these sources are estimated to be only $0.1 to $1.7 billion, with a most likely point estimate of $0.3 billion per year. This suggests that the mobile source control program, at least in its present form, does not pass a benefit–cost test. I am not the first analyst to reach this conclusion about the mobile source control program. For an excellent discussion of the economics of automotive air pollution control policy with references to other benefit–cost analyses, see Seskin (1978).

Does the vanishingly small benefit–cost ratio mean that the mobile source air pollution control program should be scrapped in its entirety? Almost certainly not. There are two avenues for improving the benefit–cost relationship for this program. The first is to examine in more detail the marginal benefit–marginal cost relationship so that changes in existing standards and requirements can be evaluated. The second is to seek ways to make this program more cost effective, that is, to increase the benefits per dollar of cost and/or to reduce the cost of obtaining a given improvement in air quality. For a discussion of policy alternatives, see Seskin (1978).

REFERENCES

Brookshire, David S., Ralph C. d'Arge, William D. Schulze, and Mark A. Thayer. *Methods Development for Assessing Air Pollution Control Benefits, Vol 2: Experiments in Valuing Nonmarket Goods*. Washington, D.C.: Environmental Protection Agency, 1979.

Seskin, Eugene P. "Automobile Air Pollution Policy," in Paul R. Portney, ed. *Current Issues in U.S. Environmental Policy*. Baltimore: Johns Hopkins University Press, 1978.

U.S. Council on Environmental Quality, *Environmental Quality—1979*. Washington, D.C.: 1979.

8

WATER POLLUTION CONTROL AND RECREATION BENEFITS

The purpose of this chapter and the next is to review and evaluate estimates of national damages due to water pollution and estimates of the benefits of its abatement. In doing so, we will arrive at a judgment as to the magnitude of benefits likely to be realized in the implementation of the Federal Water Pollution Control Act Amendments of 1972 (FWPCA–72). This law calls for all industrial dischargers to have controlled their discharges consistent with the "best practical treatment" methods (BPT) by 1977 and further to achieve the "best available treatment" technologies (BAT) by 1983. Municipal treatment systems are to meet similar requirements, secondary treatment by 1977 and the best practicable waste treatment technology by 1983. Amendments to the Act passed in 1977 allow for modifications of the BAT requirements and for various extensions of the 1983 deadline for BAT for industry. Finally, the FWPCA–72 establish the objectives of attaining "fishable and swimmable waters" by 1983 and the elimination of all discharges by 1985.

The BPT and BAT requirements apply to point sources of pollution. The principal mechanism for dealing with nonpoint sources of pollution, such as erosion and agricultural and urban runoff, is the requirement for the "development and implementation of area-wide waste treatment management plans" as required in Section 208 of the FWPCA–72. Estimation of the benefits of controlling nonpoint sources is made difficult both because of the lack of information on the effects of nonpoint source pollutants on water users and because of the difficulty in predicting the degree of control that is likely to emerge from the Section 208 planning process. The benefits of nonpoint source control will not be covered in this study.

Ideally, one would like to be able to derive estimates of the incremental benefits achieved by compliance with each stage of the FWPCA–72—that is, for BPT in 1977, BAT in 1983, and elimination of discharges in 1985. However, there are several problems in deriving estimates of incremental benefits from the studies and the data presently available. First, the FWPCA-72 is not the first effort to control water pollution. Rather, it represents a major change in those federal and state policies established in 1965. Those policies were having some effect on water quality as implementation slowly proceeded. Although there were substantial weaknesses in the 1965 law, especially with respect to incentives and the enforcement effort, it is likely that there would have been some improvement in water quality after 1972 even without the new amendments. Several of the studies reviewed in this chapter take 1972 water quality levels as the starting point for estimating the benefits of achieving full compliance with the standards established under the FWPCA-72. These studies are likely to overestimate the incremental benefits associated with the Act, since they attribute all of the subsequent improvement in water quality to the FWPCA-72.

A second set of problems concerns how to determine the incremental benefits attributable to the implementation of each stage of the FWPCA-72. First, if the benefit function is nonlinear, its exact form must be known in order to determine what portion of the total benefits can be attributed to achieving the BPT standards of 1977. Furthermore, the relative stringency of the 1977 and 1983 standards varies substantially across polluting substances and for any substance across industrial categories. The BPT requirements focused primarily on the control of the so-called conventional pollutants, organic matter, and suspended solids, while the BAT requirements are giving relatively greater emphasis to the control of metals and organic and inorganic toxic substances, such as mercury and phenols. Thus there is no simple aggregate relationship between the degree of control that was to be achieved in 1977 and that to be expected in 1983. Rather, an analysis must proceed on a case-by-case basis, looking at individual pollutants and industries. Only one of the studies reviewed here (Unger, 1975) attempts to make separate estimates of the benefits of implementing each stage of the Act. Except for this, we must be satisfied with estimates of the benefits of full compliance with the Act.

Some of the studies have attempted to estimate benefits of improvement for some base year, say 1972. Other have focused on the damages due to pollution levels actually experienced in 1972. There are at least two reasons why estimates of damages might be taken as upper-bound estimates of the benefits of full compliance with the 1983 standards. First, these standards call for strict control of discharges and in some cases will result in the elimination of certain types of discharges. And second, if the benefit function is nonlinear with decreasing marginal benefits, the first clean-up efforts will have produced the largest benefits, and the bulk of benefits will have been achieved (and damages avoided) as the 1983 standards are approached and attained.

I will proceed by estimating benefits by category of effects. In contrast with the air pollution benefits, there are substantial differences among the studies reviewed here in the way effects and benefits are classified. I have chosen to classify the benefits of controlling point source pollution in the following manner:

1. *Recreation.* These are benefits to individuals who actually use waterways for recreational activities, such as fishing, swimming, boating, and water fowl hunting. This category should also include activities such as hiking, picnicking, and nature observation, which are frequently engaged in near water bodies. However, none of the studies reviewed here attempted to estimate benefits to these activities.
2. *Nonuser Benefits.* This category includes amenity, aesthetic, and ecological benefits that are not directly associated with activities on or adjacent to the water body or with diversionary uses of the water. This category could also include preservation benefits, option values, and changes in property values that reflect households' willingness to pay to live near high quality water bodies.
3. *Diversionary Uses.*
   a. *Drinking Water and Health.* To the extent that point sources of pollution result in chemical, bacterial, or viral contamination of sources of drinking water, controlling that pollution may reduce risks to human health.
   b. *Treatment Costs for Municipal Water Supplies.* Pollutants present in intake water may force suppliers to incur higher treatment costs for reasons other than, or in addition to, the protection of health.
   c. *Household Benefits.* To the extent that point sources of pollution affect water hardness or corrosion of pipes and appliances, costs to households could be reduced by controlling these substances.
   d. *Industrial Treatment Costs.* Control of pollution may reduce costs of treating industrial process and cooling water.
4. *Commercial Fisheries.* Where pollution has reduced the biological productivity of fisheries or resulted in the closure of shellfish beds and other fishery resources, abatement can result in increased producer rents and/or lower prices of fisheries products to consumers.

The remainder of this chapter is devoted to a review of relevant recreation benefit studies and to the development of my synthesis estimate of recreation benefits of attaining the 1985 objectives of the FWPCA–72. In the next chapter, I review studies covering other categories of benefits, develop my own synthesis estimates for these categories, and discuss the relationship between estimates of benefits and costs for present policy.

METHODS FOR ESTIMATING RECREATION BENEFITS

It will be helpful first to review the conceptual basis for defining and measuring the benefits of improved water quality for recreationists. Consider a single recreation site such as a lake, park or wilderness area. There is a demand function for the use of this recreation site which relates the quantity of recreation services demanded, measured in recreation days, to the price of these services, income, and other socioeconomic variables. This demand function can also be interpreted as a marginal-willingness-to-pay or inverse demand function, relating the marginal value of a recreation day to the quantity of recreation days and other variables. An inverse demand curve can be plotted holding income, the prices and availability of substitutes, and the quality of this recreation site constant. In Figure 8.1, D_1 is the demand curve for visits before water quality is improved. Suppose the price of admission to this site is $0A per day. The actual recreational use or quantity demanded will be OX_1. The value of this recreation site to users, given the initial water quality, is the consumers' surplus as measured by area ABC.

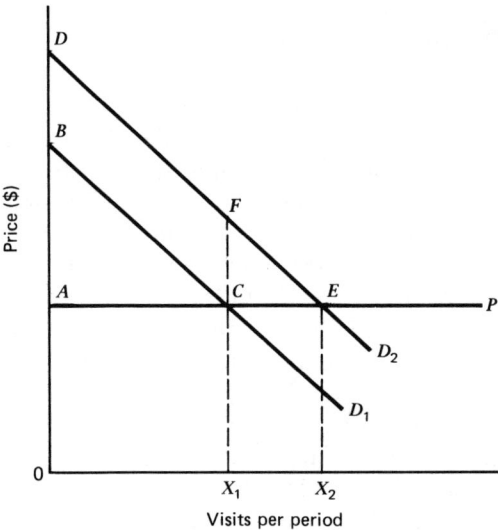

Figure 8.1. The demand for recreation and the benefits of improved water quality.

Assume that water quality is improved at this site. Users would be willing to pay more at the margin to use this improved site at given use levels; and at the given price, use would increase. In economic terms the effect is to shift the demand curve to the right. The new demand curve is shown by D_2. The net economic benefit of this improvement in water quality is the increase in willingness to pay as measured by the area between the two demand curves, *BCED*.

The net benefit can be divided into two components. The first is the increase in value to those OX_1 users who were using the facility even at the original level of water quality. This is the area *BCFD*. This area represents their increased willingness to pay to maintain present use rates at this recreation site rather than do without. In addition, the greater attractiveness of this site relative to alternative recreation sites and alternative consumption activities results in an increase in recreation days at this site equal to $X_2 - X_1$. The net benefit associated with this increase in use is the area *CEF*. This increase consists of both greater use rates by original users and new users who are attracted to this site by the improvement in water quality. In using this measure of benefits, there is no need to take into account changes in recreation use at other sites or savings in travel costs. These are all reflected with the *BCED* benefit measure. When there are simultaneous changes in quality or availability at several recreation sites, the theoretical and empirical analysis becomes more complicated. For a further analysis of this problem and other issues, see Freeman (1979, Chapter 8).

Estimating Site Demand Curves

In order to implement this theoretical approach, one must first have a way of estimating demand functions for a recreation site and, second, a way of predicting changes in the demand curve when water quality at the site changes. Of course, the problem of demand estimation would be quite straightforward if the normal practice were to charge an entry fee and if fees varied substantially across sites or over time. But the typical practice for publicly provided recreation sites is to charge a zero price or only a nominal entry fee. Without variation in the entry fee, it is not possible to estimate demand functions through normal econometric procedures.

However, it may be possible to infer how a given group of people would respond to changes in the entry price by examining data on how different groups of people respond to differences in monetary travel costs. This is the basic hypothesis of the so-called Clawson-Knetsch (C-K) travel cost method of demand estimation. What follows are a brief review of the basic C-K method and then a discussion of some problems in its application which are particularly relevant to the task of benefit estimation. The basic references are Clawson and Knetsch (1966), and Knetsch (1964). For a clear exposition and numerical example of its application, see Mäler and Wyzga (1976); see also Freeman (1979).

It must be emphasized that the C-K method is site-specific; that is, it yields a demand function for a specific recreation site rather than for recreational activities in general. However, the C-K method can be generalized and applied to the task of estimating systems of demand functions for several sites, taking into account the interrelated nature of their demands and substitution across sites. The site demand is a derived demand and depends on the ability of the site to "produce" the desired activities. While this may reduce the usefulness of the C-K method for some purposes—for example, predicting total recreation activity over time—it is precisely the site-specific nature of the method that makes it attractive for estimating the economic value of water quality improvements for particular water bodies.

In implementing the C-K method, it must be assumed that the primary purpose of the recreation trip is to visit that site. When trips involve purposes other than visiting the site, at least some portion of the total travel cost is a joint cost that cannot be allocated meaningfully to the visit to the recreation site.

The C-K method involves determining the visitation rates of different households to a given site as a function of their travel cost to the site and socioeconomic variables such as income, median educational attainment, and age. In the simplest model, travel cost is simply a function of the monetary cost per mile from the household residence to the site. In order to derive different points on the demand curve, it is necessary to assume different households will respond to changes in the price or entry fees to the site in the same way that they respond to differences in travel cost.

The simplest version of the procedure is as follows:

1. For a given recreation site, the surrounding area is divided into concentric circular zones for the purpose of measuring the travel cost from each zone to the site and return.
2. Visitors at the site are sampled to determine their zones of origin.
3. Visitation rates defined as visitor days per capita are calculated for each zone of origin.
4. A travel cost measure is constructed to indicate the cost of travel from the origin zone to the recreation site and back.
5. Visitation rates are regressed on travel costs and socioeconomic variables such as average income and median educational attainment. The regression tests the hypothesis that visitation rates depend in part on travel cost.

6. The observed total visitation for the site from all travel cost zones represents one point on the demand curve for that site, that is, the intersection of the present horizontal price line (either at zero price or the typical nominal entry fee) with the true economic demand curve.

7. Other points on the demand curve are found by assuming that visitors will respond to a $1 increase in admission price in the same way that they would to a $1 increase in computed travel cost. To find the point on the demand curve for the site when the admission price rises by $1, the estimated visitation-rate equation is used to compute visitation rates and total visits for all travel cost zones with the existing travel cost plus $1. Visits are summed across travel cost zones to determine the predicted total visitation at the higher price. These calculations are repeated for higher and higher hypothetical admission prices, and the full demand curve is traced out.[1]

This procedure involves sampling only users at the site. This sampling procedure would be adequate if the objective were simply to determine the existing demand curve. However, if the objective of the analysis is to predict how a population would respond to changes in quality or to take into account the effect of alternative recreation sites on site-specific demand, then samples should be drawn from the entire regional population, that is, those who have not visited the site as well as those who have. This would permit the inclusion in the sample of present nonusers who might shift from other sites or begin to be involved in recreation activity after an improvement in water quality.

There are a number of technical issues regarding demand curve estimation that have not been dealt with here. They include the role of travel time and on-site time in defining travel cost, congestion at recreation sites, and demand function estimation with several recreation sites. These are discussed in more detail in Freeman (1979, Chapter 8).

---

[1] Algebraically, the steps involved are: (1) Estimate for each distance or travel cost zone d:
$$V_d = V(M_d, S_d, C_d),$$
where $d = (1, \ldots, n)$ is the index of the travel cost zone; M_d is average income in the zone; S_d represents other socioeconomic variables; and C_d is a measure of travel cost. (2) Assuming no admission fee, find total visits:
$$V = \sum_{d=1}^{n} V_d$$
(3) Let increments of travel cost ΔC stand as proxies for posited admission fees. Compute
$$V_j = \sum_{d=1}^{n} V[M_d, S_d, (C_d + j\Delta C)]$$
for successive j. V_j as a function of $j\Delta C$ is the demand function for visits.

Incorporating Water Quality

To use the C-K method in estimating the benefits of improvement in water quality, one must have estimates of the demand curves for the recreation site both before and after the improvement in water quality has taken place. One possible approach is to estimate the demand curve for a recreation site before the pollution control policy has been implemented and then to reestimate the demand curve after the policy has had its effect. This kind of ex post measurement would, itself, be valuable, particularly as a check on other methods for predicting benefits. But it does not meet the real problem posed to policy analysts, that is, how to estimate benefits before the fact in order to plan for a more rational commitment of resources to pollution control. Analytically, the problem is one of estimating a multivariate demand function, with water quality at the site as one of the arguments, but where there are no direct observations on changes in water quality.

Incorporating water quality in the analysis poses two sorts of problems. The first is to determine what empirical indicators of water quality are appropriate. The second problem is how to derive the correct relationship between water quality and the demand for visits to the site. A variety of water quality indicators are affected by the presence of water pollutants. There are several questions concerning what indicators of water quality are appropriate for empirical analysis and how they should be used:

1. Should the analysis be based on objective measures of water quality such as dissolved oxygen and pH? Or should some measure of perceived water quality be derived by questioning recreationists?
2. Given the heterogeneity of water quality indicators, should the analysis disaggregate the measurement of ambient water quality into several distinct indicators? Or can an index of water quality be derived?
3. If the index approach is chosen to consolidate indicators, how are the weights for the individual indicators to be derived?

The water quality indicators actually chosen for empirical work should satisfy three criteria. The first is logical consistency. In other words, the water quality indicators should be in accord with our notions of what matters to recreationists. Second, they should be objective in the sense that they can be replicated by different observers. For example, if two observers were asked to rate the quality of several water bodies, the recorded evaluations should be substantially identical across observers. The third criterion is empirical validity. Does the water quality indicator actually help to predict recreation demand? In other words, is there a significant correlation between the water quality indicators used and the dependent variable to be explained?

Those studies that have attempted to analyze how individuals react to differences in ambient water quality have led to inconclusive results. Individuals' perceptions of water quality are sometimes difficult to reconcile with objective water quality indicators or experts' perceptions of water quality. At best, this makes it difficult to predict changes in recreation behavior associated with changes in objective water quality indicators. If recreation behavior is governed by perceptions, but it is impossible to link perceptions with objective water quality indicators, the predictive link between changes in water quality brought about by a water quality management strategy and the resulting changes in recreation behavior is broken. At worst, the use of water quality perceptions to explain recreation behavior could introduce a degree of circularity into the analysis. It is hard to tell whether people choose to recreate at a given site because they perceive that it has high water quality or whether they tell questioners that they think the water quality is high to justify their choice of that site. The ability of perceptions of water quality to explain recreation choices among alternative sites has not been established as yet. Of course this could be either because there are weaknesses in the techniques of measuring perceived water quality or because perceived water quality does not in fact matter much to recreationists.

The Regional Recreation Participation Model

The participation model is an alternative approach to the analysis of recreation and water quality benefits that involve less stringent data requirements, assumptions, and estimation techniques. These less stringent requirements can be considered advantages, but they entail the loss of ability to infer values from the empirical analysis. The approach is to estimate reduced form equations relating participation in specific recreation activities by a given population to the socioeconomic characteristics of that population and to the supply and quality of recreation opportunities available. Participation models of this sort deal only with Stage 2 in the estimation of benefits and shed little or no light on the third stage, that is, valuation. The C-K method incorporates the analysis of both Stages 2 and 3.

If reduced form population-specific participation equations can be estimated, it would be possible to predict the increase in participation to be expected with an increase in the supply of recreation opportunities or with an improvement in ambient water quality. If the value of a recreation day of a particular type could be inferred from other sources, then one component of recreation benefits can be estimated by multiplying the increase in recreation days and the assumed value per day. However, this would not capture the increased utility associated with the preexisting level of use, that is, the area *BCFD* in Figure 8.1.

A participation model of this type is used by Davidson, Adams, and Seneca (1966) as part of their study of the economic benefits of improving water quality in the Delaware Estuary. These authors use data from the 1959 Nationwide Outdoor Recreation Survey to estimate regression equations for participation in boating, swimming, and fishing. One set of explanatory variables in these equations reflects the availability of water area for water-based recreation. Actual socioeconomic data for 1960 and projected values for these variables for 1975 and 1990 are combined with the estimated reduced form equations to predict recreation activity in the 11-county area around the Delaware Estuary for those years. The variables for availability of water area are those actually observed at the time of the study, excluding the Delaware Estuary itself. This gives an estimate of recreational activities over time assuming that degraded water quality in the Estuary prevents recreation there.

It is assumed that the water quality of the Delaware will be improved sufficiently to allow water-based recreation in the Estuary. In other words, an improvement in water quality is assumed to be equivalent to an increase in the area of water available for recreation, in order to make use of the information contained in the reduced form equations. The projected increase in the availability of water area is used to predict new levels of recreational activity. The difference in the "with" and "without" predictions is attributed to the water quality improvement. Water quality enters the analysis only through a judgment as to whether or not river waters are suitable for recreation. Thus factors such as variation of water quality within the Estuary, differences in the aesthetic attributes of the shoreline and surrounding areas at different points in the Estuary, and problems of access to the water play no role in the model.

The participation approach could be used either to predict the changes in recreation at a point in time or, as in the case of the Davidson, Adams, and Seneca study, to make projections of changes in recreation over a long span of time. In the latter case, estimates are subject to all of the kinds of limitations inherent in long-term economic projections. In particular, these projections ignore the possible effects of changing tastes, increasing income, leisure time, and the impact of improved opportunities on participation rates through the "learning by doing" phenomenon.

This technique for relating water quality to recreation behavior is only as good as the data contained in the survey instrument. The survey data must include information on the availability of recreation opportunities, including types of water body, indicators of water quality, other site characteristics (such as facilities and improvements), and accessibility. Ideally, the survey should record not only levels of participation but also some measure of the costs of travel from the residence to the recreation site actually chosen.

Determining Values: Assignment of Shadow Prices

One approach to determining shadow prices is to survey users to determine their willingness to pay to use sites with a given set of attributes. The difficulties in determining willingness to pay by survey methods have been discussed above. In the absence of observations on actual values, it may still be possible to gain some feel for the order of magnitude of benefits by applying the imputed value or bureaucratic shadow price to the change in quantity. For example, Davidson, Adams, and Seneca (1966), in the study described above, made a series of illustrative calculations of monetary benefits by applying arbitrary but "reasonable" dollar values per recreation day to their estimated magnitudes of recreation activities. In some instances the disparity between benefits and costs may be so great that illustrative calculations like these will point fairly clearly and unambiguously toward one conclusion or the other. In such cases, further efforts to obtain refined estimates of values may not be warranted.

Assigning shadow prices could be an acceptable technique if there were sound bases for determining the values to be used. Some feel for a range of plausible shadow prices can be gained from a review of Clawson-Knetsch travel cost studies. Dwyer, Kelly, and Bowes (1977) have conducted such a review. However, there are several reasons why shadow prices derived for one site may not be valid for application to recreation benefits for another site or at the same site at a different point in time. First, most of the Clawson-Knetsch studies referred to by Dwyer, Kelly, and Bowes do not control for site characteristics such as water quality. Therefore they do not throw much light on the crucial question of the relationship between ambient water quality and value. Second, the demand for a given recreation site depends in part on the range of recreation alternatives in the region. The availability of alternatives differs from site to site. Finally, demand and value depend in part on the socioeconomic characteristics of the regional population. These characteristics vary among regions and over time in a given region.

The Water Resources Council, in its guidelines for evaluating water resource development projects, suggested the assignment of shadow prices for user days as a technique for determining recreation benefits (Water Resources Council, 1973). The Council suggested valuing "general" recreation days between $0.75 and $2.25 and "specialized" recreation days ("those activities for which opportunities, in general, are limited, intensity of use is low, and often may involve a large personal expense by the user" [p. 24804]) at $3 to $9 per day. These figures would have to be adjusted upward to account for subsequent inflation if they were to be used in benefit estimation now. As indicated above, in some circumstances useful information can be gained by trial calculations with tentative shadow prices. However, the danger in the Council recommendation is that the suggested prices may be misconstrued by some to be valid and accurate measures of value. The application of average values does not give sufficient weight to the concept of consumer surplus and total willingness to pay. In addition, the specification of a fairly narrow range of possible values does not give adequate consideration to the wide range of possible different circumstances. For example, total willingness to pay could be quite high where supply is restricted relative to demand, where congestion exists, or where there are no close substitutes for the recreation resource in question.

In sum, tentatively assigned shadow prices can be useful in some circumstances, but they should be seen as the last resort and be used only in the most tentative way. Furthermore, every effort should be made to allow for specialized recreation resources, the availability of substitutes, and supply–demand considerations in selecting the values to be used.

Summary

Two techniques for measuring recreation benefits associated with improved water quality have been discussed. One is based on observations of actual behavior and is capable of providing estimates of both changes in use at a specific site and values attached to use. The other is used for participation in general and must be coupled with a separate technique for determining values. If analysts have a choice of method, under what circumstances should they choose one or the other? The C-K method is specifically designed to estimate the demand for the single site or, in a simultaneous equation model, a small number of sites. It has most often been applied in the analysis of the demand for isolated parks and water bodies, such as lakes, where travel costs are significant so that most trips are made for the single purpose of undertaking recreation at the site. There is little experience with using the C-K method to estimate the demand for sites close to the population served, where travel costs are low in absolute terms and may not vary widely across users. Thus it is not clear whether the C-K method will be helpful where pollution control activities lead to increased recreation opportunities in large urban areas. The C-K method is more likely to be useful where the number of access points to the water body is limited and each access point can be treated as a separate site. But where there is general access to the water body, for example, through an extensive system of river front parks, and where the recreation activities do not require specific site improvements, for example, as with bank fishing, the recreation participation approach is likely to be more appropriate.

A REVIEW OF RECREATION DAMAGE AND BENEFIT STUDIES

The National Commission on Water Quality (1976) commissioned four studies of benefits, three of which include various components of recreation activities. Each study estimated the benefits in 1980 and 1985 of improving water quality from 1972 levels, where 1985 is the assumed date of full attainment of the objectives of the FWPCA-72. In each case, the estimates are based on projections of population, income, and other variables to the relevant year.

One of these studies is by the National Planning Association (1975). They use a model of recreational participation to estimate the increase in fresh water fishing and boating that might be attributed to projected improvements in water quality. These are the only activities for which the available data permit the estimation of the relationship between participation and water quality. The data are from the National Recreation Survey of 1972.

The model includes regression equations for probability of participating in the recreation activity and number of days per participant. Explanatory variables include income, race, sex, water quality at nearby sites, and travel cost as a measure of accessibility. It is very difficult to evaluate the model because the report contains almost no discussion of the model specification and estimation and statistical results such as standard errors, "t" values, and R^2s are not reported.

On the basis of the estimated relationship between participation and water quality, the National Planning Association predicts that participation in boating will increase by between 50 and 115 million activity days per year by 1985. Fresh water recreational fishing is predicted to increase by between 26 and 67 million days per year by 1985. Unit values of $12.12 and $10.06 per day in 1978 dollars are then applied to boating and fishing activities respectively. These unit values were apparently assigned by the Commission Staff rather than the NPA. The basis for these values is not specified. The same technique is used to estimate increases in activity levels for the year 1980. The results are shown in Table 8.1. It should be noted that this method will lead to an underestimate of total benefits for two reasons. First, some water-based activities, such as water skiing, canoeing, and sailing, have been omitted due to lack of data. And second, this technique captures only those benefits accruing to additional participation and neglects benefits due to

TABLE 8.1 National Recreation Benefits as Estimated for the National Commission on Water Quality (in Millions of 1978 Dollars)

	Millions of Dollars Per Year	
	1980	1985
Fresh water recreational fishing (National Planning Association, 1975)	$ 264–639	$ 267–677
Boating (National Planning Association, 1975)	$ 371–842	$ 603–1,399
Swimming at public beaches (Battelle Memorial Institute, 1975)	$ 173–571	$ 191–631
Marine recreational fishing (Bell and Canterbery, 1975)	$ 2,459	$ 3,997
Totals	$3,266–$4,511	$5,058–$6,705

Source: National Commission on Water Quality (1976, pp. III–286).

increased utility for existing participants. As indicated before, this omission could be significant.

The second study is by Battelle Memorial Institute (1975). They use a model of recreational participation based on data on swimming activity contained in the 1972 National Recreation Survey. The model estimates the percentage of regional populations participating in swimming activities and the number of activity days per participant—both as functions of socioeconomic variables, such as income and age. The activity days equation also includes a travel distance and cost variable which is interpreted as a proxy for availability of swimming beaches. The model is used to predict the change in swimming participation in the United States on the basis of the reduction in miles of public beaches closed to swimming because of coliform bacteria contamination. It is estimated that about 13% of the total miles of lake, river, and ocean beaches in the United States are closed to swimming either permanently or periodically because of water pollution under existing conditions. The study attempts to distinguish between net increases in swimming activity and activities diverted from other beaches because of changes in the availability of swimming sites. Estimates of unit values are not included in the Battelle Report, but rather were apparently assigned by the Commission staff. The basis for the values is not specified. Net increases are valued at $9.09 per day in 1978 dollars, while diverted activity is valued at

146   Water Pollution Control and Recreation Benefits

$3.03. The benefits associated with 1980 levels of water quality, population, income, and so on, are estimated to lie between $173 and $571 million per year, in 1978 dollars. Benefits for 1985 are estimated to lie between $191 and $631 million per year.

The third study, by Bell and Canterbery (1975), estimates the impact of changes in water quality on marine fisheries, both recreational and commercial. The results for commercial fisheries will be discussed in the next chapter. Bell and Canterbery use secondary data from a number of sources to derive relationships between water quality and biological productivity, and between productivity and the number of participants and days of sports fishing. The estimates cover ten species of fish and shellfish on the East Coast, Gulf Coast, and West Coast. A household production function model is used to derive a relationship between expenditures on fishing (for example, gear and travel) and the consumer surplus associated with the activity. Time as an input is valued at the foregone wage rate. This will lead to an overestimate of benefits if the true opportunity cost of time is less than the wage rate. In fact, some evidence suggests that the opportunity cost of time outside of the work place may be only one-quarter to one-third of the wage rate (Freeman 1979, pp. 204–209).

Bell and Canterbery estimate that implementation of the FWPCA–72 would lead to increases in marine sports fishing valued at $2.46 billion per year in 1980 and at $4.0 billion in 1985, both in 1978 dollars. These figures are also shown in Table 8.1. Adding the four components of recreation benefits covered by the National Commission on Water Quality studies gives total benefits in 1980 of between $3.3 and $4.5 billion. The range for 1985 is between $5.1 billion and $6.7 billion per year.

Heintz, Hershaft, and Horak (1976) estimate the national damages (or benefits lost) due to water pollution to four recreational activities, fishing, boating, swimming, and water fowl hunting. Estimates are derived for 1973. The data on recreation activity levels come from the 1970 surveys by the Bureau of Recreation and the U.S. Fish and Wildlife Service. Activity levels are projected to 1973 on the basis of population growth. The explanation of their technique will be framed in terms of the benefits of eliminating water pollution. We will go into their technique in some detail in order to show some of the problems that arise in attempting estimates of national benefits from the available data. These problems include very limited information on the relationships between changes in water quality and recreation activities and on the value of recreation as a function of water quality; they also include the difficulties in extrapolating from limited data on narrowly defined regions to national estimates.

The benefit measure derived by Heintz, Hershaft, and Horak has three components: (1) a travel cost savings for existing recreationists as more accessible sites become available; (2) an increase in recreation activity; and (3) an increase in the utility or welfare associated with the existing level of recreation activity.

In order to estimate the reduction in travel costs when pollution is eliminated, Heintz, Hershaft, and Horak had to obtain three key pieces of information. The first is the percentage of recreationists who shift the location of their recreation activity as water quality changes. Their source for this parameter is a survey of recreationists in Green Bay, Wisconsin conducted by Ditton and Goodale.[2] Recreationers were asked, "What would you do if water conditions deteriorated at the place you do most of your boating, fishing, and swimming?" Possible responses were:

> move to a location on Green Bay;
> move to a location not on Green Bay;
> stay in same location but participate less frequently;
> would not bother me;
> stop participating entirely.

The second key parameter is the percentage change in travel cost for those who actually shift. Heintz, Hershaft, and Horak derive this from a survey of recreationists at the Rocky Mountain National Park in Colorado. This survey is described in Walsh, Ericson, McKean, and Young (1978). Respondents were shown photographs of streams and lakes with different water qualities and asked to indicate how their plans would vary with changes in stream quality. The study shows that a given percentage change in water pollution would result in an approximately equal percentage change in distance traveled to engage in recreation activities.

The third key piece of information needed is the changes in water quality experienced by recreationists across the country. Heintz, Hershaft, and Horak use as a proxy for this a measure of the change in the number of miles of waterways classified as polluted. Thus the model does not treat water quality as a continuous variable but as a dichotomous variable, that is, polluted or not polluted.

These three pieces of information are used in the following manner:[3] It is assumed that all U.S. recreationists would respond to a reduction in pollution in the same way as those in the Green Bay sample. Travel costs per recreation day are taken from the 1970 national surveys of hunting, fishing,

[2] I do not have access to this report. The following description is based on Heintz, Hershaft, and Horak (1976).
[3] For details of the computations, see Heintz, Hershaft, and Horak (1976). A similar approach, based largely on the same underlying data, is reported in Walsh (1977).

and recreation. The percentage reduction in travel costs for those changing behavior is taken from the Rocky Mountain Park survey. And it is assumed that a 41% reduction in polluted stream miles would result in an equal percentage decrease in total travel by recreationists. The decrease in travel cost is computed by multiplication as follows:

$$\begin{bmatrix} \text{Number of} \\ \text{recreation} \\ \text{days} \end{bmatrix} \times \begin{bmatrix} \text{Travel} \\ \text{cost} \\ \text{per day} \end{bmatrix} \times \begin{bmatrix} \text{Percent of} \\ \text{recreationists} \\ \text{shifting} \end{bmatrix} \times \begin{bmatrix} \text{Percent} \\ \text{reduction} \\ \text{in travel costs} \end{bmatrix}$$

The second component of benefits, that due to the change in activity levels, is also based on information from the Green Bay Survey. The percentage responding "stop participating entirely" is taken as a measure of the change in national recreation activity levels.

Finally, the estimate of the change in utility is found by first predicting the proportion of recreationists who would not move to a different site or stop their recreation. Again, this is based on the Green Bay survey. Then, a monetary value for this utility loss is assumed. This figure, $5.75 per day in 1973, is taken from the survey of recreationists in the Rocky Mountain National Park.

The results of these calculations show that for fishing and hunting the decrease in travel cost is the major component of estimated benefits, while for boating and swimming the major benefit comes from the increased utility of existing activities. Over 40% of the total benefits come from fishing; water fowl hunting makes a minor contribution to the total. These figures can be converted to 1978 dollars by using the Consumer Price Index. Heintz, Hershaft, and Horak estimate benefits to lie in the range $3.7–$18.5 billion per year, with the most likely point estimate being $9.2 billion. This works out to just over $40 per capita for the U.S. population in 1978.

This estimate and the computations on which it is based can be criticized on the basis of both the use of the data and the underlying implicit model. There are four major problems with using data from surveys such as those from Green Bay and the Rocky Mountain National Park to estimate national benefits. First, the nature and magnitude of the change in water quality was not specified in the Green Bay survey. The question may conjure up quite different pictures of deteriorated water conditions for different individuals. Thus it is not possible to establish a quantitative link between a policy that affects discharges and water quality in a specified way and the responses of recreationists to those changes.

Second, the Rocky Mountain National Park respondents were asked about their response to given percentage changes in water quality at a single site or set of sites in that region. It was then assumed that respondents' change in travel behavior for an $X\%$ change in the *quantity* of stream miles available would be the same as their stated response to an $X\%$ change in *quality* at a given site. No justification was offered for this rather strong assumption.

Third, the questions are hypothetical; and there is no assurance that respondents would behave in the way they said they would if the postulated changes in water quality actually occurred. Responses to hypothetical questions are more likely to be accurate predictors of behavior when the respondent is presented with an accurate and detailed description of the hypothetical situation. But the vagueness of the questions makes it less likely that responses will be good predictors of actual behavior.

Finally, the surveys are specific to the locations in question, and responses are conditioned upon existing water quality in the survey area, the availability of alternative recreation sites within that general area, their water qualities, and the socioeconomic characteristics of the population. Other parts of the country will have different availabilities of substitute sites and different population characteristics. These differences must be taken into account in developing predictions of the behavior of the national population. Specifically, with respect to the travel time components of benefits, the realized travel cost savings will depend on the locations of facilities relative to user populations; and this locational pattern could vary widely across regions.

More fundamental criticisms can be directed at Heintz, Hershaft, and Horak's basic model. Unlike the model of Figure 8.1, the model implied by their method of calculation is based on the demand for participation in a recreation activity rather than for recreation at a specific site. The problem is that their treatment of the roles of site characteristics and travel cost as determinants of demand is wrong. Their model assumes a demand curve for the activity conditional on the accessibility and quality of alternative sites. The demand curve for participation when some sites are polluted is D_1 in Figure 8.2. Travel cost, presumably some average across sites, is treated as a proxy for price and taken as given at P_1. This leads to an equilibrium of OX_1 days of participation. They argue that an improvement in water quality will shift the demand curve out, say to D_2, *and* lower the average travel cost, say to P_2. If this is correct, then the benefits would be measured by the travel cost savings to original participants ($ABHI$), plus the consumer surplus to additional days of participation because of the lower price (GIF), plus the utility gain to original participants because of improved water quality ($CDGH$). These three areas correspond to their descriptions of their three components of benefits.[4]

---

[4]Their actual computation of the second component of benefits does not correspond to the model described here. The utility gain to additional participation is actually computed as a fraction of the area $ABHI$. They do not offer a clear explanation for this.

150 Water Pollution Control and Recreation Benefits

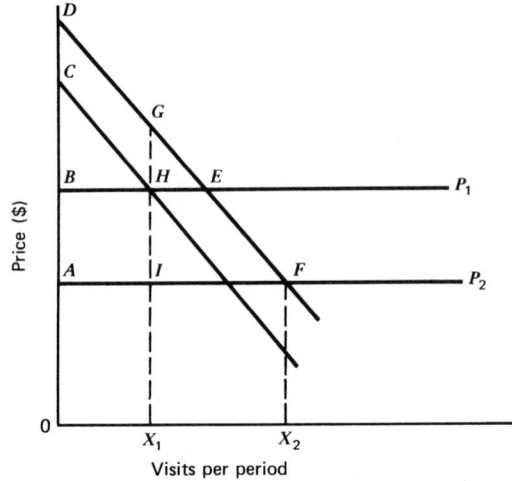

Figure 8.2. The Heintz-Hershaft-Horak model of recreation demand and benefits.

Their basic error is to treat travel cost as exogenous and as determining participation. Rather, realized travel cost per day of participation is endogenous, being determined by the interaction among demand for participation, availability of alternative sites, their qualities, and their distances from the residences of recreationists. An improvement in water quality need not decrease travel cost. It could increase travel cost if the improvement made a more distant site more attractive than closer sites being used before the quality change.

The correct model of demand for recreation participation would treat the demand curve of Figure 8.2 as an inverse demand curve. Willingness to pay would be a function of the number and quality of sites, their location, and travel cost per mile. Specification and estimation of this demand relationship would be very difficult since the function must fully capture substitution relationships among sites. The equilibrium would be where marginal willingness to pay, net of travel costs, is zero. An improvement in water quality would shift this curve out. Benefits would be measured by the area between the old and new curves.

In summary, there are theoretical and computational errors in the Heintz, Hershaft, and Horak approach to estimating benefits. And their method places excessive reliance on weak survey data that is too region specific to be used reliably to estimate national benefits. Thus their estimates of damages probably do not provide a reliable basis for determining national water pollution control benefits.

Unger (1975) estimates national recreation benefits using substantially the same data and methodology. The principal differences between his work and that of Heintz, Hershaft, and Horak are as follows:

Instead of estimating damages, Unger estimates benefits for 1977, 1983, and 1985;
Unger distinguishes between fresh water and ocean swimming and uses an estimate by Tihansky (1974) for the latter;
Unger includes an additional component of benefits for increased activity.

The benefit estimates for 1977, 1983, and 1985 reflect both changes in water quality from the base year (1970) and increases in population and income. The additional benefits for ocean swimming are quite small, amounting to only about $0.1 billion per year in 1985. Unger's total recreation benefits for all categories in billions of 1978 dollars are

1977		1983		1985	
Range	Best	Range	Best	Range	Best
$1.9–15.0	$7.0	$3.9–24.1	$12.2	$5.9–32.2	$16.8

Because these estimates are based on the same method and data (specifically, the Green Bay survey), they are subject to the same criticisms and limitations as the estimates by Heintz, Hershaft, and Horak.

Feenberg and Mills (1980) estimate recreation benefits for the years 1977, 1983, and 1985. Their estimate is based on data on water quality improvements and levels of recreation activity from Unger. The model from which their estimates are derived is based on a relationship that gives the total number of recreation visits by households with a given travel cost as a function of the average travel cost of those households. This travel cost function is plotted in Figure 8.3. Suppose that one subset of all households has a travel cost of P_1 per recreation visit. This relationship shows that total recreation visits to all sites by these households is V_1. Another subset of households with travel cost of P_2 has V_2 visits to their sites (not necessarily the same sites). Total recreation activity for all households is the sum of visits from all subsets of households:

$$\Sigma V$$

152 Water Pollution Control and Recreation Benefits

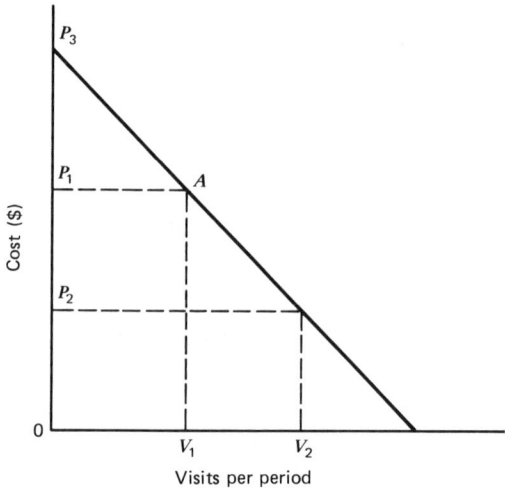

Figure 8.3. The relationship between travel costs and visits.

In order to simplify the subsequent calculations, Feenberg and Mills assume that this function is linear. Sufficient conditions for linearity are that there be a uniform distribution of the population over the range of travel costs, that the subset averages of relevant socioeconomic variables such as income be the same for all travel costs, and that individual recreation demand curves be linear.

Feenberg and Mills interpret the travel cost function as a form of demand curve (for example, p. 67). They argue that, for those who have a travel cost of P_1 in Figure 8.3, the total willingness to pay for recreation is the area OP_3AV_1 and the consumer surplus is the area P_1P_3A. The total consumers' surplus for the population as a whole is the sum of these triangular areas for all travel costs. This interpretation is valid if the conditions for linearity are met. But this interpretation need not hold in general.

For example, suppose that a region that has an average travel cost of P_3 also has low average incomes and/or low preferences for recreation. The prediction of zero visits is in part because of high price and in part because of low demand on the part of that region's residents. Further, suppose that those people in the region where travel cost is P_1 have high incomes and/or preferences for recreation. If those individuals are faced with an increase in travel costs to P_3, they would reduce visits. But because of their greater demand for recreation, they would not reduce visits to zero. And the area P_1P_3A would be an underestimate of their consumers' surplus. That area measures consumer surplus only if that group would in fact reduce visits to zero when faced with a price increase to P_3.

A Review of Recreation Damage and Benefit Studies

Given the assumption of linearity, Feenberg and Mills derive expressions for the total number of visits, average travel cost for the population, and consumer surplus, all as functions of the parameters of the travel cost function.[5] If total visits and average travel cost are known, the parameters of the travel cost function and consumers' surplus can both be calculated. Unger (1975) provides estimates of these variables for 1977, 1983, and 1985 based on observed values for 1970 adjusted for changes in prices, incomes, and population.

If water quality improves, the travel cost function will shift out, and visits and consumers' surplus will increase. The benefit is the increase in consumer surplus. Feenberg and Mills assume that the new travel cost function is parallel to the original curve. If this is granted, the only additional information needed to calculate benefits is the increase in recreation activity.

Feenberg and Mills use estimates of the increase in recreation activity for fishing, boating, swimming, and waterfowl hunting derived from the 1965 Survey of Recreation Activity reported by Unger. The percentage increases in activity and the Feenberg-Mills calculated benefits for meeting the 1985 objectives are

---

[5] If the travel cost function is $V_i = a - bP_i$, then total visits V is

$$V = \int_0^{a/b} (a - bP_i) dP_i = \frac{a^2}{2b}$$

where a/b is the vertical intercept, or P_3 in Figure 8.3. If $\bar{P}$ is the weighted average of the P_is, then

$$\bar{P} = \frac{1}{V} \int_0^{a/b} (a - bP_i) P_i dP_i = \frac{a}{3b}$$

For any P_i, consumer surplus is

$$CS_i = \frac{1}{2}\left(\frac{a}{b} - P_i\right) V_i$$

The sum for all P_i is

$$CS = \int_0^{a/b} \frac{1}{2}\left(\frac{a}{b} - P_i\right) V_i dP_i = \frac{a^3}{6b^2}$$

If V and $\bar{P}$ are known, a and b can be calculated. And this makes possible the calculation of CS. There is no simple geometric interpretation of the total CS measure.

154   Water Pollution Control and Recreation Benefits

Activity	Percentage Increase in Activity	Benefits in Billions of 1978 Dollars
Fishing	121%	$10.4
Boating	37%	1.9
Swimming	135%	5.7
Waterfowl hunting	121%	0.5
Total		$18.5

These are the benefits to the 1985 population of moving from 1970 pollution levels to the water quality expected in 1985 with full implementation of the FWPCA–72.

These benefits are large, and since they depend crucially on the estimated percentage increase in activity, this parameter deserves closer scrutiny. For each of several activities, the 1965 Survey asked recreationists, first, if their activities are restricted by the presence of pollution or not, and, second, their participation rates in days per year. For swimming, the mean participation for those not feeling restricted is 24.7 days per year, while for those feeling restricted it is 10.5 days per year. If, as a consequence of pollution control, those originally feeling restricted increased their participation rate to that of the nonrestricted group, this would be a 135% increase in their activity levels: $(24.7 - 10.5)/10.5 = 1.35$. Feenberg and Mills assume that total swimming activity would increase by this percentage on the assumption that *all* recreationists are originally restricted in their activity levels due to pollution. This assumption surely leads to overestimates of the increase in activities and benefits. Feenberg and Mills are careful to call the reader's attention to the limitations of the data at this key point in the analysis (1980, pp. 156–157).

To show the sensitivity of the estimates to the assumptions made about the increase in participation, I now present an alternative set of benefit estimates calculated on the basis of the Heintz, Hershaft, and Horak (1976) and Unger (1975) models of increased participation. Unger estimates that in 1985 there will be a 57% increase in unpolluted stream miles in comparison with the no pollution control case. This means that 36.3% of those waters expected to be clean in 1985 would be polluted without the policy. Based on the Green Bay survey, both studies predict that in areas now polluted, there would be a 45.7% increase in fishing, a 28.1% increase in boating, a 33.8% increase in swimming, and a 45.7% increase in waterfowl hunting with the elimination of pollution. If on those 36.3% of the waters now polluted an end of pollution led to a 45.7% increase in fishing, I assume that this results in a 16.6% ($.457 \times .363$) increase in total fishing activity. The assumed increases for the

waterfowl hunting. Using the Feenberg-Mills formula for calculating benefits for 1985 gives

Activity	Benefits in Millions of 1978 Dollars
Fishing	$1,177
Boating	472
Swimming	415
Waterfowl hunting	57
Total	$2,121

other activities are 10.2% for boating, 12.3% for swimming, and 16.6% for This total is an order of magnitude smaller than the estimate of Feenberg and Mills. I do not necessarily feel that this lower estimate is more accurate since it is based on what I believe is an unreliable data base for national benefit estimation, namely the Green Bay Survey.

Two studies conducted recently at Resources for the Future, Inc. (RFF) have employed versions of the participation model to estimate national recreation benefits. Peskin and Harrington (1981) use data from the 1972 National Recreation Survey to estimate the probability of a family taking one day or shorter trips for water-based recreation. Explanatory variables include socioeconomic variables such as income and family size and variables reflecting water quality within a day trip distance of the city of residence. In a second-stage equation to estimate the frequency of participation of those who participated one or more times, it was found that water quality variables are not statistically significant.

Peskin and Harrington next use the RFF Water Quality Network Model to predict the increase in probability of water-based recreation participation associated with the achievement of the BPT effluent standards. They estimate an increase of about 51.5 million visitor days of one day or shorter trip.

On the basis of studies of values of water-based recreation reviewed in Dwyer, Kelly, and Bowes (1977), Peskin and Harrington assume that each visitor day has a net benefit of $10. Thus national benefits of achieving BPT are estimated to be just over $0.5 billion per year.

Peskin and Harrington suggest two reasons why this might be an underestimate. First, although their statistical analysis does not detect such an effect, water quality improvements might also lead to an increase in frequency of participation as well as in the number of participants. They calculate that if visits per year per participant were to increase by 10%, this would double annual benefits. Also, the estimate covers only increases in day trips and does not reflect possible increases in overnight, weekend or vacation trips for water-based recreation. A third reason that this figure could be an underestimate is that it captures only the utility gains associated with increases in use and not the utility to existing users who might now enjoy a higher quality recreation experience.

The second study, by Russell and Vaughn (1981), is available only in preliminary draft form at this writing. It deals with only one component of water recreation, fresh water fishing. Russell and Vaughn break new ground in this study by incorporating a qualitative dimension of the fishing experience in their analysis. Their model is based on the National Survey of Hunting, Fishing, and Water Associated Recreation conducted in 1975 and estimates participation in each of three classes of fishing activity as functions of availability of fishing areas to support each activity. The classes of activity are cold water fishing (trout and so on), warm water fishing (bass, pan fish, and so on), and rough fishing (carp and so on). Data from privately operated fishing-for-fees areas are employed to estimate demands and unit values for these three types of fishing activity. The RFF Water Quality Network Model is used to predict the changes in availability of fishing for attainment of the BPT standards and for three more stringent levels of control, including BAT.

One somewhat surprising result of their analysis is their prediction that although attaining BAT would result in a reduction in unfishable waters of over 70%, the increase in fishable water would be only about 2%. This suggests a relatively small potential for fishing benefits. Their models predict an increase in fishing days of 30–45 million per year with the move from 1970 water quality to BAT. Different model specifications and bases for valuing fishing days lead to estimates of total fishing benefits of attaining BAT standards of between $0.2 and $1.0 billion per year. Their best estimates, in round numbers, are $0.5 billion for attaining BPT and another $0.25 billion for moving to BAT, for a total of $0.75 billion per year for the full improvement to BAT. These figures are in 1978 dollars and refer to the 1985 population, income, and so forth. A portion of these benefits represent upgrading of the quality of fishing to a category with a higher unit value, especially from warm water to cold water fishing.

There are two recent estimates of the benefits of improving recreation opportunities for specific river basins. While it is dangerous to extrapolate from one river basin, with its perhaps unique characteristics, to the nation as a whole, these studies may provide at least some support for order-of-magnitude estimates of national benefits.

Gramlich (1977) uses a willingness-to-pay survey of households in the Charles River Basin in Massachusetts to estimate the benefits of achieving swimmable water quality throughout that river. Gramlich's estimate lies in the range of $12.9 to $32.1 million per year in 1978 dollars. The best estimate is $22.6 million per year. This amounts to about $32 per family for the population within the watershed. If every family in the United States has this willingness to pay for water quality improvements in their rivers, national benefits would be about $2.2 billion per year.

In the second study, Walsh et al. (1978) showed about 600 residents in the South Platte River Basin of Colorado pictures of streams of different water quality. Unlike the Charles River, the principal source of pollution in the South Platte River is heavy metals from mining and refining activities. Recreation users indicated a willingness to pay of $64.92 per household per year for an improvement in water quality that would permit recreation activities. Users were also asked a question about willingness to pay to preserve the option of future use. Responses to this question averaged $25.89 (all values in 1978 dollars). Since it is conceptually difficult to distinguish the option value from the use value for known users, the best estimate of willingness to pay for users is the sum of these two—that is, $90.81 per year. This amounts to $6.03 per activity day. If this per household benefit were the same for the total U.S. population, national benefits would be $5–6 billion per year. However, it is dangerous to extrapolate in this way from a limited sample drawn from a region with perhaps untypical water quality problems, water-based activities, and range of available alternatives.

Nonusers were also asked their willingness to pay to preserve the existence of a natural undegraded waterway and to bequeath clean water to future generations. The sum of these responses averaged to $48.05 per household for nonusers.

The last recreation benefit study to be reviewed here was recently published by Bouwes and Schneider (1979). The authors use the Clawson-Knetsch travel cost method to estimate a demand function for visits to a small (400–600 acre) lake in Wisconsin. The demand function includes a variable reflecting the recreationists' perception of water quality. At the then existing water quality level, the value of the recreation site as measured by the area under the demand curve is $491,000 per year in 1978 dollars. This is equivalent to an average value per visitor day of $2.91. The demand curve and site value are recomputed with a postulated reduction in water quality due to storm sewer pollution. Damages (the area between the demand curves) are estimated to be $44,700 or 26¢ per visitor day. The relatively low values may reflect the availability of close substitutes and may not represent conditions in other parts of the country. The principal value of this study is its demonstration of the feasibility of using an appropriate theoretical model incorporating the influence of water quality in the estimation of recreation demands and benefits.

SYNTHESIS ESTIMATES OF RECREATION BENEFITS

We have reviewed several estimates of national recreation benefits based on different methods and data. Table 8.2 reproduces the benefit estimates from each of the major studies by category. All values are in 1978 dollars. Since the Heintz, Hershaft, and Horak estimates are of damages, they are included on the assumption that as a first approximation achieving the 1985 objectives will mean elimination of the adverse affects of pollution. In this respect they may tend to overestimate true benefits. But these estimates are biased downward in comparison with those of the National Commission on Water Quality and Unger in that they do not reflect the influence of population and income growth on recreation behavior and potential benefits.

These estimates span a range from approximately $1.5 billion per year to $18.5 billion per year. The highest estimates are those that base predictions of increased activity levels on responses to survey questions (Heintz, Hershaft, and Horak; Unger; and Feenberg and Mills). For the most part, the lower estimates are based on more recent and more comprehensive data on behavioral responses to differences in water quality (NCWQ: Peskin and Harrington; and Russell and Vaughn). I turn now to developing synthesis estimates in each category.

Consider first the category of fresh water fishing. The National Commission on Water Quality makes separate estimates for fresh water and marine sports fishing, while Heintz, Hershaft, and Horak, Mills and Feenberg, and Unger estimate aggregate fishing benefits. These latter studies use poor data and, except for Mills and Feenberg, faulty method, so their estimates must be discounted. The Commission's estimate for fresh water is based on a recreation participation model that captures only the benefits to new activity, the area *CEF* in Figure 8.1. Adding benefits to existing users (the area *BCFD* in Figure 8.1) could substantially increase the estimate. I assume somewhat arbitrarily that benefits to existing users are at least equal in magnitude to the benefits to increased activity. Thus the Commission's lower and upper bounds and most likely point estimate should be doubled to reflect this adjustment. Giving substantial weight to Russell and Vaughn's study, I estimate that fresh water fishing benefits lie in the range of $0.5–1.4 billion per year. The most likely point estimate is $1.0 billion per year.

In developing the estimate of marine sports fishing benefits for the National Commission on Water Quality, Bell and Canterbery use an únrealistic value of time. I assume that the true opportunity cost of time is one-third the wage rate. This affects only one component of their estimate. I assume that the effect is to reduce their estimate by about 25% to about $3.0

TABLE 8.2 Recreation Benefit Estimates from Various Studies (in Billions of 1978 Dollars per Year)

Study	Fresh Water Fishing	Marine Fishing	Boating	Swimming	Waterfowl Hunting	Total
National Commission on Water Quality—1985 objectives	$0.3–0.7[a]	$4.0	$0.6–1.4[a]	$0.2–0.6[a]	—	$5.1– 6.7[a]
Heintz, Hershaft, and Horak—damages	$1.8–7.5[a] ($4.0)[b]		$1.0–5.2[a] ($2.5)[b]	$0.8–5.4[a] ($2.6)[b]	$0.1–0.4[a] ($0.2)[b]	$3.7–18.5[a] ($9.3)[b]
Unger—1985 objectives	$ 7.9	$0.1	$3.5	$4.9	$0.4	$16.8
Feenberg and Mills—1985 objectives	$10.4	—	$1.9	$5.7	$0.5	$18.5
Freeman—1985 objectives[c]	$ 1.2	—	$0.5	$0.4	$0.1	$ 2.2
Peskin and Harrington—BPT	—	—	—	—	—	$ 0.5[d]
Russell and Vaughn—1985 objectives	$ 0.8	—	—	—	—	$ 0.8
Gramlich—1985 objectives	—	$2.2[e]	—	—	—	$ 2.2

[a]Range.

[b]Best estimate.

[c]Based on Feenberg—Mills model and Green Bay Survey. (See the section "A Review of Recreation Damage and Benefit Estimates" earlier in this chapter.)

[d]Total for all water-based recreation; day trips and short trips only.

[e]Willingness to pay for swimmable water; reflects all categories of uses.

billion. But even after this adjustment, the estimate appears to be implausibly high, especially relative to the fresh water fish benefits estimated by Russell and Vaughn. In 1975 only about 20% of total fishing activity took place in marine waters.[6] Thus if the impact of pollution on fishing were proportional to the level of recreation activity, one would expect marine fishing benefits to be one-fourth the size of fresh water benefits rather than 3–4 times larger. Since I am not able to discount entirely the National Commission's study, I estimate marine fishing benefits to lie in the range of $0.1-$3.0 billion per year. The most likely point estimate is $1.0 billion per year.

Turning to boating, I judge the National Commission estimates to be based on a more reliable model than the others. They can be adjusted upward to reflect benefits to existing users. However, given the nature of the activity, one would not expect the benefits in this category to be significantly larger than those for fishing. I estimate boating benefits to be in the range of $1.2 to $2.8 billion dollars per year in 1978 dollars. The most likely point estimate is $2.0 billion per year.

It is difficult to place much confidence on any of the estimates of swimming benefits. The Unger and Feenberg-Mills estimates are likely to be biased upward. A substantial portion of the Peskin-Harrington estimate of total water recreation probably is attributable to swimming. But this total is biased downward. I judge the benefits to lie in the range of $0.2 to $2.0 billion per year in 1978 dollars. The most likely point estimate is $1.0 billion per year. Waterfowl hunting benefits are relatively insignificant according to Heintz, Hershaft, and Horak. I judge the benefits to lie in the range of $0 to $0.3 billion per year. The most likely point estimate is $0 billion per year.

The estimates described here are summarized in Table 8.3. Total recreation benefits for achieving the 1985 water quality objectives are estimated to lie in the range of $1.8 to $8.7 billion per year in 1978 dollars. The most likely point estimate is $4.6 billion per year.

I do not have a firm basis for determining what portion of this total can be attributed to achieving the BPT standards for what portion has been realized by actual water quality improvements as of 1978. On the one hand, many people have argued that the marginal benefits of achieving BAT will be substantially smaller than the benefits of achieving BPT. On the other hand, as of 1978, not all point sources were in full compliance with BPT standards (Freeman, 1978, pp. 48–53). For these reasons, I will not hazard an estimate of what has been achieved by actual water quality improvements as of 1978.

---

[6] I am indebted to Clifford Russell for bringing this to my attention.

TABLE 8.3 Synthesis Estimates of National Recreation Benefits to be Realized in 1985 (in Billions of 1978 Dollars per Year)

	Range	Most Likely Point Estimate
Fresh water fishing	$0.5–1.4	$1.0
Marine sports fishing	$0.1–3.0	$1.0
Boating	$1.0–2.0	$1.5
Swimming	$0.2–2.0	$1.0
Waterfowl hunting	$0.0–0.3	$0.1
Total	$1.8–8.7	$4.6

REFERENCES

Battelle Memorial Institute. *Assessment of the Economic and Social Implications of Water Quality Improvements on Public Swimming*. Columbus, Ohio, 1975.

Bell, Frederick W., and E. Ray Canterbery. *An Assessment of the Economic Benefits Which Will Accrue to Commercial and Recreational Fisheries from Incremental Improvements in The Quality of Coastal Waters*. Tallahassee: Florida State University, 1975.

Bouwes, Nicolaas W., and Robert Schneider. "Procedures in Estimating Benefits of Water Quality Change," *American Journal of Agricultural Economics*, 61, no. 3 (August, 1979), 535–539.

Clawson, Marion, and Jack Knetsch. *Economics of Outdoor Recreation*. Baltimore: Johns Hopkins University Press, 1966.

Davidson, Paul, F. Gerard Adams, and Joseph Seneca. "The Social Value of Water Recreational Facilities Resulting From an Improvement in Water Quality: The Delaware Estuary," in Allen V. Kneese and Stephen Smith, eds. *Water Research*. Baltimore: Johns Hopkins University Press, 1966.

Dwyer, John F., John R. Kelly, and Michael D. Bowes. *Improved Procedures for Valuation of the Contribution of Recreation to National Economic Development*. Urbana-Champaign: Water Resources Center, University of Illinois, 1977.

Feenberg, Daniel, and Edwin Mills. *Measuring the Benefits of Water Pollution Abatement*. New York: Academic Press, 1980.

Freeman, A. Myrick, III. "Air and Water Pollution Policy," in Paul Portney, ed. *Current Issues in U.S. Environmental Policy*. Baltimore: Johns Hopkins University Press, 1978,

──────. *The Benefits of Environmental Improvement: Theory and Practice*. Baltimore: Johns Hopkins University Press, 1979.

Gramlich, Frederick W. "The Demand for Clean Water: The Case of the Charles River," *National Tax Journal*, 30, no. 2 (June, 1977), 183–194.

Heintz, H.T., A. Hershaft, and G. Horak. *National Damages of Air and Water Pollution.* A report submitted to the U.S. Environmental Protection Agency, 1976.

Knetsch, Jack L. "Economics of Including Recreation as a Purpose of Eastern Water Projects," *Journal of Farm Economics*, 46, no. 5 (December, 1964), 1148–1157.

Mäler, Karl–Goran, and Ronald Wyzga. *Economic Measurement of Environmental Damage.* Paris, Organization for Economic Cooperation and Development, 1976.

National Commission on Water Quality. *Staff Report.* Washington, D.C., 1976.

National Planning Association. *Water-Related Recreation Benefits Resulting from P.L. 92–500.* Washington, D.C., 1975.

Peskin, Henry M., and Winston Harrington. *Policy-Relevant Applications of a System of Expanded National Accounts: Effects of Water Quality on Recreation Behavior* (processed), 1981.

Russell, Clifford S., and William J. Vaughn. *The National Benefits of Water Pollution Control: Fresh Water Recreational Fishing* (Forthcoming).

Tihansky, Dennis P. "Recreational Welfare Losses from Water Pollution," *Journal of Environmental Quality*, 3, no. 4 (1974), 335–342.

Unger, Samuel G. *National Benefits of Achieving the 1977, 1983, and 1985 Water Quality Goals.* A report submitted to the U.S. Environmental Protection Agency, 1975.

Walsh, Richard G. "Recreational User Benefits from Water Quality Improvement," *Outdoor Recreation: Advances in the Application of Economics*, General Technical Report WO-2, Forest Service, Washington, D.C., U.S. Department of Agriculture, 1977.

Walsh, Richard G., Roy K. Ericson, John R. McKean, and Robert A. Young. *Recreation Benefits of Water Quality: Rocky Mountain National Park, South Platte River Basin, Colorado.* Colorado Water Resources Research Institute, Technical Report no. 12, 1978.

Walsh, Richard G., et al. *Option Values, Preservation Values and Recreational Benefits of Improved Water Quality: A Case Study of the South Platte River Basin, Colorado.* Research Triangle Park: Environmental Protection Agency, 1978.

Water Resources Council. "Principles and Standards for Planning Water and Related Land Resources," *Federal Register*, 38, no. 174 (September 10, 1973).

9

WATER POLLUTION CONTROL: OTHER BENEFITS, CONCLUSIONS

The remaining categories of benefits of water pollution control are nonuser benefits, commercial fisheries, and the several types of diversionary uses of water. I take each of these up in turn and conclude with a discussion of the relationship between benefits and costs of control and policy implications.

NONUSER BENEFITS

This category includes all welfare gains experienced by and reflected in the willingness to pay of people not making direct use of water bodies or diverted water. This includes what have been called aesthetic benefits, ecological benefits, preservation values, and option values in various studies in the literature. Nonuser benefits are difficult to define in quantitative terms and to measure; and because they are not linked to observable activities such as recreation, it is difficult to determine their value and individuals' willingness to pay by observation.

Two approaches to determining nonuser benefits have been employed in the literature. They are property value studies and survey questionnaires. Property value estimates may capture both aesthetics and the value of proximity for active recreationers. Thus there may be an element of double counting if these are counted as nonuser benefits and added to recreation user benefits. However, property values to not appear to be a significant component of national benefits, so this problem is relatively unimportant as a practical matter.

Dornbusch, in a series of studies culminating in his report to the National Commission on Water Quality (Dornbusch, 1975), estimates the relationship between changes in water quality and changes in property values over time. He estimates these relationships for 17 localities and uses them to estimate the national benefits for given predicted improvements in water quality. He estimates that benefits in 1980 would be $74.7 million and benefits in 1985 would be $92.5 million per year, both in 1978 dollars. However, it is difficult to know how much credence to give to these estimates. The equation estimated by Dornbusch is not derived from either of the theoretical models that have been developed as a basis for benefit calculation (Freeman 1979, Chapter 6, especially pp. 148–151). It should be noted that even if property value benefits have been correctly measured, they capture only those benefits accruing to the relatively small percentage of the population that owns property in the vicinity of water bodies.

Heintz, Hershaft, and Horak (1976) cite two willingness-to-pay surveys dealing with nonuser or aesthetic benefits. One deals with the willingness to pay of residents of the Fraser River Valley in British Columbia to preserve a local salmon fishery even though they do not expect to use it themselves. The willingness to pay is $223 per household; and this amounts to 54% of the estimate of recreation benefits per household associated with the fishery. This value may strike the reader as implausibly high. However, salmon are an especially desirable and highly valued game fish species. In any event, what is of interest here is the ratio between user and preservation values.

Heintz, Hershaft and Horak also cite a similar questionnaire administered in the southeastern United States. In this study aesthetic benefits of fish observation are found to range from 50–150% of the benefits of recreation fishing. The survey of willingness to pay for preservation and bequest motives by Walsh et al. (1978) finds a similar relationship between nonuser and user benefits. Heintz, Hershaft, and Horak use the ratio of aesthetic to recreation benefits (.54) from the Fraser River study and apply it to their estimate of fishing benefits to derive an estimate of aesthetic benefits to the United States of $2.2 billion per year in 1978 dollars.

This is a very tenuous empirical basis from which to estimate national nonuser benefits. Also, it is not clear why nonuser benefits should be related only to fishing benefits and not to all forms of water-based recreation for which people might have option and preservation values. I will use the synthesis estimate of total recreation benefits of $4.6 billion per year presented above and assume that aesthetic and ecological nonuser benefits are 25% of this. The most likely point estimate is $1.2 billion per year. To reflect the uncertainty in the estimate, I give a range of $.5–4.0 billion per year in 1978 dollars. It should be noted, however, that this approach to estimating nonuser benefits does not reflect the possibility of subtle but eventually quite serious effects that continued discharge of a variety of substances might be having on aquatic ecosystems.

COMMERCIAL FISHERIES

One approach to determining commercial fishery benefits is to estimate the quantity and value of fish catch that is lost because fisheries are closed or fishing grounds become biologically unproductive due to pollution. If this approach is used, the value of the fish lost must be a *net* value; in other words the costs of labor, fuel, and so forth that would have been expended in catching the fish and transporting them to the dock must be deducted from landed value to determine the net value of the fishery resource itself. This is because if the fishery is closed those resources can move to other productive activities; they are not lost to the economy as a whole.

The National Academy of Sciences (1979) uses this approach to estimate the impact of chemical contamination of fish and Food and Drug Administration maximum concentration levels for chemicals in fish on commercial fisheries. The Academy limits its study to the impact of contamination by polychlorinated biphenyls (PCBs). The National Academy estimated that reducing the allowable content of PCBs from 5 mg/kg to 2 mg/kg would result in a loss of landed value of about $1 million for marine fisheries and $7 million for fresh water fisheries. Lowering the allowable tolerance further to 1 mg/kg would result in the loss of another $10 million in landed values. Because of the availability of substitutes and because labor and capital resources can be reallocated, the true economic damage would be substantially less than the loss in landed value. Thus these figures must be interpreted as an upper-bound estimate of economic damages.

The second approach is to model both the biological production functions and the relevant demand and supply curves for the product or products of interest. The best example of the modeling approach is the study by Bell and Canterbery (1976) of the relationship between water quality and salt water fisheries. They use secondary data to develop biological productivity functions and use these to estimate the impact on productivity of changes in water quality. These predictions are then combined with an economic model of supply and demand in the markets for fish to predict changes in prices, quantities, consumer surpluses, and factor incomes. Increased harvests due to improved water quality lower fishery prices to the benefit of consumers and increased fishermen's incomes. They estimate that the benefits of achieving the objectives of the FWPCA–72 in 1985 would be $575 million per year in 1975 dollars (or $696 million in 1978 dollars).

Heintz, Hershaft, and Horak (1976) cite earlier estimates of damages carried out between 1970 and 1973. These are then adjusted to the 1973 base year. Damages and/or benefits are estimated to be approximately $100 million per year. These are about evenly divided between marine and fresh water fisheries. I do not have access to these earlier studies, so evaluation is not possible. Unger (1975) uses the same sources to arrive at approximately the same figure for benefits of attaining the 1985 objectives.

Because of the omission of fresh water fisheries and the impacts of some forms of chemical contamination of fish, the Bell and Canterbery figure is probably an underestimate of the total damages to all commercial fisheries due to human-made pollutants. However, it seems unlikely that these other categories would be more than an additional $100 million per year. Thus my estimate of the most likely value of benefits is $0.8 billion per year. The range is estimated to be between $0.4–1.2 billion per year.

DIVERSIONARY USES

Drinking Water and Health

Until very recently most of the concern about the health effects of polluted drinking water has been focused on bacterial and viral diseases such as infectious hepatitis, salmonellosis, and gastroenteritis. Two estimates of the benefits of controlling bacterial and viral diseases have been prepared for the Environmental Protection Agency. But they differ by more than two orders of magnitude.

Unger (1975) bases his estimate of the benefits of achieving the objectives of the FWPCA–72 in 1985 on a review of the causes of waterborne disease outbreaks in the United States compiled by Craun and McCabe for EPA. These investigators find that the reported number of cases of disease for which the cause could be traced to drinking water averaged less than 3,000 per year in the period 1960–71. Unger adjusts these figures for under-reporting and applies a value per case of $594 in 1975 dollars based on medical costs and lost earnings. He assumes that attaining the 1985 goals would eliminate waterborne diseases in the population drawing drinking water from surface sources. Because of the low number of cases attributed to drinking water contamination, the disease control benefits of attaining the 1985 goals are estimated at only $3 million per year in 1975 dollars.

Heintz, Hershaft, and Horak (1976) combine data from three other studies prepared for the Environmental Protection Agency to estimate that existing levels of water pollution induced between one and two million cases of disease and 1,600 deaths per year. These figures apparently are not derived from statistical analyses of disease rates, but rather come from data on the incidence of these diseases and some judgment as to the portion caused by drinking water contamination. The main categories of death are gastroenteritis, hepatitis, and salmonellosis. Applying unit values for morbidity similar to those of Unger, and valuing mortality at $100,000 to $250,000, Heintz, Hershaft, and Horak estimate the benefits of eliminating drinking water pollution to lie between $320 and $967 million per year in 1973 dollars. About half of this total is attributable to preventing mortality. If avoiding mortality is valued at $1 million, the Heintz, Hershaft and Horak estimate would rise to between $1.68–2.14 billion per year in 1973 dollars.

As the following calculation shows, the Heintz, Hershaft, and Horak estimate of the incidence of waterborne disease seems high. Unger estimates that in 1977 approximately 115.7 million people used municipal drinking water from surface sources. An annual incidence of one to two million cases implies that between one and two percent of this group contracts a drinking water-related disease each year. I take the Heintz, Hershaft, and Horak estimate to be an upper bound. The Unger estimate is a lower bound. Thus the benefits of controlling viral and bacterial disease transmitted through municipal drinking water are estimated to lie between $3 million and $2 billion per year. I take $1.0 billion per year as the most likely point estimate of benefits of controlling contagious disease.

Recently there has been increasing concern about the health effects of chemical contamination of drinking water. Page, Harris, and Epstein (1976) find evidence linking contamination of surface drinking water supplies in Louisiana with higher cancer mortality. Harris, Page, and Reiches (1977) find similar evidence linking drinking water contamination and cancer mortality in the Ohio River Valley. These two studies use dummy variables to distinguish between water drawn from surface sources presumed or known to be contaminated and ground water sources presumed or known to be "clean." Thus they can be interpreted as tests of the hypothesis that contaminated drinking water causes cancer. But they do not provide a basis for determining what substances are the root of the problem or for deriving dose–effect relationships and estimates of benefits of control. The National Academy of Sciences (1978) concludes that chloroform in drinking water increases the risk of death due to cancer.

Unger (1975) estimates the benefits of eliminating chemical contamination of surface waters to be $182 million per year in 1975 dollars. This figure is derived by estimating the costs of removing chemicals from drinking water supplies by activated carbon filtration. This is an appropriate basis for estimating benefits if all drinking water supplies are actually filtered through activated carbon and the sole purpose of the filtration is to remove these chemical contaminants. Elimination of the chemical contamination of surface waters would lead to a cost savings of this magnitude in municipal water supply treatment.

In fact, very few municipal systems presently use activated carbon filtration. And although the EPA has adopted regulations to require cities above a certain size to undertake filtration, the primary target is the trihalomethanes, most of which are formed by the combination of free chlorine (from disinfection) with naturally occurring organic compounds. Thus eliminating chemical contamination of intake water due to point source pollution would not much affect the need or desirability of activated carbon filtration.

The appropriate method for estimating the benefits of preventing chemical contamination of drinking water intakes is to estimate dose–response functions and apply these to present estimates of exposure. I am not aware of any quantitative estimates of dose–response functions at ambient concentrations that could be used for this purpose. In the absence of any empirical basis for estimation, this category of benefits is omitted from the totals.

Treatment Costs for Municipal Water Supplies

The presence of point source pollutants at the intake points of municipal water supply systems increases the degree of treatment required to remove suspended solids and substances affecting odor and taste. If the point source pollutants are eliminated, it would be possible to reduce municipal supply treatment costs accordingly. These cost savings should be counted as a benefit of pollution control.

Unger (1975) and Heintz, Hershaft, and Horak (1976) provide estimates of the benefits based on similar data and methodology. They use the same sources to estimate that about 40% of municipal water supply treatment costs are attributable to point source pollutants and that costs could be reduced by 40% if these pollutants were controlled at the source. The sources are Barker and Kramer (1972) and Bramer (1960). See Heintz, Hershaft, and Horak (1976), pp. III-38 and III-39.

Heintz, Hershaft, and Horak assume that 40% of estimated municipal water treatment costs in 1973 are due to pollution. Thus damages due to pollution are calculated to be $0.4 billion per year in 1973 dollars (or $0.6 billion in 1978 dollars). Unger uses a different basis to estimate treatment costs in 1977 and to project costs to the years 1983 and 1985. He estimates the benefits of meeting the 1985 water quality objectives to be $0.993 billion in 1975 dollars (or $1.2 billion per year in 1978 dollars).

On the basis of these two studies, I estimate that municipal water supply benefits lie in the range of $0.6–$1.2 billion per year in 1978 dollars. The most likely point estimate is $0.9 billion per year.

Household Benefits

Water hardness and the presence of dissolved solids in municipal water supplies may impose a variety of costs on households, for example, due to staining of fixtures, mineral deposits, and appliance damages. If the hardness and dissolved solids are due at least in part to point source pollution, then controlling these sources will reduce these costs and lead to corresponding benefits. Tihansky (1973) estimates damages to households due to mineral contamination of water. Tihansky's work is the basis of the benefit estimates of both Unger and Heintz, Hershaft, and Horak. These two studies use different bases for extrapolation and different assumptions regarding the contribution of human point source pollution to total damages. Unger estimates the benefits to households in 1985 of controlling point source pollution to be $88 million per year in 1975 dollars ($107 million in 1978 dollars). Heintz, Hershaft, and Horak estimate that damages were $346 million per year in 1973 dollars (or $508 million in 1978 dollars). Based on these two studies, I estimate that the benefits lie in the range of $0.1–0.5 billion per year in 1978 dollars. The most likely point estimate is $0.3 billion per year.

Industrial Treatment Costs

Heintz, Hershaft, and Horak (1976) and Unger (1975) use many of the same sources to estimate the impact of point source pollution on industrial treatment costs for process water, boiler feed water, and cooling water. Heintz estimates damages in 1973 to be $0.3 billion per year (or $0.4 billion in 1978 dollars). Unger estimates the benefits of achieving water quality objectives in 1985 to be $0.6 billion per year in 1975 dollars (or $0.8 billion in 1978 dollars). On the basis of these studies, I estimate that benefits to industry lie between $0.4 and $0.8 billion per year in 1978 dollars. The most likely point estimate is $0.6 billion per year.

BENEFITS AND COSTS COMPARED

The benefit estimates derived in these two chapters are summarized in Table 9.1. Total benefits to the nation of meeting water quality objectives in 1985 are estimated to lie in the range of $3.8 to $18.4 billion per year in 1978 dollars. The most likely point estimate is $9.4 billion per year. Of this total,

TABLE 9.1. Benefits in 1985 From Removal of Conventional Water Pollutants (in Billions of 1978 Dollars)

	Range	Most Likely Point Estimate
Recreation	$1.8–8.7	$4.6
Nonuser Benefits		
Aesthetics, ecology, and property value	$0.5–4.0	$1.2
Commercial Fisheries	$0.4–1.2	$0.8
Diversionary Uses		
Drinking water—health	$0.0–2.0	$1.0
Municipal treatment	$0.6–1.2	$0.9
Households	$0.1–0.5	$0.3
Industrial supplies	$0.4–0.8	$0.6
Total	$3.8–18.4	$9.4

almost 50% is attributable to recreation alone, and about 60% of this total is due to the combined categories of recreation, aesthetics, ecology, and so on. It would be more useful for policy analysis if the total figure could be allocated between the attainment of the 1977 BPT goals and the 1983 BAT goals. But the available data do not permit this.

The CEQ (1979) estimates annual water pollution control costs in 1978 to have been $10.2 billion. This figure is not directly comparable with the benefit estimates presented here because the latter refer to expected benefits in 1985. The CEQ also presents an estimate of control costs in 1987. From this it is possible to infer that annual control costs in 1985 will be between $15 and $20 billion. Benefits have been estimated to be between $3.8 and $18.4 billion, with a most likely point estimate of $9.4 billion per year. Thus, although the upper bound estimate of benefits lies above the range of estimated costs, it is likely that on balance the benefit–cost relationship for the present water pollution control program is unfavorable.

However, there are two important qualifications to this conclusion. The first is that this estimate of benefits does not include benefits to human health, recreation, or the ecology that might be realized by the control of toxic substances and metals. Yet the costs of control in 1985 include substantial costs for the control of discharges of these substances. To the extent that these substances now cause significant damages, the benefit–cost relationship of the water pollution policy present here is biased downward.

The second qualification is that the present policy contains many features that reduce its cost effectiveness. There have been many recommendations for changes in this policy that would reduce the costs of attaining a given level of benefits or increase the benefits realized with a given level of costs (Kneese and Schultz, 1975; Anderson et al., 1977; Freeman, 1978; Greene, 1979). Most of these recommendations involve altering incentive structures through devices such as effluent charges. Studies have shown that costs might be reduced by as much as 25–50% by such policy changes (Kneese and Bower, 1968, p. 158–164; and Herzog, 1976).

REFERENCES

Anderson, Frederick R., et al. *Environmental Improvement Through Economic Incentives.* Baltimore: Johns Hopkins University Press, 1977.
Barker, Bruce, and Paul Kramer. "Water Quality Conditions in Illinois," in *Statewide Water Resource Development Plan,* Illinois Department of Transportation, 1972.
Bramen, Henry C. "The Economic Aspects of the Water Pollution Abatement Program in the Ohio River Valley." Ph.D. dissertation, University of Pittsburgh, 1960.
Bell, Frederick W., and E. Ray Canterbery. *An Assessment of the Economic Benefits Which Will Accrue to Commercial and Recreational Fisheries from Incremental Improvements in the Quality of Coastal Waters.* Tallahassee: Florida State University, 1975.
Dornbusch, David M. *The Impact of Water Resource Quality Improvements on Residential Property Prices.* Report to the National Commission on Water Quality, 1975.
Freeman, A. Myrick, III. "Air and Water Pollution Policy," in Paul Portney, ed. *Current Issues in U.S. Environmental Policy.* Baltimore: Johns Hopkins University Press, 1978.
———. *The Benefits of Environmental Improvement: Theory and Practice.* Baltimore: Johns Hopkins University Press, 1979.
Greene, Robert C. "Water Pollution Controls for the Iron and Steel Industry," in James C. Miller, III, and Bruce Yandle, eds., *Benefit Cost Analysis of Social Regulations.* Washington: American Enterprise Institute for Public Policy Research, 1979.
Harris, Robert H., R. Talbot Page, and Nancy Reiches. "Carcinogenic Hazards of Organic Chemicals in Drinking Water," in *Origins of Human Cancer.* Cold Spring Harbor, New York: Cold Spring Harbor Laboratory, 1977.
Heintz, H. T., A. Hershaft, and G. C. Horak. *National Damages of Air and Water Pollution.* A report to the Environmental Protection Agency, 1976.
Herzog, Henry W., Jr. "Economic Efficiency and Equity in Water Quality Control: Effluent Taxes and Information Requirements," *Journal of Environmental Economics and Management,* 2, no. 3 (February, 1976), 170–184.
Kneese, Allen V., and Charles Schultz. *Pollution, Prices, and Public Policy.* Washington: The Brookings Institution, 1975.

Kneese, Allen V., and Blair T. Bower. *Managing Water Quality: Economics, Technology, Institutions.* Baltimore: Johns Hopkins University Press, 1968.

National Academy of Sciences. *Chloroform, Carbon Tetrachloride, and Other Halomethanes.* Washington, D.C., 1978.

———. *Polychlorinated Biphenyls.* Washington, D.C., 1979.

Page, R. Talbot, Robert Harris, and Samuel Epstein, "Drinking Water and Cancer Mortality in Louisiana," *Science* 193, no. 4247 (July 2, 1976), 55–57.

Tihansky, Dennis P. *Economic Damages to Household Items for Water Supply Use.* Washington: Environmental Protection Agency, 1973.

Unger, Samuel G. *National Benefits of Achieving the 1977, 1983, and 1985 Water Quality Goals.* A report submitted to the U.S. Environmental Protection Agency, 1975.

U.S. Council on Environmental Quality. *Environmental Quality—1979.* Washington, D.C., 1979.

Walsh, Richard G., et al. *Option Values, Preservation Values and Recreational Benefits of Improved Water Quality: A Case Study of the South Platte River Basin, Colorado.* Research Triangle Park: Environmental Protection Agency, 1978.

10

CONCLUSIONS

I have shown—I hope to the reader's satisfaction—that U.S. air and water pollution policies have produced, or will produce when fully implemented, benefits for the American people; and that there is presently sufficient information to allow the estimation of the monetary value of these benefits at least within an order of magnitude of accuracy. When these estimates of benefits are compared with the costs of pollution control policies, they show that the stationary source air emissions control program appears to be justified on economic or benefit–cost terms. This is primarily because of the likely benefits to human health of controlling suspended particulates and sulfur compounds.

The benefit–cost comparisons are not nearly as favorable for the mobile source air emissions control program or the water pollution control program. But in both cases, the benefit–cost comparison could be made more favorable by changes in the policy that increase the cost effectiveness of control efforts or that make marginal changes in standards and requirements. However, the estimates made here are not sufficiently precise or detailed to provide specific guidance to decision makers as to how to "fine tune" present policies. For that we require analyses of marginal or incremental benefits for specific substances, preferably at the regional or "problem shed" level rather than for the nation as a whole.

Are the models and techniques described in this book capable of providing more guidance to policy makers? Are detailed and accurate estimates of marginal benefits feasible given the present state of the art? Subject to several important qualifications, I believe that the answer is yes. In the cases of the quantitatively most significant types of benefits, the appropriate models and empirical techniques for benefit estimation can be identified, and the data requirements can be established. But this does not mean that gathering the data and implementing the techniques would be easy in any given regional context.

174 Conclusions

The most important qualifications are:

1. The necessary dose–response and physical damage functions of Stage 2 may not be known;
2. the appropriate economic data may be difficult and costly to gather;
3. the validity of the concept of economic value of statistical lives is still a subject of controversy, and attempts at estimation have produced a wide range of values; and
4. even where the necessary data are available, there will still remain some uncertainty and imprecision in the resulting estimates (but perhaps no more imprecision than that for present estimates of costs).[1]

AGGREGATE BENEFITS AND THE MACROECONOMY

The Council on Environmental Quality regularly conducts analyses of the impacts of environmental regulation on macroeconomic variables such as the Consumer Price Index, the unemployment rate, and gross national product. But the large-scale econometric models used for these analyses incorporate only the effect of pollution control expenditures, that is, costs; they do not incorporate benefits. This means that the effects of pollution control benefits on GNP are not accounted for. Furthermore, as is well known, many of the benefits of pollution control do not show up in the national income accounts. Therefore gross national product, even if accurately predicted by the model, would not accurately mirror the overall changes in welfare of our citizens resulting from environmental regulation.

Another macroeconomic issue is the effect of environmental regulation on productivity. Substantial attention has been devoted recently to the decline in the rate of growth of various measures of productivity in the last 15 years (Denison, 1979; Norsworthy, Harper, and Kunze, 1979). One important question is the contribution that environmental regulation has made to this decline in productivity growth by diverting resources from producing marketable outputs to the control of air and water pollution (Christainsen, Gollop, and Haveman, 1980). Focusing only on the effects of pollution control costs will give an incomplete picture of the effect of environmental regulation on productivity. Private sector firms can be viewed as multiproduct firms that employ capital, labor, materials, and energy to produce both marketable output and, by undertaking pollution control activities, improved environmental quality. To account properly for the impact of pollution control benefits on measured productivity, it is necessary to distinguish between: (1) benefits that are reflected in recorded output because they increase output or

[1] For a more extensive discussion of the state of the art, see Freeman (1979, Chapter 10).

reduce the costs of market activity, and (2) utility increasing benefits that have no counterpart in market activity.

I now consider the impact of realized benefits on recorded GNP and then show how the benefit estimates of this book can be used to adjust recorded GNP to reflect the welfare enhancing consequences of diverting resources toward pollution control activities. I will then show that this adjusted measure of GNP has grown more rapidly than the official GNP, and that the true decline in productivity growth has been less than that shown by the official statistics.

It would be helpful at this point to review the relationships between measures of benefits and changes in GNP. The benefit categories analyzed in this book can be placed in one of three groups according to their relationship to changes in GNP. They may be "cost reducing," "output increasing," or "utility increasing." The first two groups result in increases in recorded real GNP equal to the dollar measure of benefits. Thus they are "GNP increasing" benefits. But the utility increasing benefits have no net effect on recorded GNP. I now consider each of these groups in more detail and allocate the benefits of air and water pollution control as estimated here to each of these groups.

Cost Reducing Benefits

Some beneficial effects result in lower production costs or expenditures on intermediate goods and factor inputs for a given level of output. As a result, resources are freed for increasing some component of aggregate output. For example, if materials damages to producers are reduced because of air pollution control, producers can reduce expenditures on painting, materials replacement, and so forth. Provided that the freed resources are in fact reemployed elsewhere in the economy, these benefits are reflected in an increase in recorded real GNP.

Cost reducing benefits estimated here include reductions in costs for treating municipal and industrial water supplies and reductions in materials damages to producers due to air pollution. Of the total benefits due to reduced materials damages due to air pollution, just under one-third or about $0.2 billion is estimated to accrue to households in the form of lower house painting costs. This component of materials damages is allocated to the third category below.

These allocations are shown in Table 10.1. They are based on the most likely point estimates of the benefits of air pollution control and water pollution control summarized in Chapters 7 and 9. For air, I use realized benefits in 1978, that is, those benefits actually incurred because of improve-

Conclusions

TABLE 10.1. Benefits by Category—Best Judgment Estimates (in Billions of 1978 Dollars)

	Air	Water[a]	Total
1. GNP Increasing			
(a) Cost reducing	$ 0.5	$0.8	$ 1.3
(b) Output increasing	$ 0.5	$0.4	$ 0.9
Total	$ 1.0	$1.2	$ 2.2
2. Utility Increasing	$20.7	$3.6	$24.3
3. Totals	$21.7	$4.8	$26.5

[a] It is assumed that one-half of the benefits reported in Table 9.1 were realized in 1978.

ments in air quality between 1970 and 1978. For water, I somewhat arbitrarily assume that one-half of the benefits of attaining the 1985 objectives had already been realized by 1978.

Output Increasing Benefits

Some beneficial effects result directly in increases in marketable output. Benefits in this category include increased output and earnings due to reduced air-pollution-caused morbidity, the reduction in agricultural crop damages due to air pollution control, and the increased commercial fishery yields due to water pollution control. As these damages are reduced, GNP as measured by the national income accounts is increased. I estimate that $0.2 billion of morbidity benefits are in the form of increased output and earnings.

Utility Increasing Benefits

Benefits in this category represent increases in individuals' welfare, but they are not reflected in increases in GNP. These non-GNP benefits can arise in two ways. First, if a pollution reduction results in a decrease in household expenditures to maintain a given level of welfare, GNP as measured by final expenditure is reduced; but the freed resources can be reemployed elsewhere, increasing GNP. The net effect on GNP is zero; but benefits are positive. Benefits in this category include those due to reduced expenditures on medical care, reduced home painting costs, and reduced household expenditures that were caused by mineral contamination of water.

Second, some beneficial effects simply increase utility without any corresponding increase in marketable output. Benefits in this category include the utility associated with reduced mortality and morbidity from both air and water pollution, increased recreation opportunities, reduced household soiling, and aesthetic improvements. To the extent that increased recreation is accompanied by higher expenditures on equipment and travel, this results in a diversion of expenditure from other categories and not a net increase in expenditure or GNP. When an estimate of this component of benefits is included in Table 10.1, it can be seen that utility increasing benefits make up a little over 90% of total benefits for air and water pollution control combined.

As indicated above, the econometric models typically used to assess the macroeconomic impacts of environmental regulation do not take account of the GNP increasing benefits associated with pollution control policies. Thus when these models are used to make predictions of GNP in future years, their predictions will be biased downward. How large is this bias likely to be? As Table 10.1 indicates, realized benefits of air and water pollution control in 1978 are estimated to have increased recorded GNP by $2.2 billion. This amounts to about 0.10% of the $2,128 billion recorded GNP for that year. The fact that GNP predictions derived from macro models do not reflect this component of realized GNP turns out to be of very minor importance.

The most likely point estimate of what I have termed utility increasing benefits not recorded in GNP is $24.3 billion in 1978. This figure is 1.1% of recorded GNP. As a result, measured increases in real GNP since 1970 understate changes in welfare by this amount due to failure to account for pollution control benefits not recorded in GNP accounts. Of course, there are other biases in GNP as a measure of welfare that work in both directions. This downward bias in GNP may take on more importance when we consider assessing the effects of environmental regulation on the rate of productivity change. Measured productivity would be lower the greater the extent to which firms are forced to reallocate factor inputs to the production of nonmarket environmental goods. To obtain a true measure of productivity change, one must add the utility increasing benefits to whatever measure of marketed output is used in the numerator of the productivity ratio. This also means that in the era before pollution control policies became effective, measured productivity growth overestimated the true productivity growth because it failed to adjust for the growing negative output of firms in the form of external diseconomies from pollution.

Conclusions

How important are these benefits in the overall productivity measure? A commonly used measure of output in productivity assessment is aggregate private sector output. This is the sum of personal consumption expenditures, gross private domestic investment, and net exports. Between 1970 and 1978 aggregate private sector output grew from $1,244 billion to $1,692 billion (both in 1978 dollars). This is a growth rate of approximately 3.92% per year. If the 1978 aggregate private sector output is adjusted upward to account for utility increasing environmental benefits, the adjusted growth rate is 4.11% per year. If Q is aggregate private sector output and I is a measure of factor inputs, productivity, P, is Q/I. The rate of productivity change, dP/dt, is approximated by $dQ/dt - dI/dt$. If the rate of growth of output is underestimated, the rate of growth of productivity will be underestimated by the same amount. Thus, as a rough approximation, we can say that true productivity change over this period was approximately 0.19% per year higher than that reflected in the conventional measure. Or to put it differently, about one-fifth of a percentage point per year of the recorded decline in productivity can be accounted for by the failure to measure the productive output of resources diverted from producing marketed goods to producing environmental improvement.

REFERENCES

Christainsen, Gregory B., Frank Gollop, and Robert H. Haveman. *Environmental and Health-Safety Regulations, Productivity Growth and Economic Performance: An Assessment.* Washington, D.C.: U.S. Joint Economic Committee, 1980.

Denison, Edward. "Explanations of Declining Productivity Growth," *Survey of Current Business,* August, 1979, 1–24.

Freeman, A. Myrick, III. *The Benefits of Environmental Improvement: Theory and Practice.* Baltimore: Johns Hopkins University Press, 1979.

Norsworthy, J. R., Michael J. Harper, and Kent Kunze. "The Slowdown in Productivity Growth: An Analysis of Some Contributing Factors," *Brookings Papers on Economic Activity*, 1979, no. 2, pp. 387–421.

AUTHOR INDEX

Acton, Jan P., 40-41
Adams, F. Gerard, 141-143
Adams, Richard M., 89-90
Ahearne, William R., 79-80
American Lung Association, 36n
Anderson, Frederick R., 171
Asch, Peter, 63, 67

Babcock, Lyndon R., 77-78, 88
Bailey, Martin J., 37n, 42
Barker, Bruce, 168
Barrett, Larry B., 77
Battelle Memorial Institute, 145-146
Bell, Frederick W., 145-146, 159, 165-166
Benedict, H. M., 88-90
Bergstrom, Theodore C., 22
Bhagia, Gobind S., 73
Blomquist, Glenn, 40
Booz, Allen and Hamilton, Inc., 103-104, 107
Borcherding, Thomas E., 22
Bouwes, Nicholaas W., 157
Bower, Blair T., 171
Bowes, Michael D., 142, 155
Boyd, W. K., 94
Bramen, Henry C., 168
Brookshire, David S., 21, 81, 111, 115, 119-120, 129
Brown, Charles, 40n, 41
Brown, Gardner M., 115
Buttner, F. H., 94

Canterberg, E. Ray, 145-146, 159, 165-166
Carpenter, Ben H., 73
Chappie, Mike, 59-60, 67
Christainsen, Gregory B., 174
Clawson, Marion, 137

Cooper, Barbara S., 38, 49, 53, 65, 74
Crocker, Thomas D., 33, 40, 51-60, 65, 67, 70-74, 79, 89-90, 107-108
Cropper, Maureen L., 73, 122

Davidson, Paul F., 141-143
Davis, Robert K., 21
Deacon, Robert T., 22
Denison, Edward, 174
Dillingham, Alan E., 40-42
Dornbusch, David M., 163
Dwyer, John F., 142, 155

Eastman, Clyde, 21, 110-111
Epstein, Samuel, 167

Feenberg, Daniel, 151-155, 158-160
Fink, F. W., 94
Fisher, Anthony C., 56
Freeman, A. Myrick, III, 2, 4, 5, 15, 17n, 18n, 19, 21, 23, 36n, 41, 90, 110n, 111, 115n, 116n, 122, 136, 137, 138, 146, 160, 164, 171, 174n

Gerhing, Shelby, 55
Gillette, Donald G., 80, 93-94
Gollop, Frank, 174
Goodman, Robert P., 22
Gramlich, Frederick W., 156-157, 159
Greene, Robert C., 171
Gregor, John J., 62

Hamilton, James D., 89, 90, 105
Harper, Michael J., 174
Harrington, Winston, 155-156, 158-160
Harris, Robert H., 167
Harrison, David, 115, 117-120

179

180 Author Index

Haveman, Robert H., 174
Haynie, F. H., 94
Heck, W. W., 89
Heintz, H. T., 48, 64-65, 87, 89-91, 95, 146-151, 154, 158-160, 164-169
Hershaft, A., 48, 64-65, 87, 89-91, 95, 146-151, 154, 158-160, 164, 169
Herzog, Henry W., Jr., 171
Horak, G. C., 48, 64-65, 87, 89-91, 95, 146-151, 154, 158-160, 164-169

ITT Electro-physics Laboratories, Inc., 94
Ives, Berry, 21, 110-111

Jackson, Clement J., 61, 88, 102-103
Jaksch, John, 104-107
Jones-Lee, Michael W., 37n, 40

Kelly, John R., 142, 155
Kneese, Allen V., 171
Knetsch, Jack L., 21, 164
Kramer, Paul, 168
Kunze, Kent, 174

Landau, Emmanuel, 48
Larsen, Ralph I., 89
Lave, Lester B., 32, 36n, 41-61, 63-65, 67, 73-74, 77-79, 81
Lipfert, Frederick W., 62, 67
Liu, Ben-Chieh, 51-53, 65, 67, 68-70, 88, 95, 103, 107

McDonald, Gary C., 60-61, 67, 78
Mäler, Karl-Goran, 164
Mathtech, Inc., 98-100, 105-107, 122
Mendelsohn, Robert, 61-62
Michelson, Irving, 102
Miller, C. J., 88-90
Mills, Edwin S., 151-155, 158-160
Mishan, Ezra J., 37n
Mueller, W. J., 94

Nagda, Miren L., 77-78, 88
National Academy of Sciences, 23, 80-81, 88, 93-95, 107, 118-122, 165, 167
National Commission on Water Quality, 144-145, 158-160
National Economic Research Associates, 4n, 31, 33n, 34n, 41-42
National Planning Association, 144-145
Needleman, L., 40

Nelson, Jon P., 115, 119
Norsworthy, J. R., 174

Olson, Craig A., 40-42
Orcutt, Guy, 61-62

Page, R. Talbot, 167
Peskin, Henry M., 155-156, 158-160
Polinsky, A. Mitchell, 118
Pollakowski, Henry O., 115

Raiffa, Howard, 37n
Randall, Alan, 21, 110-111
Reiches, Nancy, 167
Rice, Dorothy P., 38, 45-49, 53, 61, 64-65, 74, 77-78
Robbins, R. C., 94
Rosen, Sherwin, 40-41, 42n, 56, 111, 122n
Rubinfeld, Daniel L., 15, 117-118
Russell, Clifford S., 156, 158-160
Ryan, John W., 87, 90-91, 96-98, 100, 103-104, 106-107

Salmon, R. L., 94, 96-97
Salvin, V. S., 94, 95
Schelling, Thomas C., 37n
Schneider, Robert, 157
Schultz, Charles, 171
Schulze, William D., 21, 55, 111
Schwartz, William B., 37n
Schwing, Richard C., 60-61, 67, 78
Seneca, Joseph, 63, 67, 141-143
Seskin, Eugene P., 32, 36n, 41-59, 61, 63-65, 67, 73-74, 77-79, 81, 131
Small, Kenneth A., 47, 64-65, 78, 95
Smith, J. S., 88-90
Smith, Robert S., 40-41
Smith, V. Kerry, 52n
Spence, J. W., 94
Stickney, P. B., 94
Stoevener, Herbert, 73

Thaler, Robert H., 40-41, 42n, 56
Thanavibulchai, Narongsakdi, 89-90
Thibodeau, L. A., 48, 50
Tihansky, Dennis P., 169
Tourin, B., 102

Unger, Samuel G., 133, 151, 153-154, 158-160, 166-169
U.S. Council on Environmental Quality, 2, 4n, 33-34, 130-131, 170

Author Index

U.S. Department of Health, Education, and Welfare, 75n, 76n, 80
U.S. Environmental Protection Agency, 31-34, 46, 68
U.S. House of Representatives, Committee on Science and Technology, 47

Vaughn, William J., 156, 158-160
Viren, John R., 48, 50-51, 62
Viscusi, W. Kip, 40n, 41

Waddell, Thomas E., 32, 46-48, 50, 64-65, 77, 87-88, 93-95, 102n, 115-118

Walsh, Richard G., 147, 157, 160
Water Resources Council, 142-143
Watson, William, 104-107
Weinstein, Milton C., 37n
Westman, Walter E., 24
Willig, Robert D., 17
Wyzga, Ronald, 137

Yu, Eden S., 51-53, 65, 67, 68-70, 88, 95, 103, 107

Zeckhauser, Richard, 56

SUBJECT INDEX

Acid rain, 11, 86, 107-108
Aesthetic effects, 13, 23, 102, 125-127, 129, 134, 141, 163-164, 177. *See also* Amenity values
Agriculture, 9, 10, 19, 86, 91, 107, 110
Air quality standards:
    primary, 31, 32, 33, 46-47, 78-79, 91, 105, 114
    secondary, 32, 90, 96, 105-107, 122
Allegheny County, 62, 73
Amenity values, 13, 17, 20, 121-122, 125, 129, 134. *See also* Aesthetic effects

Bacteria, coliform, 145
Benefits, 3, 26-28
    cost reducing, 175-176
    and costs, 130-131, 169-170, 173
    GNP increasing, 175-176
    marginal, 2, 18, 130, 133, 160, 173
    national, 28
    nonuser, 163-164, 170
    output increasing, 175-176
    regional, 28
    utility increasing, 175-177
Benzo-(a)pyrene, 62
Best available treatment, 132-133, 156, 160
Best practical treatment, 132-133, 155-156, 160
Bidding games, 20, 110, 129
Boating, 134, 141, 144-146, 153-155, 159-161
Boston, Massachusetts, 119

California, 90, 105
California Air Resources Board, 80
Carbon dioxide, 12
Carbon monoxide, 29, 34, 61, 77-79, 82
Charles River Basin, Massachusetts, 156-157
CHESS report, 46-47, 68
Chicago, Illinois, 79, 115

Chlorine, 168
Chloroform, 167
Clean Air Act of 1970, 5, 26, 31, 32, 48, 66, 82, 130
Cleaning costs, 19, 86, 100-108
Cleveland, Ohio, 122
Climate, 10, 52-53, 55
Confidence intervals, 5
Consumers' surplus, 135, 146, 149, 152-153, 165
Cost-effectiveness, 171, 173
Cost function, 98
Costs:
    of goods, 106
    marginal, 2, 130
    of pollution control, 26, 130-131, 170-171, 174
    of production, 91, 93

Damage function, 28, 92, 96-97, 126, 174
Damages, 3
    due to air pollution, 88-89
    due to water pollution, 132-134, 146, 157, 158, 165, 169
Defensive expenditures, 102
Delaware Estuary, 141
Demand curve:
    for agricultural output, 87
    for air quality, 116
    for cleanliness, 100-101, 104, 106
    for environmental quality, 17-18, 22
    for output, 99
    for recreation, 135-136, 138-139, 150, 152, 157
Demand function:
    for air quality, 114, 116
    for doctors, 57

184   Subject Index

for recreaton, 135-137, 139
Denver, Colorado, 122
Diet, 43, 45, 59, 62-63
Disability, 71-72
Dissolved oxygen, 14, 139
Dose-response functions, 36-37, 46, 79-80, 86, 89, 168, 174
Drinking water, 134, 166-168, 170

Ecological benefits, 134, 163, 170
Ecological impacts, 107
Ecological systems, 9, 12, 24
Effluent changes, 171
Epidemiology, 14, 43, 54, 56-57, 68, 77
Executive Order 12291, 1

Federal Water Pollution Control Act of 1972, 5, 132, 134, 144, 154, 166
Fisheries, 3, 86
  commercial, 9, 10, 11, 14, 19, 134, 163, 165
Fishing, 134, 141, 146-148, 153-155
  fresh water, 144-145, 151, 156, 158-161
  marine, 145-146, 151, 158-161
Fluorides, 87-88
Food and Drug Administration, 165
Forestry, 9, 10, 19, 86, 90, 107
Four Corners Power Plant, 110
Fraser River Valley, British Columbia, 164

Green Bay, Wisconsin, 147-148, 151, 154-155
Gross national product, 174-177

Health, human:
  and acid rain, 107
  benefits of air pollution control, 126-129
  benefits of water pollution control, 170
  effects of air pollution on, 14-15, 31, 36-82, 110-111
  effects of environmental change on, 9-10, 12-13
  water pollution and risks to, 134
  see also Morbidity; Mortality
Hedonic price technique, 111-115, 121
Household benefits, 134, 169-170
Housing prices, 102, 110. *See also* Property values
Hunting, waterfowl, 134, 146-148, 153-155, 159-161
Hydrocarbons, 29, 60-61, 78-79, 119

Illness:
  acute, 70-72, 75-76
  chronic, 71-72
  see also Morbidity
Implicit price, 106, 112-116
Industrial treatment costs, 134
Iron, 62

Kansas City, Missouri, 115

Lake Powell, 111
Los Angeles, California, 80-81, 111, 119-120
Los Angeles-Long Beach, California, 105
Louisiana, 167

Macroepidemiology, 36. *See also* Epidemiology
Manganese, 62
Market approaches, 19-20, 21n
Market effects, 9-12, 19
Materials:
  acid rain damages to, 107
  benefits of air pollution control, 91-100, 126-128
  damages to, 3, 9-10, 12-13, 86, 110, 175
  reduced costs of, 19
Medical costs, 166
Medical expenditures, 38, 42-43, 45, 71, 177
Microepidemiology, 36. *See also* Epidemiology
Minnesota, 107
Mississippi River, 107
Mobile source pollutants, 33-34, 37, 77-82, 98, 130-131
Mobile source pollution control, 96, 118-121, 173
Monte Carlo technique, 70, 103
Morbidity, 2, 9
  air pollution and, 10, 36-37, 50, 51, 53
  benefits of reducing, 176-177
  costs of, 46-47, 49
  empirical estimates of air pollution control benefits, 68-77
  interaction with air pollution and medical care, 54-55
  relationship with other categories of benefits, 125-128
  value of reductions in, 38, 42-43, 45
  water pollution and, 167
Mortality, 2, 9
  air pollution and, 10, 36-37
  benefits of reducing, 177
  compared to morbidity benefits, 72
  mobile source control benefits, 78, 81

Subject Index

relationship with other categories of benefits, 126-130
stationary source control benefits, 43-69, 77
water pollution and, 167
Most reasonable point estimates, explained, 6
Multicollinearity, 51, 60

National Commission on Air Quality, 90
National Recreation Survey of 1972, 144, 145, 155
National Survey of Hunting, Fishing, and Water Associated Recreation of 1975, 156
Nationwide Outdoor Recreation Survey of 1959, 141
New Jersey, 63
Nitrates, air emissions and health, 60, 61, 63, 78-79
Nitric oxide, 78-79
Nitrogen compounds, 61, 107
Nitrogen dioxide:
 ambient concentration, trends, 34
 mobile source control benefits, 70, 77-79, 81-82
 morbidity effects, 70
 mortality effects, 55, 60-61, 63
 and wage differentials, 121
Nitrogen oxides, 29
 and health, 78, 81
 and materials, 94-95
 and property values, 119-120
 and vegetation, 89
Nonmarket effects, 9-12
Nonpoint sources, 132

Odors, 110, 168
Ohio River Valley, 167
Opportunity cost:
 of illness, 37, 38, 53, 71
 of time, 104, 146, 158
Option value, 134, 157, 163-164, 170
Oxidants, *see* Photochemical oxidants
Ozone:
 and climate, 12
 and mortality, 61-62
 and property values, 120
 trends in ambient concentrations, 33
 and vegetation damages, 86-87, 89-91
 see also Photochemical oxidants

Panel Study of Income Dynamics, 70, 73, 122
Particulates:
 and materials damages, 12, 94

and morbidity, 70, 77
and mortalilty, 48, 50, 53, 56, 60-61, 63, 68
and wage differentials, 121
see also Suspended particulates
Philadelphia, Pennsylvania, 104-105
Photochemical oxidants:
 and agricultural productivity, 10, 87-91
 and health, 77-79, 81-82
 and materials, 94-95
 and property values, 119
 trends in ambient concentrations, 29, 33
Pittsburgh, Pennsylvania, 62
Polychlorinated biphenyls, 165
Portland, Oregon, 73
Preservation benefits, 134, 163-164, 170
Productivity:
 agricultural, 107
 forestry, 107
 growth in, 174-178
Profits, 12
Property value benefits, 125-129, 164
Property values, 20, 110-121, 126, 163-164

Recreation, 2, 3, 9, 11, 13, 14, 20, 23
 benefits of water pollution control, 134-162, 170, 177
 participation model, 140-142, 155, 158
Rocky Mountain National Park, Colorado, 147-149

St. Louis, Missouri, 115, 118
San Francisco-Oakland, California, 105
Secondary treatment, 132
Shadow prices, 23, 142-143
Smog, 19, 110
Smoking, 43, 45, 50, 55, 58-63
Socio-economic variables:
 in analysis of pollution and morbidity, 70
 in analysis of pollution and mortality, 43-45, 51, 52n, 55, 59-61, 63, 129
 in analysis of property values, 114
 and demand for recreation, 135, 137, 138n, 140-142, 145, 149, 152, 155
 and effect of pollution on cleaning behavior, 103-104
Soiling, 10, 12, 86, 100-108, 110, 125-128, 177
South Coast Air Basin, California, 81
South Platte River Basin, Colorado, 157
Stationary source air pollution control, 67, 96-97, 115-118, 130, 173
Stationary source emissions, 60

Subject Index

Stationary source pollutants, 29-33, 37, 77, 119, 121
Steubenville, Ohio, 102
Sulfate particles, 29, 31, 44, 58
Sulfates, 46, 48, 50, 59-63, 77. *See also* Sulfate particles
Sulfation rates, 116-117
Sulfur compounds:
  and acid rain, 107
  and health effects, 37, 43, 48, 52, 61, 66, 173
  and materials damages, 94-96
  and property values, 117
  trends in ambient concentrations, 29
Sulfur dioxide:
  and acid rain, 107
  and cleaning behavior, 106
  and health effects, 48, 51-53, 55, 58, 60-63, 68-70, 73
  and materials damages, 93, 97-100
  trends in ambient concentrations, 29-32
  and vegetation damages, 90
  and wage differentials, 121-122
Sulfur oxide, 50, 56, 68, 77. *See also* Sulfur dioxide
Sulfur particulates, 106. *See also* Sulfate particles
Supply curve, 87, 98
Supply function, 87
Survey of Consumer Expenditures, 106
Surveys, 3, 19, 20-21 [1]
  and nonuser benefits, 163-164
  and recreation participation, 141, 158
  and willingness to pay for air quality, 120, 129
  and willingness to pay for water quality, 156
Suspended particulates:
  and cleaning damages, 12, 102-107
  and materials damages, 95-100
  and morbidity, 68-73, 77
  and mortality, 37, 43-44, 46, 52, 55, 59-60, 62, 66

  and property values, 117, 119, 125
  trends in ambient concentrations, 29-32
  and wage differentials, 122
Suspended solids, 133, 168
Swimming, 134, 141

Toxic substances, 11, 170
Travel cost method, 136-139, 142, 157
Travel costs, 143, 147, 150-153
Travel cost savings, 146-149
Treatment costs:
  municipal water supplies, 134, 168, 170, 175
  industrial, 134, 169-170, 175
Trihalomethanes, 168

Uncertainty, 5, 77, 129-130, 174
Uniontown, Pennsylvania, 102
Utility, 12, 13, 16-17, 141, 145, 147, 156

Value of life, 23, 38-43, 56
  human capital approach, 37-38
  opportunity cost, 45, 47
  statistical, 39, 68, 174
  willingness to pay approach, 39-43, 45
Vegetation, 86-91, 107, 127-128
Visibility, 10, 110-111

Wage differentials, 20, 39-42, 45, 121-122
Washington, D.C., 79, 115, 118, 119
Water hardness, 169
Water Quality Network Model of RFF, 155-156
Water supply, 14, 107
Welfare, 12, 13, 16, 24, 147, 174-177
Willingness to pay:
  approaches to estimation, 4, 20
  and concept of benefits, 3, 13, 17-18, 28, 36
  and value of life, 38, 40-43